William Trevor: The Writer and His Work

WILLIAM TREVOR
The Writer and His Work

Dolores MacKenna

New Island Books
Dublin

William Trevor: The Writer and His Work
First published April 1999 by
New Island Books
2 Brookside
Dundrum Road
Dublin 14
Ireland

ISBN 1 874597 74 X

British Library Cataloguing in Publication Data
A catalogue record for this book is available from the British Library

**New Island Books receives financial assistance from The Arts Council
(An Chomhairle Ealaíon), Dublin, Ireland.**

The Arts Council
An Chomhairle Ealaíon

Cover design: Slick Fish Design, Dublin
Cover photograph: Geordie Greig
Typesetting: New Island Books
Printed in Ireland by Colour Books Ltd.

In memory of my parents
Jack and Úna MacKenna

Contents

Prologue

'Outside the estate gates'

By his own admission William Trevor is an outsider and has been so all his life. Born into a Protestant family in a predominantly Catholic society, son of a bank employee whose work necessitated constant changes of location, Trevor's growing up in Ireland at a particular time in history situated him at the edge. For a writer of fiction, however, this peripheral stance is an advantage, he suggests: it allows him to be all-seeing observer of people, a watcher in the wings who, although not part of the action, is an acutely interested spectator. Furthermore, the very history that determined his social and cultural inheritance significantly shapes his development as a writer and is woven into the fabric of his fictional world. For William Trevor the past is not dead. It is perpetuated and becomes part of the future. In his own words 'history is unfinished'. (CS 763)

William Trevor is a tall, shy, courteous man with clear blue eyes and a wry, humorous expression. His weather-beaten look betrays an enjoyment of gardening and walking; his hands remind one that earlier in his life he was a sculptor. An Irish accent can still be detected even though he has spent the greater part of his adult life in England. In his conversation there are occasional echoes of the old-fashioned English still spoken in parts of Ireland, and which is so typical of many of the characters he has created in his short stories and novels.

He was born William Trevor Cox, his family on his father's side originating in County Roscommon in the west of Ireland. Although Cox is a common English surname, in Ireland a majority of the people of the name are descended from the Gaelic family, Mac an Choiligh, which literally means 'son of the cock'. Through the centuries the name was anglicised to Cocks, Cox or the phonetic McQuilly.[1]

Two-thirds of County Roscommon is bounded by lake or river water, but its centre is comprised of good farmland. In the mid-seventeenth century much of the county was colonised, and the area of Cruachan or Croghan was given by King Charles I to the Lloyds, a Welsh family with strong Norfolk connections. The Coxes were among the Catholic Gaelic families of Roscommon who as a consequence of colonisation were ousted from their lands. Reduced in status as in wealth, many of those dispossessed remained in the vicinity of their old homes, eking out a living as rightless cottiers. A census of the Diocese of Elphin made at the request of the Protestant Bishop Synge in the year 1749 shows only one member of the family, M B Cox, a cottier, then resident in the arish of Killukin of which the village of Croghan – birthplace of Trevor's immediate forebears – formed part. M B Cox was a 'papist' or Roman Catholic. Fifty years later, however, the Cox family living in the same place are Protestants and are classed as 'farmers'. The improvement in the family's fortunes would certainly have been facilitated by their new allegiance to the established church, the members of which were given preferential treatment when renting farms from Protestant landlords.

Neither the family's change of status nor of religion was unusual at a time when there was a great deal of social and religious fluidity in Ireland. Industrious cottiers, even those who were Catholic, were able to lease land, but it was easier for Protestants to get good terms and long leases from a landlord. Some tenants, therefore, found it expedient to convert to the Protestant religion in order to prosper. It is possible that the Cox family of Croghan were among those who chose this course, although their names do not appear in the Convert Rolls of the time.

Another possible explanation of their conversion lies in the political situation of the time. Following an extremely fallow period in Irish politics when general elections were held only on the death of a King, the 1768 Octennial Act ensured that voting now took place every eight years. Irish politics suddenly became more interesting. The Patriot Party was formed to further the rights of the Irish Parliament in its struggle against interference from London and events were under way which culminated in the independence of the Irish legislature in 1782. But the Irish Parliament was a totally Protestant assembly, elected by and representing only members of the established church. The Penal Laws still denied Catholics both the vote and the right to sit in parliament and consequently they could take no part in these new political developments. It was tempting for any Catholic who was politically, economically or even socially ambitious to change religion. The rate of conversion to Protestantism was greatest in the years between 1772 and 1789 and farmers whose property qualifications would have made them eligible to vote – if they were members of the Protestant Church – were numbered highly among converts. In County Roscommon the number of conversions to the Protestant faith was particularly remarkable on the eve of the very hotly contested election of 1783.[2] Landlords determined to have their own candidate elected often put pressure on their tenants to join the Protestant church so that they could then command their votes. Some tenants didn't need any persuasion: they were themselves anxious to be in the political swim of things and converted voluntarily. When the election was over a number of them then reverted to their old religion.

From the extant records it is not possible to pinpoint exactly when the Cox family of Croghan became members of the Church of Ireland. But the family was undoubtedly Protestant by the beginning of the nineteenth century. Mark Cox, William Trevor's great-grandfather, was born in 1795. He and his brother, Robert, lived in the townland of Knockroe. In 1838, on the eve of his marriage, Mark signed a 31-year lease for land at Killumod, a part of Knockroe. His landlord was Edward Lord Baron Crofton, a relative of Oliver Goldsmith's family, but the lease eventually passed into the hands of the Lloyds of Croghan. By the 1860s Mark Cox and his family had moved from Knockroe to the adjacent townland of Killappoge, where he held a farm of 150 acres and built a house called Millbrook.

The long, stone, farmhouse had two storeys and was relatively roomy. It resembled many of the other houses on the Lloyd estate in design, its off-centre front door protected by a porch which opened to the side. Eight sash windows on the front looked out over a curved, gravelled avenue. All the farms around Croghan had similar entrances as it was believed locally that the twists and turns facilitated escape from unwelcome pursuit.

During the eighteenth century the Lloyd family had remained resident in England, making only sporadic visits to their Irish estates. In the 1820s, however, they decided to return to live in Ireland and Croghan House was built as their permanent home. The village grew in its shadow, all the buildings except the Catholic Church facing in the direction of the landlord's house at the insistence of the family, who did not wish to be presented with a view to the back yards of their tenants' houses.

The tenants on the Lloyd estate survived the vicissitudes of the great famine of the 1840s, at a time when much of Ireland witnessed great suffering. The Irish population had vastly increased during the first half of the nineteenth century. As a result there was tremendous competition for land. In 1845 there were nine thousand people in the parish of Croghan which to-day numbers about fourteen hundred.[3] The landlord of the day, Guy Lloyd, was a militant Protestant, and had a policy of renting his best farms to tenants of his own faith. The Coxes, as Protestants, were therefore in a more secure position than many of their neighbours. But Guy Lloyd was by the standards of the day a good landlord and even at the height of the Famine, when his own income was greatly reduced because of the inability of many of his tenants to meet their rental commitments, he continued to pay his workers and to contribute to the upkeep of the poor of the area. It is to his credit that no tenant on his estate died of famine, at a time when one million people perished from hunger and its effects, while another million fled the country. People elsewhere in the area were not so lucky and many of the starving were glad to accept food from the local soup kitchens which combined charity with Protestant proselytising. Guy Lloyd's two sisters, ardent evangelists, dispensed cash with their religious tracts, hiding the money in the leaves of prayer books to encourage their readers. His wife, Elizabeth, had less guile and is remembered locally for her generosity to all sections of the poor.[4] The fortunes of the Lloyd family in later years are mirrored in Trevor's Big House stories, particularly 'The News from Ireland' and *The Silence in the Garden*: their land was originally acquired by force, but in famine times they took care of those who depended upon them and at a later period the estate lands were sold off and the house destroyed.

The Coxes were among the more prosperous of the Lloyd tenants. When an appeal was launched for the building of a new Protestant church in Croghan in 1860, Trevor's great-grandfather's contribution was a very respectable £4 – three quarters of the parishioners gave smaller amounts. Mark Cox's eldest son, Arthur, married some months before the death of his ninety-five year old father in 1890. His wife was Mary McGarry, nearly twenty years his junior and the daughter of the steward on the Lloyd estate. The McGarrys were also coverts to Protestantism and James, Mary's father, was a punctilious employee, with the sense of duty and deference expected at the time from a man of his position and class. When Guy Lloyd was absent from the estate for a number of weeks in 1840, his steward wrote regularly to him, addressing his as 'Master' and giving him detailed accounts of day-to-day activities on the estate: 'I examined the pipes of the house. They are all right except one spot that leaks over the study window ... This day the speckled heifer calved a most beautiful bull calf.' Petty crimes were reported upon:

> On Saturday night some person or persons entered the house of James McDermott and robbed him of the two hundred of meal which you got for him with the exception of about two stones of it which he had used. He searched by magistrates order for it but could not get it ... He certainly is in want.

Also enclosed in his communications to Guy Lloyd are lists of tenants who were 'not at church on Sunday last ... nor their wives'. The letters end with the promise 'I will obey your order' and are signed 'Your obedient Servant'.[5] James McGarry, like the Coxes, may have been of the same faith as the Lloyds, but socially he did not belong in their world, while at the same time his religion kept him apart from the majority of his neighbours who were Catholic. Like Fogarty – the Protestant servant in Trevor's historical short story 'The News from Ireland':

> All he said came from a feeling he had, a servant's feeling which he'd always had in this house ... Poor Protestants as they were, he and his sister belonged neither outside the

estate gates with the people who had starved nor with a
family as renowned as the Pulvertafts.

('The News from Ireland' CS 904 -5)

By the time he married in 1890, Mark Cox's son, Arthur,
Trevor's grandfather, was the proprietor of his own farm and
independent of landlord influence. A series of Land Acts in the late
nineteenth century made it possible for relatively prosperous
tenants like the Coxes to buy out their leases. The Lloyds remained
the Big House family, but they now requested permission to hunt
on Cox land.

Arthur Cox had become a Methodist, the only one of his family
to do so, when, dissatisfied with the local Church of Ireland clergy,
a number of Protestants in the area changed their allegiance to a
travelling Methodist preacher who had impressed them. When he
married, in his fiftieth year, Arthur was still handsome, a tall man
with fine features, a full, greying beard and clear eyes which held a
gentle but steady gaze. His bride, Mary, was only thirty. She was a
good-looking woman, with large, dark eyes and a ready smile,
which revealed her happy disposition. Her confident and friendly
manner helped to bridge the age gap between herself and her
husband.

The couple's first son, born in 1891, was given his father's
name. Two years later James William (Bill), Trevor's father, was
born. There were four more children – Maud born in 1895, George
born in 1898, Harriet born in 1899 and Mary born in 1901. Arthur
Cox was a quiet, hardworking man. Older people in the village of
Croghan still remember that he liked to bathe all year round,
regardless of the weather, in the river which ran through his land.
In keeping with his religious beliefs he did not drink alcohol. He
attempted to instil into his children a love for the Bible. Every now
and then he would introduce family Bible readings at night, but
when the children's interest faltered he did not insist. He felt
strongly on issues like gambling on a Sunday and his children were
in the habit of stopping the clock sometime before midnight on
Saturday nights in order to continue a card game.

The nearby town of Boyle had a small Methodist community
but no resident clergyman. Consequently the Cox children were
baptised into the Church of Ireland and attended services at the

local Holy Trinity Church at Croghan. Mary Cox had been raised in the Church of Ireland and in spite of her husband's adherence to Methodism, he regularly attended Sunday services there with the rest of the family. Occasionally a travelling Methodist clergyman arrived at Millbrook on horseback to stay a few days. Members of the Methodist community from Boyle and its environs would gather at Millbrook and a service would be conducted in the drawing-room. Sometimes the clergyman outstayed his welcome and even Arthur's patience came to an end. 'Give Mr McIntyre two eggs for his breakfast in the morning, Mary' he would advise his wife in the clergyman's hearing, 'he has a long journey ahead of him!'

In 1901 members of the Church of Ireland formed only 8.2% of the population of the whole country including Ulster.[6] In County Roscommon, as in the rest of Ireland, the descendants of the Ascendancy class who had ruled the country since colonisation, lived in the Big House and did not mix socially with local farmers, even those who were members of the same church. The Lloyd family entertained at Croghan House, but the Coxes visited the demesne only on occasions such as Sunday School picnics. In summer they received gifts of fruit from the estate and at Christmas there were presents for the children. The relationship was one of patronage rather than of friendship. Sunday service at the Holy Trinity Church in Croghan was one of the few occasions on which farmers came into contact with the world of the Big House. There the Cox family heard the artist, Sir William Orpen, a regular visitor to Croghan House, read the Sunday Lesson. Another visiting member of the congregation was the poet and composer, Percy French.

With several families of cousins living in the area, the Coxes had their own social circle. In the previous generation, Mark Cox's brother, Robert, had five children and his son, John, who inherited the farm adjoining Millbrook also had a family of five who grew up in Croghan. By the end of the nineteenth century, therefore, there were numerous relatives settled within a radius of thirty miles, and all of them were Protestants. Arthur Cox's family also had Catholic friends, particularly in childhood, but the religious divide still existed among adults. As farmers the family encountered their Catholic neighbours in the course of their daily lives and they cooperated with them at busy times of the year, but their close friends were Protestants of their own class.

Mary Cox, Trevor's grandmother, was a woman of strong views, with a vibrant personality. Her sense of humour and her kindness ensured that her children grew up in a genial, relaxed atmosphere. Because Arthur was already a middle-aged man when they married and the more retiring personality, it was her presence which dominated the home. She could laugh at her own shortcomings and liked to remind her children of an occasion when she left Millbrook to visit Dublin. Before locking the house she decided to take in the door-mat from the hall door in case it should be stolen during her absence. Having put the mat in a safe place she then set out for Dublin leaving the door of the house open.

The Cox children attended the Bishop Hodson Grammar School at Elphin and travelled there each day by a pony and trap. A small school with only about 25 pupils enrolled, it catered exclusively for Protestants. It was run by Canon Irwin, a well-known Classics scholar, assisted by a young monitor. The five-mile journey from Croghan to Elphin was often difficult in winter. If the children protested, Arthur Cox was quick to point out 'If those little Horan girls can cycle to the Convent, you can take the pony and trap to school!' The girls of the family were more academically orientated than the boys and their mother was determined that they should have the best opportunities that could be afforded. She would often remark with a degree of perception and determination unusual in a woman of her time: 'A man can always scrape a living somehow, but a woman must have a proper means of supporting herself'. Her eldest daughter, Maud, was one of Canon Irwin's most promising pupils and so it was decided that she should go to boarding-school in Dublin. The younger girls followed and Maud later graduated from University College Galway and became a teacher, while Harriet ran a successful boarding-house and Mary the youngest, became a doctor.

As Arthur Cox became increasingly incapacitated by arthritis, he handed over the running of the farm to his eldest son. His youngest son, George, was also interested in farming but realised that Millbrook could not support two families and emigrated to Canada. Bill, Trevor's father, was a more diligent scholar and when he finished school in Elphin he became a student at the Sparkhill-Brown Business School on St Stephen's Green in Dublin. He intended to become a bank official. At this time almost a third of those employed in Irish banks were members of the Church of Ireland, a very high proportion considering the percentage of Protestants in the country.[7] Consequently Protestant influence in the banking world was substantial. Bill's first attempt to join the Bank of Ireland was unsuccessful because he failed the medical test – his chest expansion was found to be less than the regulations required. Mary Cox was not going to allow her son's plan for his future to be so easily upset, so she bought him an apparatus for muscle expansion exercises and then travelled to Dublin by train and made an appointment to see one of the bank's directors. 'You must give my son a job!' she told him politely but firmly. At the next Bank of Ireland examination Bill succeeded and in 1913 he was appointed to a branch of the bank in Dundalk.

Bill Cox, like the other members of his family, had an affable manner. Tall, with an extremely erect bearing, he might have been taken for a military man. In fact he was a very mild person and though punctilious as a banker he generally liked a quiet, easy-going life. In Trevor's novel *Fools of Fortune* Mr Quinton, Willie's father, has similar characteristics:

> My father liked a tranquil pace in all things, and time for thought ... his favourite walk was down the avenue, wrapped in the silence induced by the beech trees that celebrated Napoleon's defeat. Their branches looped and interwove overhead, their leaves held off the sky: in spring and summer the avenue of Kilneagh was as silent as a cave, which was when my father liked it best.
>
> (FF 15)

In Dundalk Bill met Gertrude Davison, a 'lady clerk' at the town's branch of the Ulster Bank. Gertrude, or Gertie, was a slight, very pretty girl with delicate features, bright blue eyes and a shy smile. Her reserved manner contrasted with the gregariousness of the Coxes and although she too came from Protestant farming stock, she grew up in County Armagh, an area very different from Roscommon, with a majority Protestant population and strongly Unionist in politics.

The Davisons came originally from near Dundee in Scotland, arriving in Ireland in the late sixteenth or early seventeenth century. The proximity of the Antrim and Down coastlines to Scotland ensured that there was a strong Scottish presence in these counties, even before the systematic colonisation of Ulster in the early seventeen hundreds. Family lore suggests that they arrived in Ireland before the departure of the illustrious O'Neills from the country in 1607. At the time the name was spelt Davidson and the story of how the second 'd' was deleted involves an encounter between the first Davidson to arrive in the country and O'Neill, one of the last great chieftains of Gaelic Ireland. The Davidsons settled in Tyrone, O'Neill's territory. Their arrival was resented and the head of the family was challenged to a duel. Davidson declined to meet the chieftain in single combat and instead it was agreed that both men's names should be nailed to a tree and each should fire three shots from a crossbow at the other's name. If O'Neill hit Davidson's name, the intruder would be obliged to move away from Tyrone and if Davidson pierced O'Neill's name, then the family would be allowed to stay. The chieftain's second arrow transfixed the Davidson scroll, shooting the second 'd' from the name. The Davidsons duly moved from Tyrone to Antrim where they made their home, and from then on the name was spelt Davison.[8]

By the time the family settled in Ireland in the early seventeenth century, the eastern part of Ulster had already begun to resemble England in appearance and character. The land was cultivated and the houses were sturdy and neat. During the following century the area became relatively prosperous as the linen industry expanded. The Davisons were pioneers in the trade and when members of the family moved south from Antrim to a richly cultivated and fertile valley in Armagh, they took with them their textile-making skills. By the beginning of the nineteenth century Thomas Davison, a linen draper, or dealer, was living with his family in the picturesque townland of Ardress, just outside the County Armagh village of Loughgall. There was a strong sense of community in the area, but demarcation lines were clearly drawn between the various religious denominations. Sectarian strife was rarely overt although Sloane's Bar in Loughgall was famous as the place where the Orange Order was founded in 1795 after a fight between a Protestant group, the

Peep o' Day Boys and their Catholic rivals, the Defenders. The bloody encounter took place at the Diamond outside the village of Loughgall.

When James Davison, Trevor's great-grandfather, married Lydia Anne Sinclair in 1846, the Great Famine was raging in the west of Ireland. In Armagh, however, the effects of local crop failure were of little significance because of the thriving linen industry. Following the family tradition, James Davison was a linen draper, and had sufficient means to build a house in Ardress large enough for his six children. In spite of their comfortable circumstances, however, the family suffered considerable misfortune. Two of their sons, Sinclair and Simon died in infancy, while a third, James, who had qualified as a doctor at Dublin's Royal College of Physicians, died of tuberculosis only six months after finishing his studies. A year later his sister, Catherine Adelaide, succumbed to the same disease.

A certain mystery surrounds young Doctor James Davison, who died before his twenty-third birthday. An Irishman, using the same name, address in County Armagh and medical qualifications, set himself up as a doctor in Australia three years after James's death. Although he practised as Doctor James Davison, this second doctor was otherwise known as John Sinclair Davison. He married in Australia, but later deserted his family and subsequently disappeared. John Sinclair Davison was never registered with the Australian Medical Board and the only Davison to qualify as a doctor at the time in Dublin was James Davison of Ardress. The evidence would suggest that the man who practised under the name of James Davison in Australia was someone who was familiar with the Ardress man and his family and was aware of his death. Perhaps he was a friend or an unsuccessful classmate, or even a relative.

Two brothers of James Davison survived to adulthood, the elder of whom, Thomas, married Jane Elizabeth Berry in 1886 and purchased a farm at Causnagh, not far from Ardress. Jane Elizabeth's mother was dead and because her father was a commercial traveller and frequently away from home, the girl was raised by two aunts who lived near Loughgall. A handsome young woman with luxuriant fair hair, Jane Elizabeth had a genteel upbringing and was a fine pianist. She was also headstrong and used to getting her own way. Whenever she made up her mind about something, she would stand with her arms clasped firmly behind her back, and there was no gainsaying her wishes. Her marriage to James Davison was happy, however, and six children were born to the couple, four girls and two boys. Gertrude (Gertie), Trevor's mother, born in 1894, was the fifth child and the third girl. For a long time she was the youngest of the family; she was eight years of age when her sister, Henrietta (Hetty) was born in 1902.

Shortly before Gertie's birth, her parents moved back to Ardress. Her grandfather was now in the last years of his life and her father, Thomas, took over the running of the linen business and also of the farm which had been built up over the years. Gradually, James Davison had acquired land and a modest amount of property, small dwellings which were leased to cottiers. An enterprising and mischievous cousin, Charles, was in the habit of charging these cottage dwellers a penny each to see them safely past the Davison linen yard, where a very temperamental boiler constantly threatened to explode. Although the family continued to produce a small amount of linen, by the end of the century the farm had become its main source of income. Like most farms in the region, the Davisons grew apples. The county's orchards had been cultivated as early as the seventeenth century by the English settlers who arrived from Worcestershire, bringing with them a knowledge of apple-growing from the Vale of Evesham.

Life in Ardress was both structured and stable, with a great belief in the importance of security. The men of the family joined the Free Masons, not because of any philosophical commitment to the society's principles, but because membership ensured protection for dependants in the event of unexpected hardships. Social life was limited to the confines of the neighbourhood, with young people 'ceilidhing' – visiting each other's houses for evenings of song and talk, but the young women were always seen home at the end of the day by a male relative. Alcohol was frowned upon and was never allowed in the Davison household. There was a strong work ethic in the family and it was expected that even the women should be self-supporting. The eldest girl, Lydia, became a school matron while her sister, Adelaide, managed a temperance hotel – both professions which often appear in William Trevor's work – and in 1915, when the Great War saw a large exodus of young men to the British army, Gertie was among the first women to be employed by the Ulster Bank.

The first two years of Gertie Davison's working life were spent in the northern town of Newtownards. In 1917 she was transferred to Dundalk and, apart from a short sojourn in Cavan, she spent the rest of her working life there, resigning from her job shortly before her marriage. In the following year, only a few months after his first meeting with Gertie Davison, Bill Cox was transferred to the Bank of Ireland branch at Mountbellew, a small town in the western county of Galway.

The couple, who were to become William Trevor's parents, continued to keep contact, but not long after their separation the country was engulfed in political turmoil and communications became increasingly difficult. Guerilla-style attacks made by the newly organised Irish Republican Army, in search of arms to further their cause of separation from Britain, led to acts of retribution against the whole population, particularly after the arrival in Ireland of a specially recruited police auxiliary force, popularly known as the Black-and-Tans. By 1920 a bitter Anglo-Irish war was raging in the country. Travel was both difficult and dangerous and meetings between the young couple were of necessity brief and infrequent. As a result there was little opportunity for them to get to know each other.

Meanwhile in Croghan, the Big House was raided by Republicans who came in search of guns and ammunition. The Lloyd family was attending church at the time and the servants were locked up by the raiders who made off undetected. The Coxes were largely undisturbed, although as Protestants they were viewed with some suspicion by the extreme Nationalists and on one occasion their cattle were driven off their land – a gesture to warn them against any opposition to the Republican movement. But since they had never been landlords, nor had ever been involved in politics, they were not considered targets by either side.

The war was still in progress when Bill Cox and Gertie Davison became engaged and as his fiancée she was now introduced to the family and visited Millbrook for the first time. She found the encounter disconcerting; the ambience at Croghan was very different from the more sombre atmosphere in which she had been raised in Armagh. Her extreme reserve and her strong sense of propriety were at odds with the somewhat lackadaisical ways at Millbrook. Her son was to inherit both his mother's shyness and his father's benevolent manner.

The Coxes' land was already beginning to show signs of neglect as young Arthur took little interest in the daily work of the farm. Instead he frittered away his time hunting, gambling and generally living beyond his means. He spent whole days away, leaving the house in his working clothes and then retrieving his good suit from the garden where he had thrown it from the bedroom window so that he could escape from the farm unnoticed, to enjoy socialising. His father was now in his eighties and bedridden. His mother attempted to keep the farm functioning, doing the usual farmhouse duties herself and supervising the single workman they could afford to employ. Eventually, however, the land was taken over by the bank and young Arthur, unable to cope with his debts, fled to Canada. The eldest daughter, Maud, a teacher, attempted to buy back the farm, with the financial support of the Bowe family of Boyle and George returned home from Canada to help his sister work it. The task proved too much, however, and the land and house were sold before the end of the decade. By then Trevor's grandfather, Arthur Cox, was dead and his grandmother, Mary, went to live with her second daughter, Harriet, in Belfast, where she died a short time later.

Trevor's parents, Bill Cox and Gertie Davison, were married in the Church of Ireland Parish Church in Howth, County Dublin, on 14 July 1921. Three days earlier a truce had brought the Anglo-Irish War to an end. The Republicans had lost large numbers of their guerrilla fighters, the British government was being increasingly criticised for its conduct of the war in Ireland and above all a majority of the Irish people longed for peace. In October talks between both sides began in London; in early December a treaty was signed and the Irish Free State came into being. A clause in the agreement allowed the six Unionist-dominated counties of Northern Ireland, including Armagh, to remain outside the Free State if they so wished. This area formed its own government and continued as part of the United Kingdom.

In Mountbellew life was peaceful for the first year of the Coxes' marriage, but in the summer of 1922 dissatisfaction with the terms of the treaty led to the outbreak of Civil War in the Free State. One morning Bill Cox found that the four wheels of his much prized Morris Cowley had been removed during the night by Anti-Treaty soldiers urgently in need of them for their own makeshift transport. He replaced the wheels but for the remainder of the war he conscientiously removed them from the car each time he returned from a journey.

The Coxes had always felt themselves to be unambiguously Irish, although they had never given active support to the Nationalist struggle. Now their sympathies lay with the Pro-Treaty side in the Civil War, as the party most ready to offer security to the Protestant minority. Michael Collins, one of the signatories of the treaty and a senior member of the country's provincial government, had already recognised their right to protection and was ready to accept their allegiance to the newly constituted Free State. In Trevor's novel *Fools of Fortune*, Collins appears as a minor character sketched in a sympathetic light as he accepts financial support for his cause from a rural Protestant family:

> I remember being surprised to hear my mother saying she had liked Collins the first time she met him ... Collins had an honest laugh, she insisted, his blue eyes had tenderness in them.
>
> (FF38)

In January 1923 the Coxes' first child was born in Mountbellew. She was christened Mary Constance but was called June in the family. The civil war was abating and finally came to an end in May 1923. Nine months later the family moved to the south of the country, to Mitchelstown in County Cork, where four years later William Trevor's personal history begins.

Part I

'Behind the lace curtains'

North of Mitchelstown lie the Galtee Mountains and to the west are the Ballyhouras: this is the country immortalised in Edmund Spenser's *The Faerie Queen* with its shadowy woods and 'gentle Mulla' – the River Awbeg. Nearby also is Bowen's Court, the home of the novelist Elizabeth Bowen. In the late 1920s Mitchelstown was very much a farmers' town, its wide squares providing ample space for buyers, sellers and their livestock on fair days. The town's castle was already a ruin, having been burnt to the ground during the Irish Civil War, but by the beginning of the 1930s the town's economy was improving, due mainly to the organisation of the local farmers' Dairy Cooperative. It was well provided with schools, banks, hotels and members of all the necessary professions. Transport to Cork City, thirty-five miles away, was readily available through a regular train service.

Trevor's first memories are of Mitchelstown. He was born there on 24 May 1928 at Upper Cork Street, in a semi-detached house adjoining the town's Police Station. It was the beginning of life in the small towns of Ireland, the first three in County Cork:

> My earliest memories are of County Cork: of sunshine and weeds in a garden at Mitchelstown, Civic Guards in the barracks next door, a tarred gate; of dark limestone steps in Youghal, and a backyard tap in Skibbereen. These three small towns, to the north, east and west of Cork City have only slight, perfunctory claims to fame. A rare breed of spider is attracted to Mitchelstown's caves; its martyrs, of 1887, are not forgotten; more recently, processed cheese put it on the map. Youghal is where Sir Walter Raleigh lived, in Myrtle Lodge by the gates of St Mary's Protestant Church. The *Skibbereen Eagle* warned a Russian Czar that it was watching his every move.
>
> To the stranger they might be three towns anywhere in Ireland: big Catholic church, old Protestant graves, a cinema struggling on, haphazardly parked cars, turf smoke

in the back streets, pubs and the Angelus, dancing on a Friday. But the county to which they belong has its own insistent idiosyncrasy, as marked in its changing landscape as in its singsong intonation. It is the county of the Blackwater and the Lee, spacious and unhurried, the most varied in Ireland. The lush farming land of neighbouring Limerick and Tipperary influences its northern boundaries. The Waterford coastline does not obediently change character when Waterford has finished with it. West Cork has been filched from Kerry.

Going back sets nostalgia right; time-worn impressions are corrected. Going back is a lesson in proportion, an exercise in give-and-take, more revelation than *déjà-vu*. Sixty years on, Mitchelstown has a beaten look that memory has failed to register, its shops economically squat, its skyline humble beneath the mountains that make it seem as if someone has sat on it. The woman in the chemist's remembers my mother. The town's doing well, the proprietor of a drapery and footwear business says, but even so the jobs in the bacon factories and the creameries aren't enough to go round. All the time the population's increasing.

(*Excursions in the Real World* 1-2)

It decreased by five in 1931 when the Bank of Ireland moved the family to Youghal, a third child, Alan, having been born the year before. Youghal, at the mouth of the Blackwater, is an ancient town, its name derived from the Gaelic *Eo-Chaille* or Yew Forest, the remains of which are still to be found beneath the surface of the hinterland. It exudes a sense of history. Rumoured to have been founded by the Phoenicians who came to trade, Youghal was later settled by the Vikings – the place where Spenser wrote the opening stanzas of *The Faerie Queen* and the town in which Shakespeare is believed to have played with a touring company from Bristol, and to have found the model for his character Shylock in the local Jewish Lord Mayor.

It had a violent history too, since it was a fortress and vital to English security in Ireland. There was always the risk of invasion from the sea, because to the south there is nothing but open water between the town and the north coast of Spain. The surrounding land also posed a threat: down the centuries it was populated by 'native' Irish who were usually hostile to the English forces in control. In the winter of 1649 Youghal became Oliver Cromwell's headquarters during his campaign to subdue the south of the country. Later, in the eighteenth century, it became a 'closed borough' totally in the power of the Protestant minority who ruled, and no Catholic could become a 'freeman' with civil rights within the town. The newly built Marshalsea or gaol was a symbol of terror to the native population who lived in the surrounding countryside. Torture was regularly used there to extract information from suspected rebels who, once they had revealed what they knew, were hanged from the windows of the Clock Tower.

In the 1930s Youghal was a depressed sea-side town which in spite of its poverty remained, at least on the surface, graceful and elegant, its buildings evoking a past which seemed ever present. In summer it was a holiday resort, its seven miles of beautiful beach particularly attracting day-trippers from the city of Cork, who came on what was known as the 'sea-breeze' train. They had the added advantage of being classed as bona fide travellers and could consequently avail of the generous licensing laws which then operated, allowing people who had come a distance of three miles of more to drink alcohol outside the normal opening times of the public houses. Farmers from the surrounding area came too, many not to bathe but to paddle at the shore and drink each morning a glass of sea-water. They were known locally as 'Olishers' from their habit of calling out to each other in Gaelic 'Ar Olais?' (Did you drink?). Along the promenade were Perks' amusements and performing Pierrots, both of which brought shrieks from delighted children to mingle with the cries of the gulls. Although Trevor's novel *The Children of Dynmouth* is set in an English seaside town, the author draws on his own memories of Youghal for details which become the texture of his fiction. Like Dynmouth, Youghal had once:

> been renowned for its lacemaking ... unspoilt, a seaside
> resort of limited diversions, its curving promenade and
> modest pier stylish with ornamental lamp-posts.
>
> (CD 7)

The ferry was a feature. Both sea and river separate the town from Monatrea and Ardmore, which lie opposite. Since there was only one bridge, this municipal ferry boat, operating under a charter granted to the town in Elizabethan times, made regular crossings. Children made the journey twice daily to go to and from school. Once again particulars of the author's real experience merge into his created world:

> He always arrived at the pier before the ferryboat had begun its journey from the quays on the other side. A couple of donkey-carts were usually there before him, their churns of milk unloaded and waiting. The donkeys would nibble the short grass, or stand patiently, until their owners returned with an empty churn from the creamery lorry .... Three girls went over to work in Renehan's fish sheds and another four to attend the convent school that Tom would continue to attend himself until he was old enough to pass into the Christian Brothers'.
>
> (SG 27)

Trevor's first experience of the classroom – in a convent school – brought him into direct contact with rural Irish Catholic life and gave him an easy knowledge and understanding of attitudes and feelings of which many people of his religion and class remained in ignorance. It also gave him his first experience of being an outsider. At six years of age he was already aware of being part of something and yet apart from it – of being an onlooker.

Together the two brothers walked along the path to the convent each morning and entered their classroom, in which the nuns had earlier eaten their breakfast. The Loreto sisters in Youghal had very little money: the convent supported itself by taking in 'lady guests' who lived and died in the care of the sisters and who were given the best rooms in the house. School fees, at £3 a term, supplemented their needs, but the school had to be housed in the rooms the nuns used themselves. So every morning after breakfast the refectory furniture was rearranged and desks were set out for the children. When their charges went home in the afternoon, the desks were removed and the sisters then had their second meal of the day.

During Religious Education, Protestant children waited in the cloakroom, and were sometimes brought to the kitchen and given little treats by the lay sisters who did most of the domestic work of the convent:

> ... on one occasion a lay sister brought him down to the kitchen and lifted him up onto a table so that he could watch the bread being made. Sometimes if they passed through the cloakroom the lay sisters would give him raisins or marzipan.
>
> (SG 33)

But outside the convent the harsher aspects of life – and death – impinged:

> Behind the town, in a henhouse on the old back road, a man shot himself. This man's life was hell, it was whispered, and the henhouse developed an eeriness that the chatter of birds accentuated. The King of England died, that old bearded face in the *Daily Sketch*, the funeral service on the wireless. Another man died, a man who used to come quite often to our house, who had the habit of very finely chopping up his salad. And the woman we bought herrings from died. But all this death seemed quite in order at the time, except for the violence in the henhouse.
>
> (ERW 5 -6)

There was a more immediate tragedy. A locally owned boat, the Nelly Fleming, disappeared without trace on a regular run from Wales to Youghal. The members of the crew were all local men and when the boat failed to return as expected, wives, parents and children of those on board gathered along the quays, from which position they could see the mouth of the bay. As the hours passed and it became obvious that all hope of rescue had gone, the shawl-clad women began to keen in the traditional manner, their wails drifting up to Clifton on the night air. From a window of the Loreto Convent a priest gave Absolution to the missing men. The whole town was thrust into mourning by the event which touched so many families.

Youghal itself died, in a way, Trevor has written, when again:

> ... the yellow removal vans – Nat Ross of Cork – carted our possessions off, westward through Cork itself and through the town people called Clonakilty-God-Help-Us, through untidy Bandon, to Skibbereen, the back of beyond.
>
> (ERW 6)

It was the Bank of Ireland's policy to move its provincial officials to another town when it promoted them. The frequency of these moves – new towns, new faces, new houses – took a toll in a marriage that was already beginning to fall apart. Childhood was not easy, Trevor recalls:

> My mother was tiny, capricious and beautiful, firm of purpose, fiery and aloof, with a sharp tongue, and an eccentric sense of humour that often took you by surprise ... My father liked to tell stories rather than jokes – stories about people or events that amused him. He smoked Sweets Aftons, drank anything he was offered, and had a flair for picking winners ... They made no bones about their shattered relationship, yet in all the quarrels that exploded, in all the accusations and recriminations, in all the brooding silences, there was never a clue to the truth that lay at the heart of their marriage's failure.

(ERW 19-20)

In spite of the beauty of its surrounding countryside, Skibbereen was not, in the late 1930s, a tourist attraction. Its several hotels catered for commercial travellers, most of whom were known to each other. But whenever a new face appeared in one of the hotels, the others, anxious to know what firm he represented, immediately asked 'Who do you do for?' As a result all commercial travellers were known as 'who-do-you-do-fors'. Skibbereen was as different from Youghal as two small towns in Munster can be, noisy with horses and carts in the narrow streets, cattle on their way to market fouling footpaths. The many pubs which opened onto the streets exuded a smell of whiskey mixed with sawdust. The journey to school was a mile and a half, through the centre of the town, past the grey statue of the Maid of Erin. Nearby an undertaker's establishment had a steady sideline trade in sweets and ice-cream. As Trevor in his late fifties remembered:

> Horses and carts rattled back from the creamery with empty churns, returning to the farms they'd come from. The green wooden shutters had not yet been lifted down from the windows of Meath's nor the red ones from Dungan's. The windows of the public houses were empty except for notices that said *Guinness is Good for You* and *John Jameson*. Padlocks secured the doors of Traynor's Picture Palace.

(SG 30)

School was a Methodist dame-school, where for the first time Trevor wrote essays under the demanding tutelage of Miss Mary Willoughby, whose efforts he has never forgotten and still appreciates. But school began to be an uphill struggle because too often there were missed weeks or months - sometimes whole terms - while another move took place: in the autumn of 1939, soon after war broke out in Europe, the Nat Ross vans came again. This time the journey was out of County Cork altogether, to Tipperary town.

Children delight in change until it happens. What was left behind in West Cork were Christmas parties and summer picnics, a lace-curtain Protestant world that was under-valued at the time, but later greatly missed. From Skibbereen:

> Twice a year perhaps, on Saturday afternoons, there was going to Cork to the pictures. Clark Gable and Myrna Loy in *Too Hot to Handle, Mr Deeds Goes to Town*. No experiences in my whole childhood, and no memory, has remained as deeply etched as these escapes to the paradise that was Cork. Nothing was more lovely or more wondrous than Cork itself with its magnificent array of cinemas: the Pavilion, the Savoy, the Palace, the Ritz, the Lee and Hadji Bey's Turkish Delight factory. Tea in Thompson's or the Savoy, the waitresses with silver-plated tea-pots and buttered bread and cakes, and other people eating fried eggs with rashers and chipped potatoes at half-past four in the afternoon. The sheer sophistication of Thompson's or the Savoy could never be adequately conveyed to a friend in Skibbereen who had not had the good fortune to experience it. The Gentlemen's lavatory in the Victoria Hotel had to be seen to be believed, the Munster Arcade left you gasping. For ever and for ever you could sit in the middle stalls of the Pavilion watching Claudette Colbert, or Spencer Tracy as a priest, and the earthquake in San Francisco. And forever afterwards you could sit while a green-clad waitress carried the silver-plated tea-pot to you, with cakes and buttered bread. All around you was the clatter of life and of the city, and men of the world conversing, and girls' laughter tinkling. Happiness was everywhere.
>
> (ERW 8-9)

All that was over. Tipperary during the first years of the Emergency – as Hitler's war was called in Ireland – seemed remote and gloomy. The war had brought isolation to the whole of the Free State, which was now virtually cut off from the outside world.

In small towns the sense of claustrophobia was particularly strong as people were forced to look inward, in the absence of any outside stimuli. In Tipperary, for example, one of the great preoccupations of the opening months of the conflict was with the new public lighting restrictions. The black-out system was something of a farce since street lighting was reduced or cut off, while private individuals were left to comply with the government's recommendations or not, as they wished. Farmers found themselves driving their cattle to market in the early mornings through unlit streets. The resulting chaos in the town eventually caused the authorities to change their policy and the public lighting arrangements were subsequently modified. Local issues became magnified as people attempted to come to terms with constraints, such as censorship and rationing, which were considered necessary in a country determined to preserve its neutrality in the midst of major hostilities. The Irish government was anxious to demonstrate its sovereignty by refusing to follow the British dominion countries into the war. Instead, in the tradition of other small European states, it chose to remain neutral.

The move to Tipperary in 1939 brought with it another educational hiatus. There was the usual period of no school at all, a couple of unsatisfactory arrangements made – the Church of Ireland national school, a failed Christian Brother who came daily to the house – and then there was Miss Quirke. She was a young Catholic girl at a loose end in a farmhouse at Oola, a few miles from the town.

> Fair-haired, pink-cheeked, she was probably little more than a school girl, although she seemed old, and wise. Her soft, solemn smile and calm voice, her unhurried movements, her modesty, her confidence, all supported this impression.
>
> Every morning she rode in on her BSA, a breath of fresh air from Oola. Often she came with brambles or sprigs of birch and oak snipped from the hedges. These were arranged on the table in front of my brother and myself and we were instructed to paint them in watercolours. Poster paint was produced; ink was mixed with glue and patterns made with combs cut from cardboard. We were told about the continental Sunday, and the Guillotine and the Champs-Elysees. We were shown pictures of *baguettes* and *ficelles*, so very different

from our own dreary pan loaves and turn-overs. Joan of Arc and Niall of the Nine Hostages were rescued from the dust that had years ago settled on them. Mathematical subjects were less distasteful than they had been. Even geography had its moments, through admittedly not many.

Patiently, without anger, errors and aberrations were corrected, a Relief nib forever dipping into the bottle of Stephens' red ink Miss Quirke uncorked every morning when she sat down. Her composure was startling the more it was in evidence, her knowledge seemingly endless. She knew why rain came down in drops. She knew the names of clouds, and how to bind a book and the exact town in America where the electric chair had been invented, and by whom, and whose life it had first claimed. She knew the names of the Chicago gangsters, and that the story of William Tell was a myth, and that it was all nonsense about St George and the dragon. She described the Famine ships that had taken the starving Irish across the Atlantic, how every day more bodies had been dropped over the side, how only the fortunate had survived. She read *Lorna Doone* aloud.

(ERW 25-6)

It was in Tipperary that Trevor, at eleven, began to read for himself. In Youghal his father had read him the fairy stories of Hans Andersen and the Grimms, in Skibbereen the Greyfriars stories. Being read to was life's second best pleasure, after going to the pictures, and it seemed that it was now finished with forever. The household possessed two bookcases – one containing the school stories of Trevor's sister, the other a varied assortment of thrillers and romances, and the works of Charles Dickens and Jane Austen, obtained with Sweet Afton cigarette papers. Among the thrillers was Edgar Wallace's *The Crimson Circle*.

This was the first book Trevor read all the way through and with the delight that reading has offered him ever since. Nothing else in the two bookcases matched its ingenuity, its tension, its marvellous denouement – until years later Dickens was somewhat tentatively approached. The shelves of the Argosy library in Hogan's newsagents – a few doors down in Tipperary's Main Street – were pillaged for thrillers and detective novels. The glittering worlds of John Creasy and Peter Cheyney, Leslie Charteris and C D H and M Cole were wonderlands of pleasure. Agatha Christie's *Ten Little Niggers* and *One, Two Buckle my Shoe* were masterpieces. A penny it cost to borrow a book; if you were flush, you could actually buy one in paperback, for tuppence, in Mackie's at the other end of the town. It was in Tipperary that Trevor first wanted to be a writer.

Here, too, he first experimented with film:

> My brother and I were given a cinematograph, an inexpensive toy that promised hours of wholesome winter fun. It came with off-cuts of films featuring Red Indians on horseback, and was lit by a tricky arrangement of torch battery and bulb. You darkened the room, turned a handle, and the Indians appeared on the wallpaper, waving tomahawks and chasing something that never came into the picture.
>
> The conjunction between bulb and battery regularly failed, or the film jammed and tore, or the repetition of the Indians' pursuit of the unknown became tedious, even when the film was run backwards. So we scraped at both sides of the off-cuts with a penknife, ridding them of the galloping Indians and leaving us with transparent strips of celluloid. On these we inscribed with pen and ink a series of grimacing match-stick figures, which jerkily changed position on the wallpaper. Inspired we added red ink to blue, and Technicolour came to our screen.
>
> [From: *Here's Looking at you, Kid! Ireland Goes to the Pictures.* p.127]

Tipperary's cinema had burnt down, shortly after its showing of *Idiot's Delight* with Clark Gable and Norma Shearer. Mr W.G. Evans, proprietor of the town's leading bicycle shop – a man of entrepreneurial genius – decided to build another. He called it the Excel, in which, according to a local newspaper report he has 'left nothing undone as regards screens, exits, furnishing and safety'.[1] In spite of this, however, when Mr Evans applied for a licence to open the premises to the public, he was refused, on the grounds that the building had been constructed without any reference to the Board of Works and in addition there were allegations that Mr Evans had not paid union rates to the labourers he employed on the job. Arguments went back and forth as local personalities took the opportunity to score against each other and the licence was deferred on a number of occasions, until adjustments to the building were carried out in accordance with the wishes of the local authorities. Eventually the doors were opened and the public flocked in to see films like *The Rains Came* with Tyrone Power and Myrna Loy. The poster promised rather fulsomely 'a modern story of fabulous India – a picture amazing in its realism ... a surging drama ... with unprecedented spectacular scenes of earthquake and flood'. It also offered Errol Flynn and Olivia de Havilland in *Dodge City* which it stated was 'photographed entirely in glorious Technicolour and set in the American Middle West, amid the ceaseless clash of reckless men and relentless nature'. For Trevor these films provided never-to-be-forgotten afternoons of wonder and excitement in what was otherwise a dreary spell in his life. In his work, he frequently refers to the films of this period, but more significantly his economy in presenting characters and his montage method of narrative, whereby brief scenes are selected and pieced together, show the strong influence which his early interest in cinema was to have on his writing. This technique has the added advantage of making his stories very suitable for adaptation to the screen.

More than forty-five years later he wrote about Tipperary's Excel Cinema in his novella *Nights at the Alexandra*. The story, set in a country town in Ireland during the war years, tells of the relationship between Harry, the fifteen-year-old son of a Protestant timberyard owner and a young English woman, whose elderly German husband builds a cinema as a present for her. The English woman becomes the focus of Harry's romantic dreams and the cinema an expression of her exotic nature. To the boy it represents all that is beautiful and luxurious:

> For the interior walls they choose the shades of amber that later became familiar to me, darker at the bottom, lightening to dusty paleness as the colour spreads over the ceiling. These walls must be roughly textured, they decree, the concave ceiling less so, the difference subtly introduced. Four sets of glass swing-doors catch a reflection of the marble steps that so astonished my father: the doors between the foyer and the auditorium are of the warm mahogany supplied by our timberyard. Long before the building is ready for it, they chose the blue-patterned carpet of the balcony, and the scarlet cinema-seats.
>
> (NA 44-5)

But the Excel cinema, Miss Quirke and Tipperary itself, were soon left behind. In the summer of 1941 – while the German

Panzer divisions were advancing into Russia and the Americans were taking over Iceland – the family moved to the Bank House in Abbey Square, Enniscorthy. This large, thriving County Wexford town, with the wide River Slaney flowing through it, overlooked by the historic Vinegar Hill, which was a rebel stronghold during the United Irishmen rising of 1798, is one of the most attractive in Ireland. In the 1940s memories of 1798 remained fresh in the folk memory of the area and in a short story called 'Autumn Sunshine', which Trevor sets in and around the town of Enniscorthy, the danger of past events being used to justify contemporary violence is explored, when a young Englishman connects the atrocities committed in late eighteenth century County Wexford with events in present day Northern Ireland.

The first six months in Enniscorthy passed without the rigours and demands of the classroom – apart from a brief attendance at the Tate School, Wexford, this proving to be wholly unsatisfactory within a couple of weeks. Boarding School – at Sandford Park in Dublin – was next on an unwelcome agenda:

> I was twelve years old on the morning of 28 April 1941, returning to boarding school by bus, from the town of Enniscorthy in the south-east corner of Ireland, to Dublin. Some time the previous January I had made this journey for the first time. I had waited with my brother outside the paper-shop where the bus drew in at the bottom of Slaney Hill. Our two trunks and our bicycles were on the pavement; other members of the family had come to wave good-bye. Too excited to say anything, we had watched the red and cream coloured bus approaching on the other side of the river, crossing the bridge, then slowing down. We had egg sandwiches and Toblerone. Our spirits were high.
>
> On this second occasion I was alone because my brother was ill. People had come to wave good-bye, bicycle and trunk were hoisted on to the roof of the bus and secured beneath a tarpaulin. A washbag and anything else necessary for the night was packed into a small suitcase known at the school as a pyjama suitcase. But everything was different also, dogged by a grim unease that the thirteen weeks following that first occasion had inspired. Journey to hell, I said to myself as the conductor handed me my ticket and my change. 'How're you doing?' he enquired, red-faced and cheery. Bleakly, I told him I was all right.

(ERW 29-30)

Hell was at its worst, first thing, when you woke up:

> You lay there listening to the noises coming from the three
> other beds – someone muttering in his sleep, someone
> softly snoring, the bedsprings creaking when there was a
> sudden movement. There were no curtains on the
> windows. The light of dawn brought silhouettes first, and
> then the reality of the room: the fawn top blankets, the
> boarded-up fireplace. You didn't want to go back to sleep
> because if you did you'd have to wake up again. 'Get out of
> that bed,' the Senior Boarder ordered when the bell went.
> 'Out at the double, pull the bedclothes back. Quick now!'
> He glared from the sheets, his acned features ugly on the
> pillow. He was said to pray before he rose.
>
> (ERW 31)

When it was founded at the turn of the century, Sandford
Park's ten acres of parkland were part of the countryside, but as the
Dublin suburbs grew on the south side of the city, the school
became surrounded by a network of streets, with red-brick houses,
shops and even a cinema outside its gates. The large Victorian
house provided accommodation for a small number of boarders –
during Trevor's time there, in the early 1940s, there were only
about twelve – and about eighty day-pupils. The headmaster, an
Englishman call A D Cordner, hailed from a military rather than
an academic background:

> Majestic in a blue suit, he was a man of considerable
> passion, the greater part of which lay in his love of cricket.
> He had two subsidiary obsessions, one for spelling-bees and
> the other for whistling the 'British Grenadiers'. The great
> nuisances in his life were the Sandford Cinema and men in
> semi-clerical dress who attempted to get into conversation
> with his boys, with the bespectacled Warren in particular.
> He had no scholastic qualifications of any kind. Once upon
> a time he'd played cricket for the Gentlemen of Ireland.
>
> (ERW 36)

In fictional form A D Cordner appears in Trevor's short story
'Downstairs at Fitzgerald's':

> Often he would pause as if he had forgotten what he was
> about and for a moment or two would whistle through his
> breath 'The British Grenadiers'. The only task he was ever
> known to perform were the calling out of names and the
> issuing of an occasional vague announcement at the

> morning assemblies which were conducted by Mr Horan.
> Otherwise he remained lodged in his own cloudlands, a
> faint, blue-suited presence, benignly unaware of the feuds
> that stormed among his staff or the nature of the sixty-eight
> children whose immediate destinies had been placed in his
> care.
>
> (CS 723)

A less sympathetic figure was the science master, H.E.
Dudgeon, thinly disguised in a number of Trevor stories including
'The Third Party':

> ... a Savonarola-like figure in a green suit, sadistically
> inclined ... in his foul laboratory, prodding at your ears
> with the sharp end of a tweezers until you cried out in pain.
>
> (CS 1139)

The chronic shortage of fuel during the war years meant that
the main school building was always cold. At weekends the
boarders gathered round a small fire in what was called 'the
lounge', listening to the strains of a violin echoing through the
building from a room at the top of the house occupied by L.N.
Horan, a master of whom Trevor was particularly fond and whose
name he retained in 'Downstairs at Fitzgerald's'.

Boredom was mixed with loneliness:

> The day boys used to come noisily up the short, suburban
> avenue on their bicycles and later ride noisily away. They
> were envied because they were returning to warmth and
> comfort and decent food, because after the weekends
> they'd talk about how they'd been to the Savoy or the
> Adelphi or even to the Crystal Ballroom.
>
> ('The Third Party', CS 1139).

Trevor hated boarding-school. In spite of the increasingly grim
atmosphere at home – 'behind the lace curtains that had been
altered to fit windows all over the south of Ireland' (ERW 23)
within a family held together for the sake of the children – the end
of each term was always a relief. Shackled by convention, the
marriage went on, long after love had drifted into indifference, into
irritation, into hatred in the end. But, somehow, shreds of warmth
survived: 'They gave their love to their children and were loved in
return, fiercely, unwaveringly.' (ERW 24)

School improved a bit as the years went on, but the gaps caused by so many interruptions and changes – Portlaoise (then Maryboro) and Galway were added in time to the list of towns – were never closed. It wasn't until, in the autumn of 1944, he entered the last of his many schools that Trevor began to want to learn, and by then it was rather too late.

> At night the lights of Dublin blinked below us, away from us to the sea. On a clear day, from halfway up Kilmashogue, you could see across to Wales. St Columba's with a reputation for aloofness, and skill on the hockey field, is set high in the Dublin mountains, established there in the 1840s by the Victorian cleric who was later to found Radley. 'Be ye as wise as serpents and as gentle as doves' had been the saint's catchphrase, as many a sermon reminded us.
>
> St Columba's in the only public school of its kind in the Republic of Ireland, small within a small minority yet with a certain *cachet*, more confident of itself now than once it was. 'That this House believes we are an outpost of empire' was a debating motion the term I arrived there for the last two years of my fragmentary education, knowing little of such delicate areas of life as art and music, the theatre and literature. My provincial accent was noticeable and was mocked. The rougher ambience of recent boarding establishments had not prepared me for the fact that pretty junior boys were called *bijous*, and that the poet Horace - laboured through with the assistance of Dr Giles's Keys to the Classics – was more interesting because of that. In all sorts ways it was at St Columba's where I first became aware that black and white are densities of more complicated greys.

(ERW 41)

The two years which Trevor was to spend at St Columba's were to prove extremely fruitful to the writer of the future. Over and over again he draws on his experiences at the school and the people he knew there as prototypes for events and characters in his writing. St Columba's is the model for the boarding-school to which Willie Quinton, the hero of *Fools of Fortune* goes, like his creator, unwillingly. In a letter to his mother Willie describes a typical day at the academy which lies 'exposed to the winds that swept across the gorse-laden hillsides'. (FF 83) Trevor's day followed the same pattern:

At a quarter past seven the rising bell is rung, and then the ten-minute bell. After the second one if you're caught in bed you are punished. Breakfast is at five to eight, and Chapel afterwards. Chapel is the centre of school life, so the headmaster says. He's an English clergyman, as round as a ball, with a crimson complexion. His wife wears blue stockings and has grey hair that bushes out from the side of her head ...

Classes go on all morning, with a break at eleven o'clock for milk. Buckets of it are placed on a table outside Dining Hall and you dip your mug in. That's a tradition here. So is flicking butter on to the wooden ceiling of Dining hall ... Classes continue after lunch and then there are games, tea and Preparation. Cloister cricket is a tradition too, but that's only played in the summer term. In class and Chapel and Dining Hall we have to wear gowns. On Sundays we wear surplices in Chapel, and the masters have academic hoods, all different colours.

(FF 82-3)

Traditionally about half of the teaching staff at St Columba's had been English, but their numbers had decreased since the outbreak of war and the implementation of a new regulation by the Irish Department of Education requiring all teachers to have a knowledge of the Irish language. The boys, all boarders, came from every part of the country. While some of their families had once been members of the Protestant Ascendancy class, most were engaged in the professions, in farming or in the business world. Big house families such as the Villiers Stewarts and the Somerville Larges sent their sons to St Columba's, but so did Jamesons, the whiskey makers. Some of the Ascendancy families might have chosen English schools for their sons had it not been for the war, but these people were now the exception rather than the rule.

Friendship began for Trevor at St Columba's. There had been friends before, in the small towns, at Sandford Park, but the friendship of adolescence had a particular potency, often enough to last a lifetime:

He is Stewart, K.J.; Kenneth Stewart; Stewart major. Long Stewart, the playful geography master has named him, not to be confused with Villiers Stewart or Goldfish Stewart, or Dull Stewart from somewhere in Antrim. His wavy fair hair is parted in the middle; his square features, unblemished by spots or acne, give the impression of having always been shaved. He is immaculately turned out. Too tall to look anything but ridiculous in the statutory school cap, he has obtained permission not to wear it: his bedside locker contains a brown felt hat. At sixteen, nothing about him is boyish. He is a masher, putting on the style.

Victoria Four-Thirty is the novel he talks about, by Cecil Roberts, marvellous. Francis Brett Young is recommended also, and Walpole and Cronin and Jamaica Inn. Later there is the discovery of Cakes and Ale and The Moon and Sixpence, then Crome Yellow and Brideshead Revisited. He has learned by heart the end of The Bridge of San Luis Rey. 'We ourselves shall be loved for a while and forgotten. But the love will have been enough … There is a land of the living and a land of the dead, and the bridge is love, the only survival, the only meaning.' As a classroom subject, only English interests him. He would like to write himself. He begins to read Rupert Brooke.

As I am, he is a small-town provincial, but the home life he talks about is vastly different from my own. He takes out girls – bank girls five or six years older than he is, who've even been engaged, girls from Sligo and Carrick-on-Shannon, girls on holiday at Rosses Point. His own town is Boyle in County Roscommon, famous for its excessive number of pubs.

(ERW 59)

There were other friends – John Gahan, Peter Somerville Large, David Hone, Michael Biggs, Ivor Earle. There was the Art Room: surprising himself – for he couldn't draw – Trevor found himself a regular presence there under the tutelage of the sculptor, Oisin Kelly:

'Oh, just get on with it,' Kelly, an exasperated art master, ordered. 'Just do it, for God's sake!'

And I did it because at least it would be a change from traipsing over the hillsides in search of a rock or a clump of gorse to sketch, or going to see what the ram was up to. What I had agreed to do instead was to carve an eagle in low relief. Anyone could, Kelly impatiently insisted.

He was wrong. If the chisel wasn't sharp enough it tore at the wood, leaving it shredded and hairy. Sharpening the chisel was a knack, and carving with it was a knack. The more you hacked the less the carefully pencilled outline resembled a proud bird of prey. Perspective disappeared. If you didn't clamp the wood firmly enough it slipped about, resisting all attentions; if you tightened the clamps they left an ugly indentation. If you dealt the chisel too powerful a blow with the trickily rounded mallet the eagle's claws weren't there any more. If you didn't look after your fingers they wouldn't be there either. Most of the time there was blood all over the place.

But there was something about the arduous, unsatisfactory activity that was appealing. When a delicate little gauge was as sharp as a razor it slipped delicately through the grain of the wood, and for an instant or two you could control it perfectly. The grain was a pattern to make use of, a means of suggesting concavity or depth, an emphasis when you wanted it to be. In time – five or six weeks –I finished the eagle and Kelly advised me simply to polish it with beeswax, but I chose instead to plaster on raw linseed oil, which had the effect of bringing out all the flaws. Kelly said I'd ruined it.

(ERW 51)

At Sandford Park, encouraged by his English master, J.J. Aughmuty, Trevor had written short stories instead of essays. 'An expert on the short story', Aughmuty had inscribed an end-of-term report, an opinion which hardened Trevor's resolve to become a writer of fiction. An unexpected talent for sculpture complicated matters somewhat. So did parental pressure to go on to Trinity College rather than into some form of journalism. *What on earth chance would your puny efforts have*, his mother wrote to him, *with so many war correspondents returning to look for work? Don't be ridiculous.* He settled for Trinity.

But now looking back, it is St Columba's he remembers more fondly and with greater vividness. He enjoyed the freedom of roving about the hills, the taste of culture, which he had not known before: the plays of W.B. Yeats and Synge performed, music, the talk of Blake and Henry Moore And T.S. Eliot. For a small-town boy, St Columba's was sophisticated, and a place to sharpen a sense of humour. It wasn't the public school which was to feature in Trevor's first successful novel *The Old Boys*, but it was while he was there that he realised school had a comic side. The dialogue of *The Old Boys* had its roots in the old-fashioned, mannered, idiom with which Trevor had become familiar in the restricted society of Protestant provincial life. The title of the novel refers to eight septuagenarians who have kept in touch since their schooldays:

'Do you recall,' said Mr Sole, tired for the moment of the subject, 'those chain letters that used to fascinate us so? You copied a letter six or eight times and forwarded half a crown to a specified stranger –'

'To the name at the top of the list.'

'And it was very bad luck to break the chain. One was warned against that.'

'An insidious business, those chains. Based on compulsion and fear. Some may have made a lot of money.'

'A chain of which I was an ardent link was begun by a British major in the Boer War. The man was dead, the letter claimed, and if I'm not mistaken there was talk of his having begun the chain as he lay expiring on the battlefield, the implication being that one insulted a soldier's memory if one did not play the required part.'

'There was a chain letter that got going at school. Burdeyon spoke of it. He likened it to current crime waves in America. "Gangster" was a great word of Burdeyon's. It was a new expression at the time, and of course he was a great one for modernity. "Gangsters! Gangsters!" he would yell, striding on to some upheaval in Dining Hall. There is a story of Swabey-Boyns' of how Burdeyon came upon him taking tomatoes from a greenhouse. "Arrest this gangster!" he cried to a nearby gardener, and Swabey-Boyns was led away on the end of a rope.'

(OB 30-1)

On his last evening at St Columba's Trevor played a part in the school's production of *Outward Bound* and then attended a ceremonial tea in the headmaster's drawing-room where other members of the staff dropped in to say good-bye:

We had planned, five or six of us, to spend that last night drinking cider in a field. But somehow, after the headmaster's party, I lost sight of the others or must have confused the arrangements, because I suddenly found myself alone, in my waterproof coat with the collar turned up. They had the cider and the two bottles of communion wine and the boxes of little cakes and the cigarettes. For all I knew they might have acquired a couple of maids as well. I ran in the moonlight, through the gardens and through the deer park and out on to the mountainside. I heard voices and I called out, and then stood still to listen for a reply. None came, and I knew that they were farther away than they seemed. I ran through the burnt gorse and I knew it was blackening my trousers and my pale waterproof coat.

I called out again, but when I stopped I couldn't hear the voices any more and I knew I must have been running in the wrong direction.

There had been a great roar in Chapel that night as we sang the end-of-term hymn. *Those returning make more faithful than before* ... Every time we had heard those words in the past we imagined the day when we would sing them for the last time, when we would roar them out because we would not now be more faithful than before, because we were not returning. I sat on a rock and looked down at the dark, scattered masses of the school. I remembered being told so often that the Chapel was the centre of school life. I remembered being told that one day I might make something of myself; more than a hint of doubt creeping into the handmaster's voice as he put forward this view ... I remembered St Patrick's Night, when some of us had risen at midnight and cycled the eight miles to Dublin. We had eaten a fried meal in a restaurant and had later called at the Shelbourne Hotel to demand whisky of the night porter. 'My father's staying here,' announced a boy we knew as Popeye Jameson. 'He'll see you right in the morning.' But the porter, although we gave him a shilling, would have no part of it.

I walked slowly, climbing a bit, away from the school and out onto a mountain road. I could no longer hear the faraway voices of my friends, and it wasn't until hours later, on the way back again, that I came across them. They were quieter now, but they had kept me some sustenance. We found suddenly that there wasn't much we could say, because already we were in the limbo. We no longer belonged to the world of school; yet we could not recognise what world it was that claimed us next.

'God, it'll be great,' one of us said, eyeing the future and assuming the best. 'Great,' we agreed; but the closer they came the cloudier seemed those halcyon days.

(Leaving School, *London Magazine*, 1964)

Trinity College Dublin was Trevor's natural destination. From its foundation in the late sixteenth century the college was the intellectual home of Irish Protestantism. For centuries Catholics were not welcome within its precincts and even after the removal in the late nineteenth century of regulations which discriminated against them, Trinity continued to be almost exclusively the preserve of middle-class Irish Protestants. Members of the Anglo-Irish Ascendancy continued to send their sons and daughters to Oxford or Cambridge and very few Irish Catholics were prepared to flout the authority of their church by attending a college which was disapproved of by their bishops because of its Protestant ethos. In addition, many young people of the Irish nationalist tradition found repugnant the college's reluctance to abandon the symbols of its former ties with Britain. The Union Jack continued to be flown over the college until 1935, 'God save the King' was played at Commencements until 1939 and the King of England continued to be toasted at college dinners as late as 1945. Before the war only eight per cent of the entire student body was Catholic even though more than eighty per cent of the students were Irish. But in spite of the fact that in the early 1940s the Catholic Archbishop of Dublin, John Charles McQuaid, imposed a virtual veto on the attendance of Catholic students at Trinity, the proportion of Catholics began to increase gradually, and by 1950 it had reached twenty-three per cent of the student population.[3]

Trevor's arrival at Trinity in 1946 coincided with an influx of ex-servicemen to the college which dramatically increased the overall student numbers and this trend continued for a number of years following the end of the Second World War. In most cases they were only a few years older than their fellow students who had entered university straight from school, but the ex-soldiers were a generation ahead in experience. Most of them had seen active service and some had suffered the brutality and privation of prisoner-of-war camps. There was a certain feeling of 'us' and 'them' between the ex-servicemen and their less experienced class-mates, who frequently resented what appeared to be the airs and graces of the ex-soldiers. The latter in turn made their presence felt, not only in the lecture halls, but also in student societies and social gatherings, where their sophisticated tastes distinguished them from their less mature companions. They had money and held wild parties called 'blinds', drank heavily in the pubs or spent evenings in Jammet's restaurant in Grafton Street, talking an army jargon which distinguished them from the ordinary students as surely as did the khaki trousers which many of them still wore. Their wartime experiences had made them cynical and opposed to all kinds of authority so they were now determined to recover the carefree youth and individuality which they believed the army had taken from them. They gave extra colour and verve to student life and ensured that the university was a more cosmopolitan place than it had been for many years. They sometimes livened up lectures by heckling and often used their ingenuity to circumvent what they regarded as tedious college rules such as those forbidding women students to be on the premises after 9 p.m. Bewley's cafés in Grafton Street and Westmoreland Street – and perhaps, more particularly, Switzer's basement café and the International Bar – were among the students' favourite haunts. Later in his story 'In Love with Ariadne' Trevor recalled these jovial, noisy gatherings:

> Students filled the café. They shouted to one another across plates of iced buns, their books on the floor beside their chairs, their gowns thrown anywhere. Long, trailing scarves in black and white indicated the extroverts of the Boat Club. Scholars were recognised by their earnest eyes, sizars by their poverty. Nigerians didn't mix. There were tablefuls of engineers and medical practitioners of the future, botanists and historians and linguists, geographers and eager divinity students. Rouge Medlicott and Slovinski were of an older generation, two of the many ex-servicemen of that time. Among these were G.I.s and Canadians and Czechs, a couple of Scots, a solitary Egyptian, and balding Englishmen who talked about Cecil Sharp or played bridge.

(CS 1176)

Trevor spent his first term in lodgings in the seaside village of Blackrock about six miles from the university. The house which was owned by a dog breeder rang with the high-pitched bark of terriers who chewed the furniture and occasionally threatened the elderly boarders. Of that time he has written:

> I met my tutor once. He was a precise man, with shiny black hair carefully brushed, a reader in law, later no doubt a professor.
>
> 'So you've changed your mind?' he commented in economical tones, his dark legal eyes betraying for an instant a hint of the sigh he successfully suppressed.
>
> 'Well, yes,' I agreed. I was attempting to extricate myself from the Medical School, in which I had erroneously landed myself.
>
> 'Actually there's no difficulty about that.' There was a cautious nod, the motion suggesting that the statement was made without prejudice, that no precedent had been established. 'The question is, what now?'

'That's what I wanted to ask you, sir.'

'You mean, you don't know what you want to do?'

'Well no, sir, actually.'

'You could try Modern Languages. Presumably you are acquainted with the rudiments of French, for instance? Or Irish?'

'It's not possible to do English on its own?'

'No, it isn't.' There was a pause. Other suggestions were put forward. Then: 'A lot of the undecided go in for the Church.'

'I don't think I'm cut out –'

'Come back when you've made up your mind.'

I never did. 'What are you doing?' people would ask me during that first term and I would say nothing, which was approximately correct because the few lectures I attended – in preparation for Littlego, an examination in general subjects, obligatory for all students – were not exacting. When, occasionally, I noticed the neat presence of my tutor in the distance I hurried out of sight.

(ERW 64)

When he returned after the Christmas holidays Trevor moved to the suburb of Terenure. The winter of 1947 was particularly cold with snow on the ground for many months. The room he rented was cheap but he had to cook his own meals. One night he found that he had set the chimney on fire and he was obliged to call on his landlady, Mrs Finnegan, for help. Together they quenched the flames and then sat together drinking tea, both happy in the knowledge that the landlady's husband, a bully, was unaware of what had happened:

... neither of us said what was uppermost in our minds: that there was something exciting about sitting there at five-fifteen in the morning, deceiving a sleeping giant.

(ERW 67)

Soon after this mishap, however, Trevor was on the move once more: he had been allocated rooms in Trinity. Anonymity was impossible now in such a social situation, and there were regulations which students were expected to abide by: they had to be present at Evening Commons in the dining-hall, attend Chapel on Sunday mornings, appear at evening roll-call and make a weekly trip to the communal bath-house. He enrolled in the History School.

Sculpture – an interest developed from his school days in St Columba's – entirely claimed his ambitions. He managed to pass the required examination at Trinity, but his interests were wholly outside the university and the life it offered. His friends were all Old Columbans. 'We Old Columbans stuck together', he has written, 'and were no doubt considered snobbish.' Desmond Hodges – working in a Dublin architects' office – had been a fellow Stackallen house perfect. So had Patrick Hackett, a medical student, and Arnold Bradshaw, a classical scholar, later to become an expert on Horace. Conor Farrington, who had not been a friend at school, became one at Trinity. Trevor designed and painted the sets for his first play, *The Outcast* – about James Clarence Mangan – in the summer of 1947.

The old Art Room companions – David Hone, Patrick Pye, Michael Biggs – were companions still. A loosely related group – with passing additions from among the students at the National College of Art – drank in Ryan's in Anne Street, often afterwards repairing to the café of the Green Cinema in St Stephen's Green, or out to Goatstown, 'on the bona fide'.

Trevor exhibited, at the annual Living Art exhibition, the Oireachtas exhibitions and in the house exhibitions that Victor Waddington, then Dublin's leading art entrepreneur, put on a couple of times a year. He cut the letters for the 1939-46 war memorial in St Anne's Church in Dawson Street. For the most part, he worked in wood, but also in clay and in lead, only once in stone, when he cut the letters for a gravestone. Midway through his four years at Trinity he attempted to leave, his plan being to study lettering with Joseph Cribb in England, and later to set up with Michael Biggs in the lettering business in Dublin. Parental opposition – even fiercer than when he had attempted to become a journalist – put paid to this. Biggs went on to become Ireland's most renowned letterer and church sculptor.

Trevor's shadowy Trinity existence continued. All he asked of it was that he shouldn't be noticed, and Trinity was as generous as it could be in this regard. Once, though, he was caught, and faced with an invitation that could not be declined:

The parties given by Professor and Mrs Skully were
renowned neither for the entertainment they provided nor
for their elegance. They were, unfortunately, difficult to
avoid, the Professor being persistent in the face of repeated
excuses – a persistence it was deemed unwise to strain.

Bidden for half past seven, his History students came
on bicycles, a few in Kilroy's mini, Ruth Cusper on her
motor-cycle, Bewley Joal on foot. Woodward, Whipp and
Woolmer-Mills came cheerfully, being kindred spirits of the
Professor's and in no way dismayed by the immediate
prospect. Others were apprehensive or cross, trying not to
let it show as smilingly they entered the Skullys' house in
Rathgar.

'How very nice!' Mrs Skully murmured in a familiar
manner in the hall. 'How jolly good of you to come.'

('The Time of Year' CS 800-1)

Trevor's standing as a sculptor was growing, more than
anything, perhaps, through his regular entries in the annual Irish
Exhibition of Living Art. This had been founded ten years earlier
when a number of young artists led by Louis Le Brocquy, Mainie
Jellett and Norah McGuinness reacted against what they regarded
as the out-of-date criteria of the Royal Hibernian Academy, which
has recently rejected works by Le Brocquy and other modern
artists. The group, therefore, set up their own alternative salon
which catered for what were then regarded as avant-garde works.
According to Anne Yeats, daughter of the poet, and a committee
member, it was the only exhibition of its kind at the time. By 1949
it was held on an annual basis and a distinctive Irish School, with
obvious European influences, was becoming evident. As well as
new names it attracted entries from established artists such as Jack
Yeats.

Towards the end of his time at Trinity Trevor went every day to
the Long Room and the Library, where the Book of Kells was
displayed. He made endless sketches of its detail and was later to
carve its three evangelists as panels for a lectern in a village church
in England (St Giles and All Saints, Braunston, near Rugby). It
was during this time that he met and fell in love with Jane Ryan, a
London born student of Modern Languages at the college.

The daughter of a higher civil servant, first in the British
Treasury and later the Home Office, she had been sent to Trinity
because of family connections with Ireland that went back to the

time when the Ryans had been landowners and solicitors in County Tipperary. Women students had been allowed into Trinity since 1904, but they were still, more than forty years later, subject to a variety of restrictions. If possible they were expected to live with their parents or a guardian while attending the college. Those who were unable to do so were permitted to live during freshman years in Trinity Hall, a university residence, situated some miles from the college in the Dublin suburb of Dartry. They were strictly forbidden to visit college rooms, whether those of professors, 'grinders' or other students except, as the regulations stated, 'on such special occasions as have received the explicit sanction of the Junior Dean and the concurrence of the Lady Registrar'. These official 'special occasions' were normally confined to Sunday afternoons. Apart from the necessary access which they had to the lecture halls and the reading rooms, they were expected to confine themselves to the special rooms in the college which has been set aside for their use. Even their examinations results were posted up separately in these rooms and the college calendar stated that 'women students are not admitted to the Assistant Registrar's office except in special circumstances'.

But rules could be broken and regularly were. This newest of his friendships thrived, both before and after Trevor graduated in 1951. In August of the following year, in Barnes parish church, in London, the two were married – in spite of vociferous disapproval from within both families. With two Corgi motor-scooters – as used by parachutists, now wartime surplus being sold off cheaply – they set out to spend the rest of the summer on Achill Island.

Trevor's abiding hope had always been that he would not have to leave Ireland. But long before he married, it became clear that it would not be realised. Employment for graduates in the new Republic of the early 1950s hardly existed. After Achill, the parachutists' motor-scooters crossed the Border into the North – the first gentle step of emigration – where Trevor and Jane had both found employment in Elm Park, a preparatory school in County Armagh.

> The stationmaster at Killylea spoke of porridge in the plural. 'I'd rather have salt on them than sugar,' he used to say.

As small as a railway station can be, the railway station was a mile and a half from the village. Trains were not frequent, a couple a day. The stationmaster was on his own there, which may have accounted for his becoming out of touch with established speech. 'You can't beat the green Chivers' jelly,' he would say if you were waiting for a train, 'with a good dollop of cream on them'. One way or another the stationmaster told you a lot about the food he ate.

When you set off from the railway station to the village you noticed after about five minutes the gates of an avenue on your right. If you passed through them instead of continuing to Killylea you found yourself eventually at Elm Park. It was a gaunt, grey, good-looking Georgian house with a semi-circular sweep in front of it, and cropped lawns and shrubberies. It had belonged to one of those Anglo-Irish families that were rarer in Ulster during the Ascendancy's heyday than they were in the rest of Ireland.

Such houses have been down on their luck for most of this century, and Elm Park was no exception. As a preparatory school, its great conservatory was a place where afternoon drinks were given out – Quosh and Mi-Wadi and Kia-Ora – depending on the brand each of its twenty-two boys had handed in at the beginning of term. Its spacious bedrooms were dormitories, its double bathrooms useful on communal bath nights, the dining-room perfect for end-of-term theatricals. The ubiquitous white paint of wainscoting and doors was chipped and bruised, ceilings were dappled brown from dried-out damp. Rickety, well-inked desks and a varnished cupboard furnished the drawing-room. No claret aged softly in the cellars; Dinky cars made a dirt track round a summer-house.

(ERW 83-84)

This part of County Armagh was where Trevor's mother had grown up, before the island was partitioned. The family farm, run by Trevor's uncle, Willie Davison, lay about twenty miles north-east of Elm Park. Armagh was now a border county, adjoining the Republic to the south. Trevor remembers the early 1950s as a quiescent time in political cross-border activity, partly because the IRA has not yet recovered from the wide-scale internment of its members during the period of the Second World War, which has left it disorganised. In addition the Catholic minority of the North had begun to benefit from the British Labour government's recently introduced legislation creating the foundations of a social-democratic welfare state. Improvements in education, health care, housing and social welfare payments meant that the average person in Northern Ireland was now financially better off than his or her counterpart in the Republic. The only illegal movements in the region were made by petty smugglers, intent on getting their hands on supplies of cheap cigarettes or alcohol.

Early in 1953 Trevor won the Irish section of the international Unknown Political Prisoner competition, sharing the prize with Frederick Herkner, professor of sculpture at the National College of Art. (The story – no doubt apocryphal – was told among his students of his escape from Nazi Germany in a packing-case; how, placed upside down at Dublin docks, he had slipped coins through the cracks in a successful effort to attract attention.) Herkner's maquette was in bronze, Trevor's in wood – a figure in the expressionist style, the head and upper part of the body clearly depicting a human form but without any detail or personalisation. Both went on view in Dublin and later in the Tate Gallery in London, where Trevor won a further award. The overall winner was the British sculptor, Reg Butler.

Elm Park was Trevor's introduction to the prep-school world, since he had not been to a preparatory school himself:

> ... a world of gossip and small vendettas, of starched white undermatrons' uniforms, Kennedy's Latin primer, *Paul est le fils de Monsieur et Madame Lepine* ...
>
> (*Old School Ties* 91)

Still within it, he moved to England in 1953, spending two years at Bilton Grange in Warwickshire before deciding to attempt to make a living from sculpture. Abandoning the bleak midlands for the West Country, he undertook commissions for church carvings, had his first one-man show in Dublin in 1956, his second in Bath in 1958.

For the Dublin exhibition he rented the Dublin Painters Gallery from the Society of Dublin Painters, rooms formerly occupied by the well-known Irish artists John Butler Yeats and Walter Osborne. On the day on which it opened – 31 July 1956 – a photograph in *The Evening Press* showed him standing beside one of his exhibits – a work in wood entitled 'The Risen Christ'. Two days later a review described the artist as 'a painstaking perfectionist who is prepared to go to endless trouble to achieve his often startling effects'.[4] The exhibition covered a wide range of styles from the intricate Celtic interlacing of a piece called 'The Devil appearing to Christ in the Wilderness' to a geometric shaped 'Death of St Andrew' and the totem pole effect of 'Head of a Clown'. Since the works included pieces in wood, terra-cotta, metal and even embroideries, the reviewer remarked on the diversity of styles which he said ran 'the whole gamut of techniques from John Haugh to Giacometti'. Other connoisseurs like Dorothy Walker noted that Trevor's exhibition had a certain 'English' flavour to it, that he was obviously being influenced by the time he had spent working outside Ireland.

By the end of that decade Trevor's work had become abstract and he was no longer happy with the effect. He began to consider other means of subsidising his slender finances. The idea of writing an autobiographical novel had been lurking at the back of his mind for some time. In 1958 *A Standard of Behaviour* was published, its author's objective purely to make money. But as the sixties approached it was apparent that some other source of income was necessary. He was fortunate, at thirty-one, to get a job in a London advertising agency:

> Notley's ... was the only one that had held out any hope when I tentatively wrote to a number of them to offer my services, A mammoth concern in St James' might have taken me on if I'd agreed to six months' selling in Selfridge's and another six months on the road. At J. Walter Thompson's I failed the writing test. Only Notley's welcomed my ignorance of the commercial world and of the craft for which I was presenting myself. On 11 January 1960 I reported there for duty.
>
> (ERW 99)

Here it was that he wrote his first short stories. 'The Nicest Man in the World' was published in the *Transatlantic Review* in 1962, 'The General's Day' in the *London Magazine* the following year. Notley's – dubbed a 'nest of singing birds' – was a haven for poets who would otherwise be as impecunious as Trevor had recently found himself. Peter Porter was there, Edward Lucie-Smith, Oliver Bernard, Peter Redgrove, Gavin Ewart. Porter became one of

Trevor's closest friends and has remained so since; Ewart later wrote what he called 'The William Trevor Poem':

> How are you off for sex
> and that class of thing?
> Let me warn you against the flex,
> it's a type of electric string.
>
> Now would you care to imbibe?
> The blacks don't understand stout
> and potations of that tribe
> or pushing the boat out.
>
> Inside the bicycle shed
> a certain suggestion was made,
> you wouldn't believe what was said
> in the way of denoting a spade,
>
> and that variety of talk
> is insulting a decent man;
> you want to take care where you walk,
> hurry on if you can,
>
> some females are out to tempt,
> and adopt an abandoned pose,
> but remember they're not exempt
> from disease, in their shameless clothes.
>
> You should lead a healthy life
> and keep your thoughts on the shelf
> or before you can say knife
> you'll be betraying yourself.

(*Encounter*, March 1977)

In his novel *The Love Department* which Trevor set partly in an office, the hero, whose name is Edward Blakeston-Smith, is intrigued when he hears his office colleagues mutter strange, incomprehensible phrases:

> As he perused the letters, Edward was aware that his mind was registering words that the letters did not contain. The words seemed to be in the air, and at first he thought he must be imagining them. Then it seemed to him – an odd fact, he thought – that his colleagues were issuing them, muttering the words, or shooting them out in a soft,

staccato manner that made Edward jump. As he listened, concentrating on what he heard, he reflected that a conversation among ghosts might be quite like this.

'His dog prowls,' remarked one clerk.

'Now, red mechanic!' said another ...

Two of the clerks began to argue about a king. 'Sweet king beribboned,' the first one said, but the other quietly objected, questioning the suitability of ribbons as a decoration for a king. 'Medals, surely?' he suggested.

'You don't put ribbons on the monarchy, I mean.' The first clerk narrowed his eyes. 'I put what I like on the monarchy,' he said. 'Any frigging object I fancy.' He spoke then of his veins, stating in a clear, low, whisper that there were trespassers in his veins by night. 'Neck death,' said the other clerk. 'Eat your meat!' Both clerks laughed gently. 'Smiling mortician,' said one, and both were solemn again ...

'Holy citadel,' said a third clerk, a worker who had not yet spoken, one with a black beard. 'Oh, cherished Roman!'

'Look here,' said Edward. 'What's going on in this joint?'

(LD 19-20)

Later he learns that the clerks are poets and that they are merely quoting from their works.

Almost overnight, Trevor ceased to be a sculptor. Something was missing in his abstractions; suddenly, he realised he didn't like them. What he was writing interested him more.

The Old Boys was written almost entirely in Notley's time. So were many short stories. But when he was halfway through *The Boarding-House* Trevor was already a part-time copywriter at Notley's and by 1967, when his first collection of stories – *The Day We Got Drunk on Cake* – was published he and Notley's had parted company. 'I resigned minutes before they would have sacked me.' Two sons had been born; the family moved back to the West Country, where Trevor has lived ever since. He returns regularly to Ireland, mainly to the provincial Ireland of his past, to County Cork, to Galway, to the Nire Valley between the Monavullagh Mountains and the Comeraghs. He gardens, walks, travels in Italy and France, spends long periods in the Alps and the Ticino, and for forty years conducted a correspondence about imaginary comic characters with his oldest English friend, Michael Streat. Family and friendship are still the most valued elements in his personal life, his long marriage increasingly his most precious relationship.

Part II

Chapter 1

'How shall we prove we are not dead?'

With the publication of *A Standard of Behaviour* in 1958 the writer William Trevor was born. His decision to adopt a *nom de plume* by using his two Christian names marked a new beginning. Like many of Trevor's later novels *A Standard of Behaviour* deals with a tragicomic confined world, in which a large cast of characters, predators and victims, live disorderly lives. Most of them are inhabitants of a boarding-house, an institution which in one form or another occurs in Trevor's work as a place where diverse characters can be gathered together. The doyenne of the boarding-house is Mrs Lamont, who wishes to be surrounded by creative people who might one day become famous or at least infamous:

> 'I like to live always within the possibility that someone in my house may at this very moment be attempting to cut off his ears.'

But Mrs Lamont likes to set parameters for the kind of activity in which her lodgers might engage:

> ... violence should be, so to speak, house-trained: screaming and blood on the chair-covers were quite unforgivable.
>
> (SB 12)

The young people who drift in and out of her house look to Mrs Lamont as their 'patron saint' (SB 52), as they experiment in a world which seems to offer no restrictions. Many of them would have been at home in a novel by Evelyn Waugh – an author whom Trevor admired and read avidly. They teeter between artlessness and corruption in the shady sphere in which they move.

All of the characters are eccentric and while most of them are aspiring artists, none achieves success in his or her field. The religious but utterly unscrupulous homosexual, Nigel Townsend, is a painter of some merit, but he declines to have his talent tested because he fears failure. He is the plausible exploiter – a figure who continues to materialise in Trevor's work. In this case the victim is the stage-German, Otto Hasenfuss, who becomes the group's stooge, duped into paying for all their excesses. David Aldridge is a sculptor whose seeming ineffectuality hides a violent streak: he rapes a girl whom he claims to love and then abandons her. Meanwhile his sculpture exhibition only prospers after it has been deliberately vandalised in order to attract attention. Edmund Archer is an obsessive poet without any talent while Virginia de Witt is studying, without any enthusiasm, to be an actress: 'After a year or so I shall try something else, I suppose.' (SB 43) she remarks without compunction.

The setting of the book might be England but there are several indications of the author's Irishness: topographical details which evoke Dublin, the atmosphere of the race-course and the particularly Irish quality of some of the dialogue:

> The man in the tweed cap sought us out and apologised.
> 'I've just beaten hell out of McLagen', he said, 'behind the stables. I left him pleadin' mercy from a pile of straw with the horses urinating on him. The dirty thieving louser.'
>
> (SB 36)

The book is narrated in the first person by an unnamed young man, one of Mrs Lamont's lodgers, who is rather aimlessly pursuing a post-graduate degree at the university. The plot involves the narrator's love affair with Virginia, whom he loses inexplicably to Archer. When Virginia leaves Archer the would-be poet kills himself and subsequently both the girl and the narrator find new partners. The novel can be seen as a bildungsroman, in that it records the progress of the narrator's mind as he passes through a variety of experiences into maturity and the recognition of his identity in the world. A young writer's book, it parallels Trevor's own stage of development as he finds a distinctive voice and an original style.

Although the work is picaresque in form the principal events revolve around four parties which occur at intervals and which as the narrator remarks 'mark time'. (SB 55) The occasions also trace the protagonist's moral decline as he consciously adjusts his own standard of behaviour to that of the artistic world which he inhabits. The first is a school party at which the boys who are about to leave get drunk on communion wine and other beverages and attempt to seduce the school maids. Only the rather stolid Archer achieves his goal – an early indication of his later success with Virginia.

During the second party, a fancy-dress ball, Peggy Lamont, one of Mrs Lamont's wayward daughters, tries to engage the narrator in some discussion about the futility of her life. She is uneasy about:

> 'The prospect of going on and on, like a vegetable who doesn't quite know whether it wants to be an animal.'
>
> (SB 53)

He brushes away her attempts at communication and reflects that the undemanding relationship which exists between the members of the group serves only to 'lengthen the present limitlessly into the future'. (SB 55)

The next event, a nude party held in the boarding-house, allows the process of self-discovery to continue. At such a function the narrator muses 'human ugliness is at its height'. (SB 63)

Such indeed is his self-disgust and his abhorrence of the occasion that he recognises that there is a just comparison between himself and the Lamont's dog:

> We seemed suddenly to be creatures of alarmingly similar circumstances: he, a jester to perform and amuse at the snap of a finger, and I as tame and docile as a captured slug.
>
> (SB 67)

This party in particular allows the author to introduce some of the hilariously inconsequential dialogue which would later become a feature of his writing:

I wandered about the room listening to snatches of conversation, filling the crevices of my teeth with nuts, and drinking.

'... He played the part of the commanding officer, if you remember ...'

'... add the kidney when the meat's nearly cooked'

' ... I really do hate him. I really do. I find him, if you know what I mean, utterly repugnant ...'

'... I looked down and I saw them. Dead as doornails. Hell I said to myself...'

'... always out of a tin, my dear, always'

'... I remember him standing there at the doors of the opera house with nothing on except his cache-sexe ...'

I shifted my position slightly. A man was saying quietly, confidentially: 'My wife says I'm the worst she's ever slept with.' His companion, a small stout woman, purred sympathetically.

(SB 69)

The final party, to celebrate the marriage of Virginia and Archer, with its echoes of the school-leaving episode which opens the novel, brings the narrator to the nadir of his misery. He survives it by adhering to the 'standard of reasonably intelligent behaviour' (SB 102) on which he had prided himself but which has so often been compromised in the company of his friends. The book ends as he picks up the threads of his career and finds a new woman friend. He has discovered that lowering his ethical standards is ultimately unsatisfactory and now he must begin the painful process of rediscovering his own moral identity.

Trevor's first experiment in the world of literature did not immediately spur him on to further efforts. It would be four years before his next work – the first of his short stories – was published. During that time his parents at last separated after almost forty years of marriage. Over the years virtually all communication had ceased between the couple – a circumstance often reflected in depressing accounts of the middle-aged and elderly couples who so frequently appear in Trevor's work – characters whose only communication is through bitter and futile bickering and who otherwise live alongside each other in silent desperation.

'The Nicest Man in the World' involves a couple, Adam and Mary Anne Raleigh, who are in their eighties. They have been happily married for sixty years. As Adam approaches death, at his request his friends visit him to make their farewells. After the funeral Mary Anne becomes worried because she has not been able to identify five of Adam's last visitors. They are all elderly women and she comes to the conclusion that they have been secret mistresses of her husband's. Her worry becomes an obsession which destroys the happy memories she had had of her marriage. When she questions them about their relationships with her husband they deny any impropriety. An amusing passage in which two of the women talk on the telephone informs the reader that they are in fact Mary Anne's old schoolmates whom she had forgotten. The exchange offers a foretaste of Trevor's genius for deadpan comedy. One of the ladies, Lady Taggart, has never mastered the art of using the telephone and she fails to speak directly into the mouthpiece. Consequently her voice registers as:

> ... a muffled roar, so that one could not escape the impression that Lady Taggart was specifically signalling for aid, that she lay in some unhappy plight, buried beneath her garden or wrapped, by mischance, in a carpet.

(TR 137)

The ensuing dialogue allows the author to exploit to the full the comic potential inherent in an interchange based on a series of non-sequiturs. Matters are resolved for Mary Anne when she recalls her late husband's belief that there has to be some badness in the world 'to balance the niceness, the charm, the humour, the kindness'. (TR 139) With his new understanding she can calmly look forward to death. The wisdom of old age and its vulnerability are themes which Trevor explores in greater depth in his subsequent work, in short stories such as 'Broken Homes' and 'The Tennis Court' and in the novel *The Old Boys*.

'The Day We got Drunk on Cake' was first published in a magazine called *Town* early in 1964. It involves four young people, two men and two women, who set out for an afternoon on the town. The moving spirit behind the expedition is Swann, a man who believes in 'getting the best out of life'. (CS 120) The two women, Margo and Jo, are 'a smart pair who drew pictures for the glossy magazines'. (CS 121) The narrator character, Mike, is persuaded to leave his office and join in the escapade, even though he is preoccupied with thoughts of Lucy, a girl with whom he is in love. In the course of the evening Mike telephones Lucy seven times as he wends his way through a series of pubs, clubs and restaurants, eventually ending up at a party. Through the dialogue that takes place on the telephone it becomes obvious to both Mike and the reader that Lucy is entertaining another man in her flat, but she remains polite and reasonable even when the calls become repetitive and absurd, due to Mike's increasing state of intoxication. At one point when he returns from the telephone he finds his companions eating rum cake:

> When I got back to the others I found them laughing in an uproarious manner. Swann said the cake they were eating was making them drunk. 'Smell it,' he said. It smelt of rum. I tasted some: it tasted of rum too. We all ate a lot of the cake, laughing at the thought of getting drunk on cake.
>
> (CS 126)

Meanwhile Mike finds himself drawn into a farcical situation with Margo who wishes him to challenge her husband for an explanation of his curious habit of entertaining several old ladies in his home on the pretext that they are having a never-ending meeting. Another comical and equally inconclusive telephone call is made and Mike is convinced that 'everything had been more or less resolved'. He is left with the regret that eventually his love for Lucy will fade and that the day will only be remembered 'as the day we got drunk on cake'. (CS 132)

The story has all the ingredients which were to become typical of Trevor's early work – the quirky humour, the preposterous characters, dialogue which is sprinkled with archaisms and literalisms and the Chekhovian notion that the inevitable must be endured.

Following closely on the publication of 'The Day We got Drunk on Cake' came two other stories 'In at the Birth' and 'A Meeting in Middle-Age' which both appeared in *Transatlantic Review* in the spring of 1964. They are of particular interest, not only as examples of the author's early work, but because they introduce themes and character types which reappear periodically throughout his oeuvre. In the former story 'In at the Birth' for the first time Trevor takes a step away from realism and creates a fantastic 'other world' which suggests a dimension beyond quotidian experience. The story begins with a play on the conventional opening of a fairy-tale:

> Once upon a time there lived in a remote London suburb an elderly lady called Miss Efoss.
>
> (CS 103)

It would seem at the outset that Miss Efoss's world is a replica of the ordinary world. The first sentence indeed reflects the two levels on which the story works, the suggestion of distance of time and place is undermined immediately by the modern setting, for this is a world of cinemas, television sets and polite glasses of sherry. The fantasy element comes neither from the era in which it takes place nor from the location of the story, but rather from the inclusion of a marvel – an inexplicable event. While the details of Miss Efoss's life in suburban London establish its authenticity for the reader, Miss Efoss is hardly a conventional elderly spinster. She is:

> ... a spry person ... she read at length ... she preferred the company of men and women forty years her junior ... She had loved and been loved. For a year or two she had known the ups and downs of early family life, although the actual legality of marriage had somehow been overlooked. Miss Efoss's baby died during a sharp attack of pneumonia; and shortly afterwards the child's father packed a suitcase one night. He said goodbye quite kindly to Miss Efoss but she never saw him again.
>
> (CS 102)

Miss Efoss babysits for a young couple called Mr and Mrs Dutt. There is nothing untoward in the arrangement except that Miss Efoss is instructed by the couple never to enter their child's bedroom, since they maintain that Mickey is of a nervous disposition and would be upset at seeing a stranger. At first Miss Efoss accepts this condition though she considers it foolish. Later when she discovers that the Dutts have lied to her about other things she decides to see Mickey for herself. She enters the forbidden bedroom:

> It was brightly painted, with a wallpaper with elves on it. There was a rocking horse and a great pile of coloured bricks. In one of the far corners there was a large cot. It was

very large and very high and it contained the sleeping figure of a very old man.

(CS 109)

The babysitter tells nobody of her discovery, nor does she return to the Dutts' home. A year later she meets the couple again and they tell her that Mickey has died:

> 'They have all died, Miss Efoss', Mr Dutt said. 'One by one they have all died.'

(CS 110)

Their misery has a hypnotic effect on Miss Efoss and soon after her encounter with the bereaved couple she begins to decline into old age. Eventually she sells her belongings, packs her case and arrives at the Dutts' house. The element of compulsion is emphasised as we are told that 'it dawned upon Miss Efoss just what it was she had to do'. (CS 111) Her arrival at the Dutts' home is expected:

> 'Perfect, Miss Efoss, perfect, said Mr Dutt. 'Beryl's child is due this very night.'

(CS 112)

The atmosphere of eeriness is augmented by the pictures flashing silently on the Dutt's television screen as Miss Efoss makes her way upstairs to the baby's room. She assures the smiling couple that she knows her way.

As Miss Efoss literally and allegorically enters second childhood in the Dutts' home, the story is lifted beyond the realms of realism. She has become a kind of living ghost, entering the 'other world' of the Dutts, a couple who earlier in the story had seemed merely eccentric, but who are now revealed as both creators and custodians of this 'other world'. It is a world which does not assault the reader in the way that some science fiction, magic or dream worlds do. It is all the more sinister because it seems at first to be identical to the real world and consequently the reader's entry into it is almost imperceptible. The path of reason is found to have taken a peculiar but almost indiscernible turning.

Just as 'In at the Birth' prefaces the idea of a dimension beyond the rational which Trevor repeatedly returns to in his stories, so 'A

Meeting in Middle Age', the other story he had published in the spring of 1964, introduces a character who becomes a familiar figure in Trevor's work – the overpowering middle-aged woman whose predatory facade masks an inner loneliness. Mrs da Tanka is meeting Mr Mileson with the purpose of providing legal evidence of infidelity so that her third husband can divorce her. Mr da Tanka is 'a person of importance, in the public eye' (CS 4) and consequently is not prepared to provide the evidence himself. He does agree, however, to finance his wife in the matter. Mr Mileson is a bachelor 'childless, the end of a line' (CS 1) who lives alone in a bed-sitter, his single sexual experience an act of fornication with the maid in his parents' house, thirty years earlier. The story is revealed through dialogue interspersed with and frequently undercut by the thoughts of the two characters. Only occasionally does the authorial voice intrude. The focus shifts back and forth between the two main characters as they journey by train to their destination, each absorbed in separate worlds.

At the hotel Mrs da Tanka drinks immoderately and a heated exchange between the pair follows. As they share a double bed they each retire into their private recollections of the past. Ironically they are closer at this moment than either can guess, she with her memories of a rural childhood, he with similar memories in an urban setting, but almost immediately they mentally go their separate ways. Their only physical contact ends in a misunderstanding: as Mr Mileson tries to assault her, Mrs da Tanka mistakes the gesture for an attempt at an embrace and rebuffs him.

The story's final section recalls the opening scene as the couple return to London by train. Although their taunting of each other continues there is another moment of convergence, again triggered off by memories of childhood. Mention of cowparsley, a flower Trevor frequently uses as a symbol of innocence, establishes a brief moment of rapport. This lonely middle-aged pair are drawn together and momentarily a meeting of minds occurs:

> The silence struck between them, and Mr Mileson knew by instinct all that it contained. She saw an image of herself and him, strolling together from the hotel, in this same sunshine, at this very moment, lingering on the pavement

to decide their direction and agreeing to walk to the promenade.

(CS 13)

Again the moment is fleeting, lost in their mutual distrust, and the story ends on a down-beat as each returns to a life of loneliness.

'A Meeting in Middle Age' was awarded second prize in a short story competition organised by *Transatlantic Review*. Trevor's talent as a writer was beginning to be recognised.

The short story from which *The Old Boys* developed was partly inspired by Trevor's father-in-law, C N Ryan, who was very proud of his public school career and liked to reminisce at length about it. The novel is primarily a sardonic yet genial study of old age. The title applies in all its meanings to the eight septuagenarians who form the committee of their school's Old Boys' Association. Their Machiavellian struggles merely perpetuate the tyranny of their school days and demonstrate that they have reached old age but not maturity. Their stunted development is an indictment of the institution in which they spent their formative years, but the book focuses rather more on their sterile existences as old men, and on their essential loneliness, than on the futile feuds which continue to occupy them in their declining years.

The Old Boys' committee is preparing to elect its next President from among its members and Trevor uses the ensuing fight for position as a hook upon which to hang a group portrait of old age. The prime candidate for the presidency is Mr Jaraby and his arch-enemy is George Nox. Their antipathy dates back to their schooldays and the plot revolves around Nox's attempt to prevent Jaraby's election. This is interspersed with amusing and pathetic accounts of the preoccupations of the other committee members, accompanied by flashbacks to their schooldays.

In boyhood the committee members had all come under the jurisdiction of the same housemaster, Mr Dowse, a sadistic, misanthropic pervert who imposed a regime of brutality on his charges. Jaraby, a housecaptain and one of the master's favourites, allied himself with the system and in turn imposed it on weaker and younger boys. Such is the extent of Jaraby's admiration of Dowse and his identification with him that he imitates his savagery and as a result earns the lifelong enmity of Nox. Jaraby's position

as housecaptain was the high point of his career. His wife remarks
to a visitor:

> 'We do not talk much about the School unless my husband
> is here. He returns to those days. They were his most
> successful.'
>
> (OB 144-5)

In old age Jaraby sees the presidency of the Old Boys'
Association as an opportunity to recapture the prestige and power
which he had so enjoyed all those years ago when he was
housecaptain.

In his private life Jaraby tries to apply the same tyrannical
authority which he learned so well from Dowse. He indulges his
prejudices and obsessions, brow-beating shopkeepers and refusing
to allow Australian produce in the house because of his dislike of
the way Australians speak. Subjected to his father's regime, Basil,
the Jarabys' son, has become at forty years of age a social misfit
with eccentric and even criminal tendencies. He is forbidden the
house by his father, but his mother continues to champion his
cause as she plans his return home. According to his father Basil's
greatest crime to date is his poor performance at his father's Alma
Mater. Mrs Jaraby defends her son and castigates the institution
which intimidated him:

> 'He was afraid of the place. It was you who rose to great
> heights and won the prizes. He was to do likewise. He
> tried, God knows, but a frightened child can achieve little.
> ... Your own ghost was at that school. And you were here
> at home. What chance had he to escape?
>
> (OB 67)

Jaraby's relationship with his wife is central to the novel. She
refuses to bow to his will and both parries his verbal assaults and
thwarts his bullying tactics. Commenting on the book some years
after it was written, Trevor made this clear:

> For me the most interesting thing about it is the marriage
> you see there. It's a failure and we look at it in old age
> because they're not the kind of people who would ever
> have got divorced, and that for me is the heart of
> everything I see in the [story]. In a way there's a longing
> that she has to go back to the past and for him to love her

again. He happens to have an obsession about school ...
It's much more about how two people can't come together
at all really and yet stay together for a lifetime.[1]

Earlier in her marriage Mrs Jaraby had been more submissive, but as she grows older, she grows bolder in her opposition to her husband. She is inspired by her determination to have her son living at home once again – a resolution which emanates as much from her loneliness as from her maternal feelings. At first she uses subterfuge to achieve her aims, but later she employs more grisly methods. Since Basil breeds budgerigars he is prevented from returning to his parents' house by the presence of Jaraby's vicious cat, Monmouth, a creature greatly loved by its owner but as loathed by Mrs Jaraby as it would have been by Trevor himself. In her husband's absence Mrs Jaraby drugs the animal, then drowns it in the bath-tub and consigns its body to the dustbin.

If the Jarabys once loved one another they have ceased to do so before the novel opens. The reader is presented with an old couple joined together in rancorous wedlock and engaged in verbal combat to the death. Their conversation is artificial and mannered, with a formality which both belies and bears out their relationship. Most of the characters adopt the same speech rhythms as do the Jarabys. When Mrs Jaraby mentions their son, her husband upbraids her:

'Obedience is my due. I will demand it: refrain please from
these references to one who is a near-criminal.'

(OB 40)

Meanwhile Miss Burdock, a minor character, orders Mr Harp from her house in the following words:

'Be gone, please. Promptly and without further argument
vacate the space you stand in.'

(OB 57)

Sometimes the characters seem to speak from the inner recesses of their minds as though they are revealing themselves through a stream of consciousness rather than addressing each other. This aspect of the book places it in the context of the *nouveau roman* of the 1960s in which characters frequently indulge in a series of interior monologues that have all the vagaries of the natural mental process. The reader is expected to make sense of what appears to be a series of disjointed and illogical declarations. A passage in which Mr Jaraby talks to himself illustrates the process

> 'She takes no care to purchase goods at the right time and in the right condition. I have myself to see to the vegetables and fruit. She will not stand up to the shop people and say: "Split the produce in half that I may see inside." How else to know if an apple or a grapefruit is worth its money? I get the better of the shop people; why cannot she? It is all embarrassing. She will not see a doctor. A doctor would give her tablets. She should have sedatives day and night; no one can come to the house without noticing that something is amiss. This wild talk. No one could stand this talk. Did Cridley and Sole not note it and shake their heads? Do they not perhaps discuss it and pity me in my distress? They will say it, all of them, soon: "Jaraby's wife knows sanity no more." They may condemn me even for not having her seen to or taken away, yet my hands are tied; I can do nothing, since she will recognise no shortcomings in herself. There was madness in that family, her mother had staring eyes, her father drank. There was a lad at school hanged himself from a tree.'

(OB 62-3)

Authorial comment is again kept to a minimum and it is through the rather strange dialogue that the characters reveal themselves. The narrative voice echoes the tone which the characters use, shifting key to suit the different relationships, acerbic when relating the petty foibles in which the old people indulge, less ironic when the author wishes to engage the sympathy of the reader for the loneliness which almost all experience at some stage in the book.

Apart from Jaraby's son, Basil, all the Old Boys appear in the book either as schoolboys or as old men. We know nothing of their middle years. As the General remarks 'an old man grows to be an infant' (OB 99) and there are implications of second childhood even though the phrase itself is never used. Like children the old people speak their minds without inhibitions. Jaraby's arch-enemy is George Nox who bears a grudge against him from schooldays. Nox's sole object in serving on the Old Boys' committee is to prevent Jaraby's election as president. He hopes to be able to reveal something discreditable about Jaraby's life and has hired a private detective with the object of unearthing a scandal which will compromise his enemy. For Nox there has been no state of existence other than old age. As he reviews his life he feels he had:

> ... never been young; that all his life had been a mere preparation for the state he now found himself in, that was his realm and that was no imposition.

(OB 53)

In childhood he had been forced to come to terms with loneliness. It had taken its toll 'but would not return' (OB 53) Now he lives only for vengeance which he sees as a logical and justifiable aim.

Some of the old boys had managed to maintain genuine friendship since their schooldays. Mr Sole and Mr Cridley live together in a boarding-house, where they are bullied by the landlady, Miss Burdock, as they once were by Dowse at school. They alleviate their boredom in harmless, childish and humorous ways but they never directly challenge authority, and only oppose Jaraby's election when others have ceased to support him. A less sympathetic picture of emotional retardation is seen in Mr Swabey-Boyns. As a boy he was sly and malevolent and he continues to be so in old age. When he fancies himself slighted he retaliates with ingenious vindictiveness. In hospital when he thinks the nurses are laughing at him, he uses his nail-scissors to clip little holes in the sheets. The most endearing member of the committee is Mr Turtle. He is gentle and inept and an easy prey to manipulative characters like his aptly-named housekeeper, Mrs Strap, and the tyrannical Miss Burdock. He is ashamed of his weakness and his attempts to buy friendship are motivated as much by generosity as they are by loneliness.

Their names often give an indication of the characters' traits. Sir George Ponders, the outgoing president of the Association, is a thoughtful man and with General Sanctuary he forms the centre of sanity in the novel. Both men have been successful in their lives and have no need to carry petty resentments into old age. The General is a refuge of truth. In his schooldays he was the only boy who refused to be intimidated by Dowse and even threatened to report his viciousness to the authorities. When challenged, Dowse acted with the typical bully's cowardice and threw himself on the mercy of his victim. The General's courage which he manifested throughout his life continues to earn him respect in old age.

The middle section of the book covers the events of the Old Boys' Day at school during which Jaraby continues to canvass for his own election to the presidency. Comedy and pathos coincide as Jaraby tries to persuade a doctor to declare his wife insane while Turtle dies during a performance of *The Mikado*. General Sanctuary and Lady Ponders discuss the subject of old age and its compensations. The vicissitudes of middle age are past, they agree, and old age brings liberation. Above all old people have gained the freedom to speak their minds.

Both Sir George and General Sanctuary have had power and responsibility during their lives and are now happy to relinquish it. By contrast Jaraby and Nox are still striving for the illusions of power, for the presidency of the Association carries no real authority. Ironically Jaraby's failure to secure the position is caused, not by Nox's efforts to discredit him, but by the behaviour of his son. Basil had always taken a perverse delight in wrong doing and his paedophilic tendencies eventually lead to his arrest while he is staying at his parents' house. The ensuing scandal leads to Jaraby's rejection by the committee, in spite of the fact that General Sanctuary ably pleads his cause, arguing that the sins of the child should not be visited on the father. In his speech the general underlines the real issue: the members fear that their decision will be reversed by the Headmaster and the school Governors. Their lack of power is starkly revealed: 'You cannot bear to see the underlining of your impotence.' (OB 185), the General upbraids them as he resigns in disgust. At first Jaraby cannot accept what has happened. When the truth eventually dawns on him the effect is devastating. He reacts by denying his son. Old and defeated, bereft of power and of his child, he lacks the tragic dimension of a Lear only because he lacks his insight and self-knowledge.

The book closes on a chilling note of black comedy as Mrs Jaraby describes a future in which husband and wife will be 'like animals of prey turned in on one another' (OB 190). In a brilliant final paragraph the bleak language of suffering is interspersed with touches of the Absurd. Mrs Jaraby's closing exhortation urges her husband to 'Cast gloom aside' and asks 'How shall we prove we are not dead?' (OB 191) Her question sums up the futile and frenetic efforts of her husband and his committee colleagues who engage in power politics and intrigues and vendettas which are but gestures of defiance against the real and inevitably victorious enemy, death.

The Old Boys was published in March 1964 and it met with immediate critical acclaim. Several reviews remarked on the authenticity of the characters and the strange dialogue also attracted comment.[2] It was described by one commentator as 'the language of the Foreign Office'.[3] Newspaper interviews followed. Trevor defended the 'staccato dialogue'[4] spoken by his characters. He disagreed with those which saw the book as an attack on the English public school system. Years later in discussing this view of the novel in the *Daily Telegraph* he was emphatic in declaring:

> It wasn't anything of the sort. It was about a group of men who'd been to a public school but wasn't an attack on a system. I ought to know, I wrote the bloody thing.[5]

The Old Boys quickly became a vogue novel in Britain, was subsequently published in the United States and several European countries, was televised and adapted for radio. It won the Hawthornden Prize in 1965. Alastair Sim, the actor/director who was then at the height of his career, read the novel and wrote to Trevor asking if he would think of writing a play. The writer agreed to begin work on a stage play which would be adapted from a short story and which Alastair Sim would both star in and direct.

Chapter 2

'A farce in a vale of tears'

By the mid 1960s Trevor had become a highly productive writer. In the late spring of 1965, a television adaptation of *The Old Boys* was screened by BBC2, a new novel *The Boarding House* was launched and a stage play *The Elephant's Foot* opened in Nottingham and moved to Newcastle-upon-Tyne. An article in *The Guardian* newspaper entitled 'Gentle Gerontocrat'[1] was not surprising for in *The Elephant's Foot* Trevor once again chooses an elderly couple as central characters. Colonel and Mrs Pocock, both in their seventies are living separately, she in the family home in south-west London and he in a boarding house in Epping. Once a year, at Christmas, they come together in order to entertain their grandchildren. The children's father – the old couple's son – no longer visits them. As they prepare the celebration meal, the Pococks' behaviour is typical of any elderly pair who have shared for many years the joys and sorrows of life together. In a manner reminiscent of Samuel Beckett's Vladimir and Estragon in *Waiting for Godot* they pass the time in talking of other days, discussing their ailments, bickering over the vegetables and, in the Pococks' case, squabbling about the forgotten ingredients of a cake. Into this ordinary scene comes an interesting duo – Mr Freer, who purports to be a journalist, and his scruffy, younger companion, who is introduced as a photographer called Tiger. These two have come, they say, to take photographs of the elephant's foot umbrella-stand owned by the Pococks, claiming that they heard of its existence during a visit to Switzerland. Trevor says that the genesis of the plot arose from an idea which both fascinated and appalled him – the notion that somebody might come to the house, be welcomed as a guest and then refuse to leave. Freer, the more genial of the two strangers who enter the Pococks' home uninvited, is a wonderful talker and soon makes himself at home. He drinks the Christmas sherry, while Tiger gets sick on a bed upstairs. The mystery of the real purpose of the strangers' visit is eventually solved when Freer reveals that he and Tiger have come instead of the Pococks' grandchildren who do not wish to spend yet another boring Christmas with their grandparents. Freer then suggests that the old people should adopt Tiger as their son and he offers to sell his young companion to them for a sum of money, advising them that they need him as much as he needs them. In this fact lies the pathos of the piece. Tiger is obviously a sad, lonely boy, but the old people are just as pitiable. Their relationship can only survive if they have a common focus to sustain it. As the curtain comes down, there is some indication that the estranged couple may come together again.[2] Thus the play ends on an up-beat and ultimately delivers a message of hope. Its underlying tragedy is balanced by comedy and yet it is the tragic element of the piece which lingers most in the mind.

Once again Trevor's distinctive use of language in the play attracted attention. One reviewer thought it 'rather like the old nostalgic letters and articles one can still find in corners of *The Times* on quiet days'.[3] Not only the elderly Pococks indulge in the formal archaisms characteristic of Trevor's people; even the intruder, Freer, speaks in the same fashion. Just as they do in an Oscar Wilde play, characters of different social status and age all converse in the same idiom.

The setting of Trevor's next novel *The Boarding House* (1965) offers enormous potential as a location in which to gather a miscellaneous collection of characters, and provides an ideal setting for the observation of lonely and eccentric individuals whom fortune has thrown together. The possibilities inherent in such a situation allow the writer to observe what happens when a group of people with very different views find themselves in the same company. The scope for farce is limitless. In all likelihood the people will quarrel, but the novelist may decide to twist the situation slightly in order to produce a different outcome. The most unlikely characters may live together in harmony and this in turn provides an opportunity for equally interesting results.

Like the author, the proprietor of the boarding-house, Mr Bird, brings his people together as an experiment. The house itself is 'a turreted confection in red brick, with untended gardens at the front and rear' (BH 8), situated in a Victorian street in London SW 17, an area being demolished gradually by the developers of the 1960s. On his death Mr Bird wills his house to two of his most unsavoury residents, Nurse Clock and Mr Studdy. The nurse's actions are motivated solely by self-advancement, while her co-inheritor, Mr Studdy, is a conman who spends his time devising schemes for petty fraud and blackmail. In addition the pair dislike and distrust each other. As the plot unfolds the secret anguishes, ambitions and dreams of all the residents are disclosed, and presiding over all, even after his death, is the faintly sinister figure of Mr Bird.

The Boarding House is typical of the writer's early work. Once again the characters speak in an eccentrically formal way. 'I delight myself by talking in this manner,' (BH 130) Mr Bird observes and he might well be speaking at this point for Trevor as author. Writer and character also share the same attitude to the residents of the boarding-house. Neither lacks compassion, but both are essentially mischievous. In this novel the writer appears to view his creatures in god-like fashion as he manipulates them, seeming to be in turn amused by their antics and moved by their predicaments. Mr Bird adopts a similar mien in dealing with his paying guests. Clearly mirroring the author's stance he views the boarding-house as his creation, referring to it as 'a place of my own invention' (BH 66), in which he has:

> studied the condition of loneliness, looking at people who were solitary for one reason or another as though examining a thing or an insect beneath a microscope.
>
> (BH 118)

The eight residents of the boarding-house are a motley bunch of oddities consisting of the lonely, the shy, the guilt-ridden, the self-sacrificing, the sexually deviant and the predatory – familiar Trevor types. The arrival of Gallelty, the kitchen-maid, completes the household. Mr Bird now removes himself physically from the scene by dying, but in bequeathing the place to two arch-enemies, Studdy and Nurse Clock, the former proprietor ensures that trouble will follow. Mr Bird's will has been made with deliberate malice and he is amused by the notion of what is likely to happen after he is gone. 'I built that I may destroy,' (BH 212) he claims on his death-bed and after his demise circumstances are set in motion which culminate in the eventual destruction of the boarding-house.

In his lifetime Mr Bird kept a notebook in which he recorded details of the lives and personalities of his tenants. These brief case histories appear at intervals throughout the book, each one revealing its subject to the reader, while at the same time disclosing the equivocal nature of its compiler's mind. The 'Notes' were undoubtedly meant to be read one day, but ironically they perish undiscovered in a fire and Mr Bird never succeeds in communicating his observations to the wider world. Even his death-bed request made to Nurse Clock to convey to a newspaper an account of his dying sensations is ignored.

While he is still proprietor of the boarding-house, Mr Bird lives at the top of the building, and from there he is in a position to observe the little group of people which he has gathered around him. He is a student of human nature and he recognises both the misfortunes and the shortcomings of the people who share his home in Jubilee Road. At first glance the residents seem to be stereotyped eccentrics: the failed lawyer, Tome Obd, whose pride prevents his return to his home in Africa but does not protect him from an unrequited passion; Mr Venables whose life is bounded by fear and pain; Miss Clerricot whose frustrated sexuality leads her to misinterpret the attentions of her boss for whom she is merely 'a listening box ... a wireless in reverse' (BH 184); the gangling misfit, Mr Scribben, with his obsessive interest in train recordings; Major Eele with all his conventional prejudices and his penchant for pornographic films and black belly-dancers; the lonely spinster, Rose Cave, whose mother continues to dominate her life even from beyond the grave. But the reader soon discovers that the boarding-house is not peopled by stereotypes at all. In the course of the plot the author allows the characters to be viewed from several different angles, hitherto unseen facets of their lives are revealed and eventually they are discovered to be real people with individual griefs and preocupations. Many of them are perceptive enough to be aware of their predicaments and these experience moments of illumination which allow them to see clearly the pathos of their lives.

These epiphanies do not undermine the book's comic vein. *The Boarding House* deals with a tragi-comic world. Like Mr Bird, Trevor has studied the human condition but through his microscope he sees not insects but human beings who are vulnerable and his lens is tinted with compassion. As a result the characters are never merely absurd and each makes a claim on the reader's sympathy. Yet the tone of the book remains light and the language sufficiently stylised to ensure that the comic element is almost always in the foreground. On the other hand it is only occasionally that the humour becomes extravagant and farcical, as for instance in the scene in which Mr Bird's clothes are being given away to a charitable organisation for refugees. Due to Studdy's interference several items of clothing belonging to the residents are mistakenly included and misunderstandings and cross-purposes ensue. The contrast between the confused action and the clipped account of incongruous detail provides a delightful piece of comedy. But the laughter is never really cruel and the characters retain both dignity and credibility.

Nurse Clock and the devious Irishman, Studdy, emerge as the most overtly complicated characters in the novel. As a young woman the nurse had attended a charm-school, but had been assured by its owner, a charlatan himself, that she totally lacked the commodity in which he dealt. As a result she takes her revenge upon the world by cultivating elderly patients who are in no position to resist her officiousness. Her ambition is to gain control of the boarding-house so that she can, in defiance of Mr Bird's will, get rid of the tenants and turn the building into an old people's home. Her plans might seem at first to be altruistic, but the indifference with which she treats the dying Mr Bird and the more open cruelty which she manifests in her treatment of the elderly Mrs Maylam indicate her true nature.

For a time an uneasy alliance exists between the nurse and her partner, Studdy. The collusion between the two of them could never have continued because they are both manipulators. Studdy's ineptitude, however, leaves him vulnerable to Nurse Clock's more efficient ruthlessness and he is about to abandon his claim on the boarding-house when it is set alight by the demented African Tome Obd. The Irishman is an opportunist, a swindler, whose wickedness is, however, the stuff of comedy rather than of tragedy, if only because of his incompetence. He is the first of a line of similar characters who appear in Trevor's work. He specialises in attempted blackmail but his victims are more than a match for him. As a result of his machinations he is on the point of fleeing from the boarding-house on the night on which the fire occurs. But his luck does not desert him and eventually he finds himself:

> ... better off than anyone else because he had lain down in the clothes he wore, thinking he would shortly be on his way. He had carried his suitcase from the burning house and placed it against a lamp-post.

(BH 282)

The fire, in which the African is burnt to death, brings the book to what might have been a macabre and even arbitrary ending. Tome Obd's unrequited love, which accounts for his sudden fit of pyromania, is only indirectly connected with the main plot, which focuses on the tripartite struggle between Nurse Clock, Studdy and the other tenants for control of the boarding-house. It does, however, demonstrate the author's perfect control of his material as he treads a fine line between pathos and comedy. At the novel's conclusion Trevor cleverly broadens his view by using a wider lens and Mr Obd's death recedes into the background and fades into the over-all resolution of the plot. By this strategy the author maintains a tactical blend of compassion and distance.

The serious concerns of Trevor's next novel *The Love Department* are also coated with the gloss of humour. While the book draws on the experience the author gained of working in an office during the years he spent at Notley's, it is primarily an investigation of marriage among the middle-aged, middle-class, inhabitants of the London suburbs of the 1960s. The plot illustrates how romantic love is betrayed, but once again it is the tragi-comic aspect of the situation upon which the author focuses. At the end of the book its hero, Edward Blakeston-Smith, describes his adventures as 'A farce in a vale of tears' (LD 294) and this phrase aptly describes the tone of the work.

As the novel opens Edward has taken refuge from the world in a home run by religious brothers. He is endeavouring to escape from the inane advertisements and slogans which assail him from the country's billboards. On impulse he leaves his retreat and goes to work in the 'love department' of a London daily newspaper. The director of the department – which caters for lonely hearts – is Lady Dolores Bourhardie, a person of minuscule stature, who specialises in answering letters from women with problem marriages. At the time Edward joins her staff, a number of Lady Dolores's clients are victims of the attentions of Septimus Tuam, a man who uses his charm to seduce married women and who is consequently regarded by Lady Dolores as the arch-enemy of love. She welcomes Edward, an obvious innocent, as a heaven-sent antidote to the wicked Tuam.

Tuam's intended victim, as the story begins, is Eve Bolsover, a bored housewife from Wimbledon. His seductive technique is to sidle up to a woman and tear her stockings with the tip of his rolled umbrella. He then calls around to the lady's home with some new hosiery. Once he has gained entrance, none of the women can resist his advances. Edward is instructed by Lady Dolores to track down Tuam and to thwart him in his nefarious intentions. The chase which ensues develops into a farcical battle between good and evil as the guileless Edward blunders along in the wake of Tuam, the libertine, whose main interest the reader soon realises is not actually sexual. His chief concern is to add to the considerable sum of money which he has to date accumulated from his philandering.

Tuam's victims are middle-age, middle-class women. Their husbands are successful men, but the wives lead boring lives and feel neglected in their comfortable, suburban homes. Many of the husbands are equally unfulfilled. James Bolsover, Eve's husband, has spent years striving for success in the business world, success which is signified by a seat on his company's Board of Directors. Once his goal is achieved, James finds the experience disappointing. He describes it to Eve:

> 'Eight fat men with glasses,' he said, 'whom I had imagined to be men of power and cunning, sit yawning and grumping over the red baize of that table. They're fifteen years my senior, and they're fair in this: they see I've done a stint and so reward me. I may now relax in my early twilight and talk with them of how I heat my house, and exchange news of meals eaten in restaurants, and tell them stories they haven't heard before. They do no work, yet imagine otherwise ... It passes the time on a sleepy

afternoon while the underlings do the work. It's my reward
to say the underlings are worthless. Well, some of them
are.'

(LD 47-48)

A completely contrasting figure is James's elderly father, whose
life is nearing its end. In his prime he had run a successful market-
garden and his marriage had retained its magic down through the
years. Now he looks forward to death as a romantic opportunity to
renew his relationship with his deceased wife.

For the bored wives who are Septimus Tuam's prey, their
seducer embodies the romance which they feel is missing from
their lives. He seems to be the ideal partner – helpful, attentive and
appreciative – rather like the ideal men who appear on the
advertisement hoardings which so terrify Edward Blakeston-Smith.
Edward, with the perception of the pure-hearted, fears this unreal
world:

> He had feared most of all the men and women who played
> around with cigarettes or chocolates, people who eyed one
> another in a peculiar manner. Men leaned forward, sticking
> chocolates into women's mouths, or lighting cigarettes for
> them. They were the giants of the hoardings, standing in
> the sunshine, in speedboats or on rocks, up to their tricks.
> They performed on waterskis, balancing butter in the air;
> they ate and they smoked, they smiled over bedtime drinks
> or glasses of hard liquor. They had green faces or purple
> ones, and brown skins, and teeth as white as toothpaste.
>
> Edward had complained of the size of the men and
> women and of their insincere teeth.

(LD 8)

Edward's pronouncement towards the end of the book that
'there's no love on the hoardings of Britain' (LD 243) is borne out
by the lives of those who strive for this impossible world. Trevor's
experience at Notley's gave him a particular insight into the cult of
unreality which advertisements promulgate. Eve Bolsover, whose
first name indicates that she is Everywoman, has come to the
realisation that the fairy-tale marriage which she had hoped would
last for ever has become spiritually and emotionally dead.
Boredom has bred bitterness and has left her vulnerable to
Septimus Tuam's dubious charms.

Meanwhile James Bolsover has become so disillusioned by his position on the Board of Directors, that he welcomes the conspiracy between his subordinate, Mr Lake, and his secretary, Miss Brown, to have him dismissed from its membership. One of the book's subplots deals with the machinations of these two and their relationship with each other. Lake is an ambitious but limited young man who wished to further his own career at James Bolsover's expense. He has sublimated all sexual desire into a determination to achieve his purpose and is consequently oblivious of the thwarted passion which Miss Brown feels for him. The impact of Lake's wickedness on the reader is mitigated, however, not only by his victim's willingness to suffer, but also by the inflated quality of the language used:

> 'I have young blood to offer,' said Lake to Miss Brown, standing by the window of her office. 'What can hold back the tide of my business success? I have business acumen of an unparalleled quality.'
>
> (LD 72)

Meanwhile the narrative voice concludes in a tone which echoes the cadences of the King James edition of the Bible:

> And Miss Brown's heart thumped and tumbled inside her, and her love was greater than it had been a minute before.
>
> (LD 72)

The comic effect is achieved by the contrast between the elevated tone of the dialogue and the ordinariness of the subject matter. It is a device which Trevor uses frequently. The same tone is adopted by Mr FitzArthur, another husband cuckolded by Septimus Tuam, when as the injured party he demands that his wife assure him of her future fidelity:

> 'Tomorrow I come in person for my final answer. I am to hear from your lips, madam, whether or no the scoundrel is naught in your heart.'
>
> (LD 29)

The plot of the novel is largely picaresque, punctuated by occasional farcical episodes. One in particular, which involves an abortive dinner party, is a comic masterpiece. It features another favourite Trevor character, the spiteful charwoman, who uses every opportunity to cheat and denigrate her employer. The guests who attend the party are also of the caricatured types generally found in farce and their broad humour and physical horseplay ensure that the party ends in uproar and confusion. Lady Dolores might also belong in a typical farce, but this is only one element of the novel and although she may seem at first glance to be a caricature, she is later discovered to be a complex character. She is fifty years of age and although only four and a half feet tall she has 'never been classified as a dwarf' (LD 13). More realistically developed versions of her character appear in Trevor's later work. She likes to manipulate others and her real aim is to seduce Septimus Tuam herself. She intends that he should fall in love with her so that she can exact revenge for all the women whom he has mistreated. On close examination we can see that her motives are as complex as her character and she is neither wholly altruistic nor completely vindictive. In fact she longs to be loved herself. Her desires are revealed in a scene which she imagines with Tuam:

> There was an explosion that was soundless in the love department, and her ears were filled with the words she had read about. 'I love you,' said Septimus Tuam.
>
> (LD 293)

She is both revered and feared by others. Edward's admiration of Lady Dolores turns to dread when he believes that her malign influence is driving him to murder Tuam. For Edward, Lady Dolores becomes a 'contemporary witch' (LD 219).

Edward's ineffectual pursuit of Septimus Tuam leads him through the streets of suburban London, allowing him to become involved in the book's subplots and to draw all the strands of the story together. In the process he discovers and denounces other miscreants such as James Bolsover's enemy, Mr Lake, and the charwoman, Mrs Hoop. Edward emerges as the catalyst who voices the moral sensibility of the novel.

Fate lends Edward a hand in settling scores and causing the downfall of the villainous forces. Having successfully foiled the plans of both Mr Lake and Mrs Hoop, only Septimus Tuam continues to elude him. Scared that he will kill Tuam, Edward decides to abandon the pursuit. As he cycles off, he throws away a pair of gloves which he has received as a present from Lady

Dolores. His gesture of defection has dramatic results. A man darts into the roadway to retrieve the gloves and a taxi, swerving to avoid the man, mounts the footpath and kills Septimus Tuam. The tragi-comic nature of the death scene confirms Edward's statement that he has indeed participated in 'A farce in a vale of tears' (LD 294).

The balance between the author's comic intent and his moral concern is delicately maintained, and humour continues to camouflage his moral preoccupations. On close examination it becomes obvious that even the putative villain, Tuam, cannot be held entirely responsible for the fate of his victims. Although three women were rumoured to have died for love of him, it was the circumstances of their lives which really ruined them and Tuam was merely the immediate instrument of their undoing. Septimus Tuam proves to be no worse than any of the petty confidence tricksters who feature in Trevor's books.

The novel is rooted in reality, yet it occasionally soars into the realms of the fantastic. The characters, too, range from the completely credible to the allegorical. Edward, the central character, inclines to the mystical, his extraordinary innocence confounding all corruption – albeit purely by accident. The book closes with Edward's return to the sanctuary of St Gregory's monastery, where he prays for 'the preservation of love within marriage'. (LD 290) The Bolsovers too find salvation. James has gladly quitted the business world and has taken over his father's market garden, where Eve, reassured by Edward's promise of prayer, joins him in an attempt to re-establish their lost Eden – the garden symbolising spiritual growth and renewal. In spite of the rich comic elements, however, this time the novel ends on a dying fall. In this it previews Trevor's later work which frequently leaves the reader with a vague feeling of sadness. A delicate balancing act has been achieved between tragedy and farce and between realism and fantasy. But the tragic element, which has hovered beneath the surface in *The Old Boys* and become more perceptible in *The Boarding House*, looms larger still in *The Love Department*.

Chapter 3

'The best things are complex and mysterious'

With two successful novels to his credit, Trevor returned to the idea of publishing a collection of short stories. *The Day We Got Drunk on Cake*, a volume of twelve stories, a number of which had already appeared in magazines, was published by the Bodley Head in 1967. The stories have certain features in common: the characters are largely defenceless people who are either very old, very young or emotionally vulnerable. They have difficulty in coping with the truth, the nature of which is seen to be far from simple. Some characters cannot perceive it, others cannot accept it and generally those who have the courage to voice it are not believed. When occasionally it is revealed, there are brief moments of illumination, but these are quickly extinguished and the situation settles back to its former state. There is disappointment and frustration, but finally there is acceptance.

Some of the strongest stories in the book feature the breakdown or loss of self which occurs when people cannot communicate with the world about them. Instead they establish alternative versions of reality into which they retreat. In 'The Original Sins of Edward Tripp' Emily Tripp begins to behave strangely on the day of her mother's funeral. Emily and her brother Edward have shared the same house since childhood, the time at which the 'sins' mentioned in the title were committed. Edward had teased her sister with mischievous acts which despite their apparent childishness may also suggest a proleptic sexual violation:

> From her own private flower-bed he had pulled her pansies, roots and all, when he was five years old; and with a pair of scissors he had cut through the centre of the buds

of her roses. 'I have played a trick on you,' he used to say, sidling close to her.

(CS 171)

Other transgressions included giving away her books, setting fire to her doll's house and killing her guinea-pig. Reviewing the past from the vantage point of middle-age, Edward realises that the cumulative effects of his 'tricks' have distorted his sister's mind. They have

> ... fallen like a blight upon her nature in the end, wrenching some bit of it out of shape, embittering the whole.

(CS 172)

Emily's delusions lead her to create a world which is full of murder and mayhem. She draws Edward so far into her warped creation that he too teeters on the brink of insanity. His position might be tragic, were it not for the ironic humour which permeates the story. Edward accepts what happens as his just punishment and prays for forgiveness, hoping that one day his sister will:

> ... smile as once she had smiled as a child, offering him her forgiveness while saying she was sorry too, and releasing in sumptuous glory all the years of imprisoned truth.

(CS 179)

The stories 'In at the Birth' and 'The Hotel of the Idle Moon' also open up for the reader strange and puzzling worlds, albeit approached from different angles – the former exploring the mysterious realms of second childhood, the latter parodying early horror films. In each case the tone is only semi-serious, but the stories demonstrate the absurdity of confining the search for meaning to the realms of rationality. The writer invites us to break away from the restrictions of reason and to accept an augmented world in which we are forced to review all our assumptions and consider the view of Miss Efoss, the central character of 'In at the Birth', that 'The best things are complex and mysterious'. (CS 111)

Gothic writers of the nineteenth century liked to explore the perversions which occasionally erupted from beneath the surface of the apparently 'normal' mind. In their works they expressed the prevailing views of their age on the constitution of the mind and its capacity for evil. In Anglo-Irish literature there is a strong tradition of Gothic writing: Charles Maturin, Sheridan LeFanu and Bram Stoker were all Irish and all masters of the mode. Trevor never consciously chose to follow in their footsteps, but when his interest in the nature of evil led him, in his early work, into a territory which Gothic writers had also trodden, he instinctively adapted the machinery of Gothic writing to the twentieth century. Instead of the remote castle beloved of the nineteenth century writer, Trevor uses the village, the suburban street and the boarding-school as enclosed worlds in which to show that the heart of post-existentialist man is just as dark as that of his nineteenth century antecedent and as the victim of evil forces he remains as vulnerable as ever.

The ordinariness of evil is a theme which Trevor develops in depth later in his writing. The most heinous acts are performed by people who, he believes, as children were like anybody else. Conversely the potential for evil is within each one of us. 'A School Story' and 'Miss Smith' are among the darker stories in the collection, the first dealing with a boy who is driven demented by a mistaken sense of guilt while the second demonstrates how an ordinary if not very attractive child becomes capable of a horrific crime.

James Machen is described by his teacher, the eponymous Miss Smith, as 'like a weasel wearing glasses'. She claims that he gives her 'the creeps'. (CS 135) Initially the child makes several attempts to win his teacher's approval but she rebuffs him and he becomes obsessed by her. When his final effort to win favour fails, James seeks revenge on his teacher. Miss Smith, now married and happily caring for her infant son, finds that strange and unaccountable accidents befall her child, culminating in his disappearance on his third birthday. When all hope of finding the child has receded, James appears and offers to show Miss Smith her missing baby. A tremendous sense of the macabre is achieved in the final paragraph of the story as the little boy skips along laughing at the side of the distraught mother:

> On the heavy air his laughter rose and fell; it quivered
> through his body and twitched lightly in his hand. It came
> as a giggle, then a breathless spasm; it rose like a storm
> from him; it rippled to gentleness; and it pounded again
> like the firing of guns in her ear. It would not stop. As they

walked together on this summer's day the laughter would
continue until they arrived at the horror, until the horror
was complete.

(CS 141)

The unspecified nature of 'the horror' echoes Marlowe's cry in
Conrad's *Heart of Darkness*, its undefined nature far more terrifying
than anything more specific could be. There is no humorous relief
in this story, no ironic detachment. This is sombre realism at its
scariest.

Now that his first collection of stories had been published,
Trevor was busy working on another stage play. *The Girl*, originally
written for ABC Television, opened at The King's Head, a small
theatre in the London suburb of Islington. Echoing Trevor's earlier
stage play, the plot involves another intruder figure, a young girl
called Felicity, who arrives at the home of a childless couple, Mr
and Mrs Green, and announces that she is Mr Green's daughter,
the issue of a brief encounter which had taken place seventeen
years before. Mr Green admits the infidelity, but denies that the girl
is his daughter.

Felicity is in search of a father and she is drawn to Mr Green,
fascinated by everything about him, his home, his hobby of making
papier mache models of royal figures. At the same time she
exploits the situation, seeming to be about to withdraw her claim
and leave, but then threatening that she will take to the streets as a
prostitute. Eventually she admits that her visit is part of a game, 'a
lark'. (TG 19) Her dead mother had bequeathed her a list of men's
names. Any one of them might have been her father. She is in the
habit of calling on a different man from the list each Friday night,
knowing that he will not be able to hand her over to the welfare
authorities until the following Monday morning. This time,
however, she is convinced that she has found the right man and
she wants to stay with the Greens. Any hope she has of being
allowed to do so is destroyed by the arrival of the girl's friends, a
bunch of teenagers who proceed to throw a party in the Greens'
house. The young people are insolent and wantonly destructive,
behaving with the same callousness as do the youngsters who
wreck Mrs Malby's house in the story 'Broken Homes'. In spite of
Felicity's pleadings the young people abuse and rob the adults.

When they finally leave there is a moment of great pathos as the girl offers to make good the damage which they have done:

> **Felicity:** *(rising)* I'll pay back the money. I'll pay back every penny. I'll clear up the mess.
>
> **Mr Green:** *(violently angry)* Clean up the mess? Pay back the money? If you hadn't come here insinuating your way into the house nothing would have happened. What d'you think it's like, for God's sake, to have a half-witted girl saying she's your daughter and bringing a gang of thugs to break the place up? Why d'you imagine we should want you here? Why? Great God, d'you think we're mad?
>
> *(Felicity [who has gone out] enters with her coat and carrying her haversack)*
>
> **Felicity:** *(very quietly)* Someone must be my father, sir. Someone.
>
> (TG 33)

The girl departs quietly and sadly, convinced that she has been turned away by her father. The Green household will never be the same again. The truth about Felicity's origins remains uncertain, but Mrs Green is convinced that the girl is her husband's daughter and she is haunted by images of his infidelity. As the curtain falls the adults try to gather up the broken pieces of Mr Green's models, symbols of their former lives, now irrevocably damaged.

A homeless orphan, Felicity is a marginalised character, who is both victim and catalyst. She provokes trouble and the same time engages sympathy. She exposes the weaknesses of others, but also reveals her own vulnerability – the quality which ultimately defines her. It is the pathos evoked in the play which dominates the memory. Characters fail to connect and an opportunity for the development of human understanding is lost.

The havoc wrought by those who ruthlessly expose the lives of others is explored by Trevor in his first recognisably 'Irish' work, the novel *Mrs Eckdorf in O'Neill's Hotel* (1969). The book is set exclusively in Dublin and it involves the author's reflections on the métier of the writer as a person who uses his own and other people's experiences as the raw material of his work. Mrs Eckdorf is the kind of writer who relentlessly follows her intuition in an attempt to reveal the secrets of the victims of her investigations.

Born in the London suburb of Maida Vale, Ivy Eckdorf, a resident of Munich, has a traumatic past. Deserted by her father, scandalised by her promiscuous mother, shocked by a teacher's homosexual advances, she has had two unconsummated marriages. The effects of the emotional damage she has suffered can be seen in her conduct as a professional photographer. She specialises in human tragedies and as the book opens she is on her way to Dublin in pursuit of another catastrophe. She has already exploited the case of a Mexican priest who has lost his faith; she has retraced and photographed the route taken by a murderer in Colorado and she has exposed the incestuous relationship in a Marrakesh family whose hospitality she had accepted. 'A picture tells a story,' (MEOH 12) she declares, but the story as she interprets it is not necessarily true.

The focus of Mrs Eckdorf's attention is a run-down family hotel, about which she had heard a vague tale from a ship's barman who had once visited Dublin. She intends to compile a story about the hotel's deaf-and-dumb owner, Mrs Sinnott, and her family, and to publish her findings in a coffee-table book. The occasion she has chosen as the centre of her investigation is the old woman's ninety-second birthday.

The Dublin through which Mrs Eckdorf travels is an authentic city of the 1960s – with its combination of dilapidation and development. The photographer has scant regard for the citizens of the capital. As she passes through St Stephen's Green she photographs an old beggar-woman:

> She photographed the woman, explaining to her that her face would now travel all over the world. She spoke harshly when the beggar-woman again asked for alms. 'Get off to hell,' she ordered angrily.
>
> (MEOH 70)

'You're local interest to me,' (MEOH 70) she tells a pair of card-sharpers she encounters in Bachelor's Walk, her reactions as mechanical as the click of her camera.

Before the advent of Mrs Eckdorf, the only official residents of O'Neill's Hotel are Mrs Sinnott and her son, Eugene, along with O'Shea, the porter. A pimp called Morrissey and Agnes Quin, a prostitute, are unofficial guests. Visitors to the hotel include

Eugene's estranged wife, Philomena, and her son, Timothy John. The young man is the centre of his mother's world, but he spends his time fantasising about a shop girl with the unlikely name of Daisy Tulip. Mrs Sinnott's daughter, Enid, and her selfish husband, Desmond Gregan, also come within the orbit of the old lady. Finally there is Father Hennessy, a local priest, who is preoccupied with the lives of the saints. His ambition is to disentangle truth from myth in his work as a hagiographer. In this he is a foil to Mrs Eckdorf, whose object is to use her camera to construct myths and then to deliver her versions of events to the world.

Unlike Mrs Eckdorf, Mrs Sinnott has experienced real love in her life. The old woman has known sadness too – her young husband had been killed in Ireland's War of Independence – but in old age she dwells more and more in the happy past and has a benign attitude to the present. People confide in her, communicating with her by writing in red exercise-books which she keeps for the purpose. A perfect listener, she allows people to unburden themselves without fear of remonstration. She is the passive but wise character who is an objective observer, rather like the author, viewing the world as it is, but forbearing to pass judgement.

Mrs Sinnott's spirit pervades the seedy hotel. Her ageing body blends with the decaying building, but her memory and perception are active and although she cannot communicate through speech her insights set events in perspective. Her conversation notebooks reveal much about the lives of those who visit her. Bit by bit the reader pieces together the past and understands the present in terms of what has gone before. Gradually the picture is completed as past, present and even glimpses of the future lend it dimension and perspective.

The 'secret' of O'Neill's Hotel which Mrs Eckdorf finally discovers is that twenty-nine years earlier, Philomena, then an employee at the hotel, had been seduced by Eugene, and had given birth to his son, Timothy John. Mrs Sinnott had arranged the marriage of the couple, but when the union proved unhappy she equally arranged a separation and established Philomena and Timothy John in a bungalow of their own. Enid had been shocked by her brother's behaviour and had married Mr Gregan in order to escape the situation. These events are unknown to Timothy John and have either been forgotten or forgiven by the other participants in the drama. Mrs Eckdorf, however, refuses to accept this version of events. Instead she imposes her own interpretation, imagining that tragedy had only been ameliorated through the goodness of Mrs Sinnott – God's agent in the affair.

Father Hennessy attempts to disabuse Mrs Eckdorf of this notion. In a pivotal exchange between them, the priest accuses her of defining the lives of others in terms of her own life. The man who wishes to unearth the ordinary lives of the saints from beneath the obscuring burden of mythology refuses to acquiesce in Mrs Eckdorf's invention of 'a God to suit her own needs'. (MEOH 264) The priest is appalled by Mrs Eckdorf's ability to invent what she cannot know and to use her invention to draw a metaphysical conclusion. He urges her instead to seek real faith, but this undramatic approach has no appeal for the compiler of coffee-table books, who wishes to express herself in a grandiose gesture of forgiveness by washing the feet of those whom she fancies have wronged her. Father Hennessy, recognising the inherent pride in her gesture, attempts to dissuade her from this action, but he only succeeds in infuriating her. In her anger she reveals the shallowness of her new-found charity and equanimity: 'God is a disease in all your minds ... My photographs will illustrate a myth,' (MEOH 264-5) she threatens as she leaves the priest's house.

The loss of her newly-created God precipitates Mrs Eckdorf's decline into insanity. In a final dramatic gesture – the kind of scene she would have wished to photograph – she throws her belongings, including her camera and all her clothing, into the River Liffey. The remainder of her life is spent in a mental institution, where she is visited in reality by Father Hennessy and in her imagination by the other people of the hotel. She began by being a callous figure, but at the end she is pathetic and yet strangely content. For Mrs Eckdorf, who in her madness regains her 'private poor man's God' (MEOH 303) who consoles her 'at least there was a happy ending'. (MEOH 304)

Mrs Eckdorf in O'Neill's Hotel is one of Trevor's most complex books. It concerns itself with the operation of God's grace in the world. Using the general framework of the religious novel – as exemplified by the work of François Mauriac, Evelyn Waugh or Graham Greene, all writers whom Trevor admires – it presents a conflict between secular and divine values in which the divine unexpectedly triumphs. Usually in a novel of this kind the activation of grace demands sacrifice on the part of the protagonist and results in catastrophe on the human level. Following this general outline the book explores the conflict between Ivy Eckdorf's exploitation of people as subject-matter for her books and the peace she finds as a result of what she perceives to be the manifestation of God in one of those people. This God whom Ivy Eckdorf finds in Mrs Sinnott's room affects her life, both magnificently and catastrophically. She had come to Dublin to exploit a supposed tragedy, but finds in the shabby world of O'Neill's Hotel a deity who heals the tragedy within herself. The place in which she first attains this beatific vision of peace and love is a street bearing the name of the apostle Thaddeus, also known as Jude, patron of the hopeless, among whom she had been numbered up to the point of her encounter with God. The cost which Ivy Eckdorf pays for her miracle of grace is the loss of her sanity – which was always precarious anyway – and the blessed state which she enters insulates her from the ugliness that had hitherto hardened her. In the asylum she lives in a heaven of her own and is 'the happiest woman they had ever admitted'. (MEOH 302)

The paradigm of the religious novel serves as a basis of the plot of *Mrs Eckdorf in O'Neill's Hotel*, but it is not necessarily the most notable aspect of the book. The cast of characters, each of whom enhances the reader's view of Mrs Eckdorf, is unforgettable. Other characters view the photographer from different angles of distortion – for one she is a restorer of the past, for another a racing tip – each projecting his own obsession and adding to the reader's picture of the lady from Maida Vale.

While Mrs Eckdorf is in search of the secret of O'Neill's Hotel, the notion of quest is played out on a farcical level by a minor character, the Liverpudlian Mr Smedley, engaged in a pursuit of his own. An outsider like Mrs Eckdorf, Smedley's ambition is to find the 'facilities' which Dublin might offer a 'Man of vigour'. (MEOH 94) He meets only disapproval and hostility and is informed that:

> ... no such persons were permitted to exist in this city of godliness and decency.
>
> (MEOH 144)

As result he concludes that:

> ... of all the cities he had ever visited this one was the most unfriendly, the most unenterprising, the rudest, the ugliest and the stupidest.
>
> (MEOH 144)

The irony of the Liverpudlian's situation is underscored by the fact that his quest is paralleled by the stratagems of the pimp, Morrissey, who is simultaneously trying to peddle his wares – and with as little success.

Three decades after it was written, the theme of the novel has become increasingly pertinent. The author returns to the same idea in a later story called 'Events at Drimaghleen' (CS 1086) – and again raises questions about the nature of truth, the tension between the duty to search for it and reveal it and the harm done by the exposure to the public gaze of people's hidden lives. For Mrs Eckdorf the price of tampering with people's secrets is insanity; for Mrs Sinnott, who receives voluntary confidences and returns compassion, there is love and peace; for Father Hennessy there is the need to continue his work of demythologising the past. At a time when the intrusiveness of the press is being clearly condemned, yet the need for transparency in public life is strongly demanded, when investigative journalism has been responsible on the one hand for uncovering serious cases of injustice and on the other for engaging in witch-hunts which victimise the innocent as much as the guilty, these subjects are remarkably relevant.

Like Mrs Eckdorf, Miss Gomez, the figure at the centre of Trevor's subsequent novel *Miss Gomez and the Brethren* (1971), is a woman with a mission who acts as a catalyst in a foreign city. As an abused orphan she too had a traumatic childhood in her native Jamaica. She comes to London to earn her living in a variety of jobs – as cereal packer, shop assistant, night-club stripper and prostitute. The chance reading of a newspaper advertisement brings her in touch with the Church of the Brethren of the Way, based in Tacas, Jamaica, with which she corresponds in her search for the meaning of life.

The London which she finds has much in common with Mrs Eckdorf's Dublin. Crow Street where she works is

> an area of demolition, a wilderness of wastelands in which hundreds of houses had already been destroyed.

(MGB 37)

Miss Gomez becomes a cleaner at the Thistle Arms, a pub managed by Mr and Mrs Tuke. Mrs Tuke exists on a diet of gin and peppermint mixed with trashy novels, a cocktail which helps her to forget temporarily the sordidness of her life. Her physically unattractive husband has become withdrawn since he discovered that he is not the father of Mrs Tuke's daughter, Prudence, and has transferred his affections to his Alsatian dog, Rebel. The lodgers at the Thistle Arms are the deaf octogenarian, Mr Batt, and a young Irishman called Alban Roche, recently released after serving a two-month jail sentence for a Peeping Tom offence. Prudence Tuke is in love with Roche and helps him look after the pets in a shop he inherits on the death of its original owner. The shop no longer has any customers and is due for demolition, so Roche and Prudence must look for alternative accommodation.

Each of the characters is engrossed in private obsessions. Consequently there is little communication between them and misunderstandings arise. Out of her loneliness Miss Gomez too creates an obsession – a mission to prevent a sexual crime. She sees herself as a divinely appointed instrument whose intervention will save Prudence Tuke from Alban Roche, whom she believes intends to rape and murder the girl. In a climactic scene midway through the novel Miss Gomez confronts Mr and Mrs Tuke in the presence of Mr Batt and Mrs Tuke's lustful Irish admirer, Atlas Flynn: 'We're all cripples ... There's something the matter with each and every one of us ... Terrible things are in all of us.' (MGB 132), she warns them, revealing all their foibles and begging them to pray together and reason with the man she is convinced intends to harm Prudence. Like so many Trevor characters, however, her listeners believe neither her warnings, nor the truth about themselves.

The crime which Miss Gomez prophesies is not committed. Instead Prudence and Alban Roche begin a new life together. A bloody act of violence does take place but its victim is Rebel, Mr Tuke's dog, who is killed and eaten by stray cats. The scene is powerful in its horror as it plays out dramatically the savagery which lurks beneath the surface of life.

The events of the novel seem to discredit both Miss Gomez's powers of prophecy and her faith. She makes a visit to Jamaica to meet the founders of her church, only to find that the Brethren of the Way are the invention of a seedy Englishman, who before his recent disappearance had been living off the donations of wretched people who depended on him to provide some purpose to their lives. While Miss Gomez is distressed to find that the Church of which she was a member has been an illusion, she quickly changes her allegiance to the Assembly of God Church, because she believes that:

> God worked in that mysterious way ... weaving a cobweb among all His people, a complexity that was not there to be understood while his people were any living part of it ... Her faith was defiant in adversity ...

(MGB 291)

Like the other characters she needs her private world to help her through the difficulties of life. But her religion is not purely an escape. It is the means by which she seeks enlightenment. Even as a child in Jamaica she had looked for answers to the riddle of life and at that point had come to the conclusion that 'The God thing was a confidence trick'. (MGB 14) Later when she follows the Brethren she is not content to carry out their instructions to allow prayer alone to solve problems. Instead she confronts people with the truth about themselves and attempts to intervene in their lives. She may be misled, but the effects of what she does are positive.

Ultimately Miss Gomez's message is that all people are capable of evil – a theme which appears early in Trevor's work and to which he returns frequently and in various ways throughout his writing career.

While it might seem at first that Miss Gomez's belief in God's 'complicated patterns' (MGB 131) has been misguided, her advice to fight against fate is justified by the subsequent lives of Prudence Tuke and Alban Roche. Other characters too reach a degree of self-knowledge and some seek new dreams or adapt old ones to suit new circumstances. Miss Gomez may find that organised religion is as unsound as the people involved in it and the mystery of life may always elude her, but her determination to continue the search, while it shows a certain naivety, also reveals the confident tenacity of the human spirit in its effort to cope with an absurd universe. A subtle optimism permeates what might otherwise have been a pessimistic theme.

The novel has a serious purpose as it probes the deepest loneliness of its characters and the foolish methods by which they try to stave off despair in their lives. Yet it is a very funny book as the author undermines even the most sober scenes with a touch of the grotesque. On the occasion on which Miss Gomez delivers her sombre message to the assembly in the hallway of the Thistle Arms, for example, the crisis is subverted by the deaf Mr Batt's misinterpretation of what is happening and by the arrant racism of the vulgar Mrs Tuke:

> Mr Batt's eyes were screwed up, fixed on the packet of Embassy Gold cigarettes that Miss Gomez still held in her left hand. He wondered if she'd stolen the cigarettes from the bar and decided that she had … An argument had broken out, which was still continuing; it was more serious, naturally, than just smoking on duty …
>
> 'The Reverend Lloyd Patterson is the founder of my Church, Mrs Tuke –'
>
> 'Your bloody Church can get itself stuffed. You're an ignorant savage, Gomez, with your slimy plants and your rubbishy Church. You're not fit for a civilised country.' …
>
> 'You're completely ridiculous,' she shouted. 'The first time I saw you I said to myself you were completely ridiculous. A negroid in glasses, I said –'
>
> 'God is present in this hall, Mrs Tuke.'
>
> 'I don't care who's bloody present. You come over here and then you imitate white people. Ridiculous they look on you, those leathers you wear. Everything about you is ridiculous. You have teeth like bloody tombstones. You have softening of the brain –'
>
> 'Please listen to me, Mrs Tuke.'
>
> 'We've listened enough to you. We're sick and tired of standing here listening to you. You're a smutty-minded creeping Jesus. You've got God on your stupid brain-box –'
>
> 'There's an emptiness in you, Mrs Tuke, that God could fill: I have had that written from Tacas. God is important, Mrs Tuke, in all our lives; I'm trying to explain that to you.'   (MGB 135-6)

The God whom Mrs Eckdorf and Miss Gomez find at the end of their quests is, after all, the God of human compassion and endeavour. The heroine of Trevor's next novel, *Elizabeth Alone* (1973), is not consciously in search of God, but in the process of the book she too debates the nature of the deity and through her experiences reaches an understanding of the miracle of humanity.

In *Elizabeth Alone* Trevor ventures into a female sanctum which is rarely explored by male writers – the gynaecological ward of a hospital – a location in which the normal divisions of society have little meaning and in which the vulnerability of the human condition is emphasised because of the patients' illnesses. Three women are having hysterectomies while a fourth is desperately trying to prevent yet another miscarriage.

Elizabeth Aidallbery, the central figure, would seem at first to be in the least desperate situation, in spite of the recent break-up of a love affair which caused her divorce. There is, however, little purpose to her life. Her eldest daughter, Joanna, has grown away from her and is under the influence of her hippy boyfriend, Samuel, and his dubious mentor, Mrs Tabor-Ellis. Elizabeth feels guiltily that the younger children will follow a similar path.

Looking back at her life from the vantage point of forty-one years, Elizabeth can make little sense of it:

> She saw mistakes, mainly made by herself. She saw her life
> as something that was scattered untidily about, without a
> pattern, without rhyme or reason.
>
> (EA 8-9)

Guilt is the emotion which haunts Elizabeth. She first experienced it at twelve years of age when she found that she was unable to weep at her father's death. Later it coloured her relationships with her husband, her children, her lover and her mother. Guilt persuaded her to marry a man many years her senior. Later she came to resent her husband when she realised that he had chosen her as his wife so that she could flatter his ego. The same residual guilt is now turned towards her mother whom she loves dearly, but who has recently become a voluntary resident of the Sunshine Home for the elderly.

The action of the novel occurs among the families and friends of the four patients, who come from different backgrounds and who are unlikely to have met in their ordinary lives. Now in the confined world of the Mary Atkins Ward of the Cheltenhan Street Hospital they communicate their hopes, dreams and worries to each other.

While Elizabeth's relationships form the main plot, they are reinforced by the experiences of the other women in the ward. Sylvie Clapper has cut herself off from her family of petty criminals, but ironically has fallen in love with Declan, a young Irishman of great charm but doubtful integrity. Lily Drucker, in danger of a miscarriage, broods over the schemes her jealous mother-in-law will concoct to regain possession of her son, Kenneth, Lily's devoted but ineffectual husband. Finally there is Miss Samson, with a disfiguring birthmark on her face, whose once-solid faith in God has been recently shaken.

The resilience of these women is shown as they cope with a world which exploits them materially and emotionally as they come to terms with their destinies. The sense of liberation which they eventually achieve is a central theme of the novel. It is reinforced symbolically by the somewhat contrived figure of the woman who parades daily outside the hospital, carrying a banner attached to a sweeping-brush handle which reads 'Liberation Now'. (EA 25) No one ever discovers the cause of the woman's protest but her message is pertinent to the four women in the Mary Atkins Ward. Another endorsement comes from the autobiography of the foundress of the hospital, the Victorian Lady Augusta Haptree, which the patients are reading. Excerpts from the book, which chronicles Lady Augusta's loveless marriage and her determination to fulfil herself through her work, punctuate the activities of the characters as would a Greek chorus. Lady Augusta's observations underscore the plight of all women and in doing so universalise the theme:

> I am angered sometimes, she read, by the exploitation of women, not in the factories, of which we nowadays hear much, but in the homes which they themselves have helped to make. And I am angered by women's folly in encouraging that exploitation and by accepting without protest the status of mindless creatures. (EA 76)

The theme is reinforced in other ways too. A framed adage which reads 'Strength groweth through Affliction' (EA 91) hangs on the wall of Miss Samson's boarding-house and Elizabeth finds herself agreeing with the wisdom encapsulated in a sign in the window of an employment bureau which advises its readers to 'Start Living'. (EA 330) For those who would accept these messages, however, there is first a painful road through a landscape of incredible bleakness. On the journey the characters draw strength from each other and the main protagonists eventually find an answer to their existentialist questions.

Post-operative dreams reveal the women's deepest anxieties. In Elizabeth's dream past and present mingle in a surrealist landscape. She feels guilty about the failure of her marriage, her inadequacy as a mother and her part in the nervous breakdown of her lover's wife. The figure of her childhood friend, Henry, intervenes to console her and the other women in the ward reassure her – 'They were all happy enough, they said, really and truly'. (EA 123) This dreamed statement is later echoed by Elizabeth herself when she in turn reassures Miss Samson '… we're just ordinary women. We're not particularly unhappy'. (EA 328) Sylvie's dream reveals her guilt about an abortion, while Miss Samson's nightmare destroys her belief in a good God. As a result the very basis of her acceptance of her affliction founders. Unable to pray she loses faith in the goodness of both God and man and becomes at this point the embodiment of suffering woman.

In the days following her operation Elizabeth receives a number of shocks. Her daughter Joanna decides to join Mrs Tabor-Ellis's commune, Henry her childhood friend dies in absurd circumstances and her former husband announces his planned marriage. The effects of these events cause Elizabeth to have a relapse and there follows a nightmare sequence in which she is again overwhelmed by feelings of guilt and fear. This time, however, a comforting Jesus – like presence attends her:

> In the room a man stood near to Elizabeth, a man she couldn't properly see … He was a man who loved her and smiled away her guilt. He listened, he forgave her, he did not cease to love her … He was a man like a ghost because she could not quite see him and was more aware of him with other senses.   (EA 284)

On her release from hospital, Elizabeth lapses into a mood of depression and languor, broken only by sensations of panic. She avoids contact with other people and only accepts Miss Samson's invitation to coffee under duress. In one of the most important scenes of the novel, Elizabeth listens to Miss Samson's agonising discourse on the nature of God. The older woman confides to her reluctant guest the full depth of the abyss of despair into which she had been plunged by her doubts about her faith:

> 'Sometimes He's here,' Miss Samson said 'and some-times He isn't. Sometimes I'm certain when I pray and sometimes I keep seeing Mr Ibbs instead. All the loveliness has gone ... The wound of doubting is the worst thing of all for a Christian.' Miss Samson touched her face. 'This isn't a wound at all.'
>
> (EA 319-20)

Miss Samson's view of the world has changed. She can no longer find justification for the hardships and pain which life has inflicted on women – Elizabeth, Lily, Sylvie, the woman with the banner or even the long dead Lady Augusta Haptree. Neither can she accept her own affliction with her former patience. In a passionate outburst she questions the goodness of a God who allows humanity to suffer:

> 'Why does He make it so hard for people? Why create His silly world in the first place? What kind of thing is He? ... He gives us human cruelty. And people throwing bombs about ... He permits all that. You remember it when your faith's in doubt. Floods and earthquakes. And marriages between two people He calls His children in which everything goes wrong. Men murder their wives and wives their husbands.
>
> (EA 324-5)

Miss Samson's agitation draws Elizabeth out of her own lethargy. The older woman had wanted God to perform miracles, to right the wrongs in people's lives. She accepts now that this will not happen, yet at the same time she feels a kind of consolation, just as Elizabeth experienced from the comforting presence by her hospital bed:

> 'I thought God spoke to me. I wasn't sure Mrs Aidallbery, but I thought He did. I thought God tried to comfort me

because I'd become so agitated ... I thought He was
explaining to me Mrs Aidallbery, but I couldn't quite hear
Him. I don't know if I'll ever hear Him properly again.'
(EA 327)

The certainty of Miss Samson's faith is gone but her
extraordinary compassion for others has reawakened Elizabeth to
life. Miss Samson's miracle has occurred – the miracle of the
human spirit. Elizabeth is able to reassure her benefactress that she
and the other women are resilient, that they 'had lives that should
not be wept over'. (EA 328)

Elizabeth does not reach an understanding of God – she has not
sought to do so – but she does gain an understanding of life. She
has drawn strength from a fellow sufferer and is ready to 'Start
Living' (EA 330) again. She prepares for Easter, a feast celebrating
renewal, which she had previously planned to ignore. As the book
closes, Elizabeth, working happily in her garden, remarks to her
daughter that she is 'happy enough alone' (EA 336) and the full
significance of the book's title becomes clear: Elizabeth can cope
on her own, accepting life's mysteries, good or evil. God's nature
and purpose may not be intelligible to mankind, but people support
each other in the business of living. Elizabeth's final act of weeding
in her garden has a symbolic significance. She lives in a flawed
Eden where imperfections must be acknowledged and tackled. For
Trevor's characters acceptance is usually offset by action. In
Chekhovian style their resilience enables them to surmount
suffering so that they achieve heroism, not in any dramatic fashion,
but in their bearing of the ordinary tragedies of life.

Metaphysical questions concerning the nature of God and his
relationship with his creatures in their everday lives have always
interested Trevor. Religious themes arise quite naturally in the
course of his work, reflecting the preoccupations of the characters
and their circumstances rather than any didactic purpose of the
author. Ivy Eckdorf, abused herself and the exploiter of others,
finds her own private God and a heavenly retreat in her insanity.
Miss Gomez, another victim of circumstances, in spite of
disappointment persists in her search for a spiritual meaning to her
life. Elizabeth Aidallbery, a woman whose life has been less
dramatic and more 'ordinary' than the others finds hope in human

compassion. The mystery of God remains, but the complexities of the human condition have been explored.

In a review of *Elizabeth Alone* Francis Stuart wrote:

> The exterior world or community can only be effectively explored by an artist whose own psyche is being revealed in the process.[1]

Trevor would not claim to be a particularly religious person, but he describes himself as a 'God-botherer', someone who is curious about the hereafter. This is, he would argue, part of his Irishness. Religion is deeply ingrained in Irish people of his generation, whatever their persuasion. As a writer he particularly enjoys the imaginative challenge of developing in English characters a spiritual life which might more readily be expected to be part of an Irish psyche. In his desire to explore new creative territory he enjoys the opportunity to grapple with the technical challenge of implanting an Irish consciousness in a non-Irish character.

As the 1970s progressed, however, Ireland and Irish problems were to preoccupy Trevor increasingly and to feature more prominently in his work. He had been living outside the country for twenty years – long enough to acquire the distance necessary for a fresh perspective on his homeland. Irish characters had featured widely in his novels and stories, often in a minor capacity, sometimes playing more important parts, but generally eccentric and amusing, winning but subversive agents in an English world, rather like the 'stage Irishmen' of previous centuries. Now he was ready to engage more deeply with Ireland, its present and its past.

Chapter 4

'We are the stuff of history'

It is the landscape of the mind which is of importance to a writer; where he actually lives is irrelevant. He can travel in his imagination to any place and create a context for his characters. William Trevor continued to live in England and although he visited Ireland frequently, by the early 1970s he had gained sufficient distance from the country to enable him to write about it with the objectivity of an outsider, but with a native's appreciation of its social and political complexities.

In common with other countries of the Western world, Ireland had experienced great social changes during the 1960s. There was relative prosperity with increased employment and a higher standard of living for all. The rate of emigration began to fall significantly and the population of the country grew for the first time since the Great Famine of the 1840s. There were new faces in the political arena and the first signs of co-operation between North and South appeared when the Taoiseach of the Irish Republic, Sean Lemass, and the Prime Minister of Northern Ireland, Terence O'Neill, met together first in Belfast and later in Dublin. It was a time of optimism and many Irish emigrants felt that the hour had come to return home and be part of this new phase in their country's history.

As the decade came to an end, however, serious rioting was taking place in Northern Ireland, with Civil Rights demonstrators demanding equal treatment for the Catholic minority, clashing with police and Loyalist supporters. The British army was called in to restore order, but the level of discontent increased as people in Catholic areas claimed that the army was treating them unfairly and turned instead to the Provisional IRA for protection. Violence escalated on both sides of the political divide and a campaign of shooting, bombing and destruction got under way. It was to last for the next thirty years.

With the situation in Ireland claiming the attention of even the international press, the focus of Trevor's writing turned increasingly towards the country in which he had grown up. His interest was not directly concerned with the political events which were happening there, but rather with the unrelenting feud behind the politics, the legacy which history has bequeathed to the island and its people. It is the human aspect of what are euphemistically called 'The Troubles' which Trevor explores. It is never his intention to be didactic:

> What interests me is people, and if one is interested in people one cannot be uninterested in the mentality that can, on a pretext, wipe them out ... How do we understand the people who pulled the trigger, who plant the bomb? Just as the bomber has to avoid looking at the humanity in his victims, we have to seek the humanity in the bomber. We don't have to be sympathetic with the bombers, but unless we find a way to see them as ourselves, the whole thing makes no sense.[1]

The writer's first reference to the Troubles in Northern Ireland came in a short story published in the mid 1970s called 'The Distant Past'. The story records the decline of an anachronistic Protestant Anglo-Irish family and its values, alongside the rise of the Irish Catholic bourgeoisie. The Middletons, a brother and sister (their name taken from a town in County Cork) are the last of a line. They have seen their estates fall into decay and have adjusted to the fact that in church they pray now for the welfare of the President of Ireland instead of for the British Royal family. The harmless trappings of British imperialism which they strive to maintain are treated with indulgence by their Nationalist neighbours. Old wounds have healed and Anglo-Irish and Irish have become friends, a phenomenon which is seen as 'the result of living in a Christian country' (CS 352). As the story unfolds the irony of that statement becomes clear.

The outbreak of the Troubles in Northern Ireland shatters the peaceful co-existence which had reigned in the area where the Middletons live. Even though the fighting is more than sixty miles away, tensions begin to mount between people who up to now had tolerated each other's differences. Items which symbolised the Anglo-Irish past – the portrait of an officer of the Irish Guards, the family crest, the Cross of St George and a miniature Union Jack – once regarded as amusing souvenirs of another era now appear to be objects of provocation. The Troubles reverberate through people's lives, even at a distance, and a new sadness is born.

Again in a short story called 'Another Christmas' Trevor demonstrates the cost of political turmoil in human terms. Although the characters are not themselves involved in the Troubles, their lives are, nevertheless, affected by events taking place in Northern Ireland. Dermot and Norah are Irish but they have spent most of their adult lives in London. In their home, pictures of Irish scenes and of the Virgin Mary pronounce their Nationalist and Catholic allegiances. The greater part of the story involves a conversation which takes place between husband and wife as they prepare for a Christmas from which their old friend and landlord, Mr Joyce, will be absent for the first time. The previous August the couple in the company of Mr Joyce had watched a television account of an IRA bomb attack in England. The landlord had condemned the outrage and Norah had wholeheartedly agreed with him. But Dermot had said that:

> they mustn't of course forget what the Catholics in the North had suffered. The bombs were a crime but it didn't do to forget that the crime would not be there if generations of Catholics in the North had not been treated as animals.
>
> (CS 519)

Dermot had added that it 'didn't do to avoid the truth' (CS 519) and Mr Joyce had not replied.

Dermot refuses to recognise his part in his friend's estrangement. Neither will he accept his wife's suggestion that he should apologise to Mr Joyce. Norah realises that her husband's intransigence rules out compassion, a virtue which in the circumstances, the story suggests, would have been more appropriate than honesty:

> Everyone knew that the Catholics in the North had suffered, that generations of injustice had been twisted into the shape of a cause. But you couldn't say it to an old man

who had hardly been outside Fulham in his life. You couldn't say it because when you did it sounded like an excuse for murder.

(CS 520)

The tone of the story is deliberately low-key, yet as it progresses it becomes clear that the writer is dealing not only with diverse political and moral opinions but also with complex human emotions. As it concludes the reader knows that the relationship between husband and wife has changed radically. The wounding of their own relationship and the death of their friendship with the old man are mirrored in the increasing isolation in Britain of Irish immigrant families like theirs. Norah reflects that one day Dermot may find himself ostracised from a community which has become suspicious of the Irish. She feels that this would be understandable because:

it was a man with an Irish accent in whom the worst had been brought out by the troubles that had come, who was guilty of a cruelty no one would have believed him capable of.

(CS 521)

The theme of collective guilt is one which Trevor investigates very fully in his 'Irish' work. Beginning with this story which demonstrates the legacy which groups such as the IRA have bequeathed to Irish citizens, in particular those resident in Britain, he goes on in later work to investigate the inheritance of complicity which lies with the descendants of the people who colonised Ireland and caused the divisions in its society.

While the political situation in Northern Ireland continued to deteriorate throughout the 1970s, its tragic consequences became something of an obsession in Trevor's work. Speaking on a radio programme in 1981 he explained his feelings:

As an Irishman I feel that what is happening in Ireland now is one of the great horrors of my lifetime, and I find it difficult to comprehend the mentality, whether Irish or British, that pretends that it will somehow all blow over. It will not. There will be more death, more cruelty, more fear, more waste. The nightmare will go on ... Compassion is thrown to the winds, distortion rules.[2]

Yet the writer's stories generally offer a message of hope. 'Never to despair' (CS 688) is the precept which Attracta, the Protestant teacher, sets before her pupils in the story which bears her name. This story among others manifests how the human capacity for forgiveness makes it possible for people to have hope no matter how adverse the circumstances.

Ireland's chequered history is reflected in the images which decorate Attracta's classroom. Portraits of England's kings and queens hang alongside pictures of Irish Nationalist heroes. The action of the story occurs in the mid 1970s and it is arguably Trevor's most complex exploration of the nature of reconciliation.

Attracta is sixty-one years of age and has spent her life teaching in the town in which she grew up. Her mind is thrown into disarray when she reads a newspaper account of the death of a young English girl called Penelope Vade. The girl's soldier husband had been murdered by Northern Ireland terrorists and his severed head packed in a biscuit tin and posted to his wife at her home in Hazelmere. With almost superhuman generosity Penelope Vade had forgiven the murderers and had travelled to Belfast to join the Women's Peace Movement. Incensed by the gesture which won her publicity, seven of the terrorists had raped her. In despair she committed suicide. Attracta is haunted by the girl's story because to a great extent it echoes her own and yet differs greatly from it.

When she was an infant Attracta's parents were killed in an IRA ambush meant for Back-and-Tan soldiers. The organisers of the ambush were a local Protestant Nationalist, Devereux, and his Catholic mistress, Geraldine Carey. Horrified by the innocent deaths for which they were responsible, the two guerrillas abandoned both their military activities and their illicit relationship. Devereux sought expiation through his dedication to the child, Attracta, to whom he becomes, ironically, a father figure. Geraldine Carey atones for her violent past by withdrawing from the world, working as Devereux's housekeeper and living a life of extreme piety. The plot is melodramatic and even macabre, but Trevor's concern is to show the people behind the situations.

Attracta remained unaware of the details of her parents' death until Mr Purce, a bigoted Protestant, revealed the facts in an effort to alienate her from Devereux. She realises, however, that her life had been happy because those who had hurt her had repented and sought reconciliation. Penelope Vade, on the other hand, had offered forgiveness but her gesture had been met with further violence. Recognising all this Attracta wonders if she has not taught the wrong things to her pupils. Instead of historical events she should have spoken of local people and their lives. In an effort to rectify her omission she reads aloud to the children a newspaper account of what happened to Penelope Vade and her husband and tells her own story in painful detail. The children are unimpressed and wonder why their teacher:

> ... didn't appear to understand that almost every day there was the kind of vengeance she spoke of reported on the television.
>
> (CS 689)

Attracta's message is misinterpreted and her resignation is diplomatically sought. Yet her life had demonstrated that 'monsters did not remain monsters for ever'. (CS 689) Perhaps the mass of its theme lies heavily on the short story, but the writer has chosen to confront a weighty issue. Human beings are capable of great evil but there is comfort in the fact that they can also repent and make atonement. Hope for the future lies in man's ability to forgive the past and apply its lessons to the present.

More than half of the stories in Trevor's fifth collection *Beyond the Pale* (1981) have an Irish connection. They deal not only with the effects of the violence in Northern Ireland, but with the coercive power of all history. The political dimension continues to play an important part, but it is the violence of the individual, often masked by gentility, which is most impressed upon the reader. The title story of the volume treats of Anglo-Irish relations on a political level but the impact of the 'hell that frightens us' (CS 770) is experienced by the characters as individuals.

Four English bridge players come year after year to holiday in Northern Ireland, ignoring the 'unpleasantness' (CS 751) which is part of the everyday life of the area. Trevor cleverly uses the device of casting the least perceptive character, Milly, as narrator. Her self-delusion allows wonderful scope for irony as the story is told in the fashion of diary entries. Glencorn Lodge, the hotel to which the bridge players come, is owned by an English couple. It provides a haven for those who do not wish to confront the reality that is Northern Ireland and who insist that:

> Nothing has changed at Clencorn Lodge, all is well with its Irish world.
>
> (CS 750)

Milly is accompanied by Strafe, her lover, by Strafe's wife, Cynthia, whom she describes as 'small and ineffectual' (CS 753) and by Dekko, a rich, ageing bachelor who cultivates the company of young women, but whose schoolboy humour and puerile preoccupations cast doubt upon his sexuality.

The violence from which the foursome initially manage to isolate themselves is borne in on them by the arrival of a red-haired man:

> uncouth-looking ... not at all the kind of person one usually sees at Glencorn Lodge.
>
> (CS 752)

Cynthia, whom Milly describes as 'an imaginative woman' (CS 755) is disturbed by a story the man tells of his relationship with a girl-terrorist, a childhood friend. He confides that he has murdered the girl because:

> He hated the violence that possessed her, yet he was full of it himself; he knew he couldn't betray her with anything but death.
>
> (CS 766-7)

The man's subsequent suicide causes Cynthia to indulge in an uncharacteristic outburst as they all sit among the 'sponge-cakes and little currant scones'. (CS 760) Dispelling their cosiness, she forces all of them to admit the existence of a world of terror and injustice which they had considered beyond the pale which they had erected about themselves. Cynthia echoes the author when she reminds the others that

> History is unfinished in this island: long since it has come to a stop in Surrey.
>
> (CS 763)

Cynthia's hysterical honesty forces her fellow-countrymen to confront political reality and to acknowledge the face of humanity in violence. At the same time she compels them to accept the truth about their complicated and sordid relationships: her husband's infidelity, Dekko's homosexuality and Milly's 'viciousness'. (CS 770) As a result confusion runs through their comfortable world, just as 'Confusion ran through Irish history ... like convolvulus in a hedgerow'. (CS 763)

Trevor maintains that the only real division between people is between those who use their imaginations and those who do not. Distinctions of sex or nationality fade in face of this one great chasm which exists between people of different casts of mind.[3] The petty, vain pretensions of the three unimaginative characters are related to the larger issues which the writer tackles in his 'Irish' work: the refusal or inability of people to acknowledge that the basis of the Northern Troubles lies in the compelling power of history. People have been wronged and this must be remembered. But vengeance is a double-edged sword which strikes back at those who use it. The power of forgiveness must be stronger than the force of memory if the circle of violence is to be broken.

In 'The Mourning'[6] a story written in the late 1990s, at a time when peace in Northern Ireland seems at last to have some prospect of success, Trevor not only places the Troubles within the broader context of Irish history but also demonstrates the way in which human compassion can rise above its historical confines and celebrate humanity. Liam Pat Brogan at twenty-three is the last of six children to leave the parental home in County Cork to travel to England in the hope of bettering himself. A young man of limited intelligence, he is an easy prey for not only those who flirt with violence, but for those who are prepared to use it without any compunction in order to attain their ends.

Liam Pat's first taste of abuse is at the hands of Huxter, the bullying English foreman at the building site where he works. Loneliness and racial prejudice force him into the company of another Irishman, Feeny:

> ... a wizened-featured man with black hair in a widow's peak. He had a clerical look about him, but he wasn't a priest.   (NY 70)

The society of his new friend and other Irishmen to whom he is introduced makes life scarcely tolerable for the labourer, who dreams of returning home. A few brief but telling details paint a picture of his isolation:

> Liam Pat was homesick for the estate, for the small town where people said hello to you. Since he'd been here he'd eaten any old how, sandwiches he bought the evening before, for breakfast and again in the middle of the day, burger and chips later on, Bob's Dining Rooms on a Sunday. He hadn't thought about that before he'd come – what he'd eat, what a Sunday would be like. Sometimes at Mass he saw a girl he liked the look of, the same girl each time, quiet-featured, with her hair tied back. But when he went up to her after Mass a few weeks back she turned away without speaking.
>
> (NY 72)

In his vulnerable state, Liam Pat is persuaded to act as a bomber for the IRA. He resents the treatment he receives as an Irish immigrant in Britain. Now he is stirred by vague patriotic emotions evoked by Feeny's oratory and his own imprecise memory of history lessons and armchair nationalism. Of more importance is the feeling that the mission he is undertaking is lending a sense of importance and purpose to his life and providing him with feelings of confidence and excitement. Unquestioningly he carries out orders, packing explosives in a sports bag and taking it onto a London bus. The story avoids all melodrama but tension builds up as the young man takes the bus across London, trying to keep a grip on reality as he proceeds towards his target in a trancelike state – the repetition of the word 'dream' adding to the soporific effect. His humanity is stirred, however, by an encounter with two young girls, likely victims of an explosion. Their casual friendliness stirs something within him and the *déjà vu* feeling he is experiencing begins to shatter. He ceases to be an automaton and remembers the death of another young man involved in just such an undertaking, recalling his own father's angry reaction to the presence of 'the lads' (NY 80) – a euphemistic term for the Provisional IRA – at the boy's funeral. Realising that he has been a pawn in a political game Liam Pat finds the courage to abandon the sports bag which falls 'with hardly a splash into the river'. (NY 80)

Liam Pat has retained his capacity to empathise with another person. In making this imaginative leap he shows himself capable of independent thought and action. He will never be the 'Poor bloody hero' (NY 80) which the other young man became and he will carry with him a feeling of mourning for the rest of his life. That mourning to which the title of the story refers is not only for the 'bomber who might have been himself' (NY 80) but for the self who might have been a bomber. He will never walk 'with the stride of Michael Collins' (NY 80) but neither will he be the dupe of terrorist manipulators.

Once again it is human dilemmas rather than political issues which are at the centre of the story. The vulnerability of the lonely, the effects of isolation, the need to belong, to find dignity in purpose and to romanticise the past – these are all part of a universal predicament. Even the most unlikely characters in certain circumstances, the story illustrates, can be drawn into violence. Ultimately, however, the human spirit is seen to triumph over bitterness, as it does over patriotic cant and lust for glory. Liam Pat's courage will never be articulated in history books or anywhere else for that matter, but his ability to recognise a common humanity with bomber and victim alike shows that it is possible for people to come back from the edge, a circumstance from which one may draw comfort and which encourages hope for the future.

In the same year in which *Beyond the Pale* was published Dublin's Abbey Theatre staged Trevor's play *Scenes from an Album*, opening on 13 August 1981. It was to be the author's first exploration of the decaying Big House, a theme beloved of Anglo-Irish writers from Maria Edgeworth and Somerville and Ross to contemporary Irish writers such as Aidan Higgins and Jennifer Johnston. As the title suggests *Scenes from an Album* consists of a series of four *tableaux vivants*, designed to convey a sense of history as seen through the experiences of one family, the Malcolmsons. The action which takes place in County Tyrone covers four centuries. The first scene is appropriately a battlefield, 'strewn with dead soldiers'. (SA 6) The year is 1610, the Irish have been defeated in war and the English Captain Eustace Malcolmson is surveying the land he has lately been granted. He plans to build a house there so that 'the past shall be buried'. (SA 6) His family will bring peace to the land. In order for this to happen, however, the present tenants of the area must be driven away. With a naivety which becomes characteristic of his descendants, Captain Malcolmson informs his lawyer:

> Do not be harsh: explain the circumstances of the law to them.
>
> (SA 7)

He further expresses his good intentions:

> I feel at peace with this subject people and would wish my family in some distant future to love them as their own.
>
> (SA 7)

Ominously the stage directions associate the building of the house with the arrival of Orangemen. Ranks are formed as the establishment of the family in Ireland coincides with the birth of sectarianism.

The second scene moves the action to the year 1907 and takes place in the garden of the Malcolmson house. The family in the early twentieth century consists of three children, Honoria, Annie and young Eustace. A Catholic gardener, Rafferty, entertains the children with stories from Irish history. They are as enthusiastic about his tales as they are about his romance with the deaf house-maid, Barbara. Rafferty's proposal to Barbara, who is a Protestant, recalls the religious strife which has continued through the centuries:

> You're deaf and I'm a Catholic. These are just facts, Barbara. We love one another is the thing that matters.
>
> (SA 11)

Being born into a particular religion, the play suggests, is as arbitrary as coming into the world with a physical handicap.

The penalties for those who try to cross the sectarian divide are disclosed in the third scene. It is the summer of 1919 and the setting is the drawing-room of the Big House where the arrival of Eustace and his fiancée from London is expected. The dialogue reveals Honoria and Annie as eccentric women, whose barbed wit barely conceals an edge of suppressed hysteria:

Annie: Remember we have known our brother at close quarters, Mother.

Mrs Malcolmson: And so have I for heaven's sake!

Honoria: There was a time when he was twelve when he wept because he could not win at bagatelle. There is that side to Eustace, too.

Annie: Pools of weeping all over the back of a chair. Fists pressed into his cheeks. No one is perfect. Isn't that so, Mr Tyson?

Tyson: No, no, Miss Annie, no one is perfect: you are right. Though of course we strive toward a perfect state.

Annie: People are speckled: it's pointless to strive toward a perfect state.

Tyson: No striving is pointless, really. What I mean, Miss Annie –

Annie: Quite so, quite so. Mother, how do you see Eustace's fiancée, if not as we do? Tall as an Amazon? Teeth missing, red-winged? A country girl, a tap-room wag?

Mrs Malcolmson: Cease your nonsense, Annie.

(SA 13)

Eustace's sisters are adamant that he shouldn't marry, that the family should be allowed to die out and the estate be returned to the descendants of those dispossessed by the seventeenth-century Malcolmsons. Annie tells Dottie, Eustace's fiancée, why they believe that this should happen. Rafferty's parents had been burnt to death because their son had planned to marry a Protestant. Driven to insanity by his loss Rafferty had shot Mr Malcolmson because, as Annie explains 'our kind were responsible for everything'. (SA 24) Every week the sisters visit Rafferty in the lunatic asylum as a gesture of forgiveness. Their mother meanwhile has refused to employ Catholics on the estate, but her son confides to his fiancée his plans to change all that:

> I shall return to the tolerance of my father, and my grandfather. Protestants and Catholics shall again work side by side on my land and in my house. That is my gesture, a forgiving gesture too, maybe, though less eccentric than my sisters.

(SA 26)

The act ends with the funeral service of Mrs Malcolmson, who died content in the belief that the family line is secure with the marriage of her son. But as the Reverend Tyson reads the funeral prayers, the Orangemen reappear and in an expressionist ritual offer their services to Eustace. Appearing in a spotlight, he becomes a symbolic figure, representing not only a family, but a country which is the focus of political and sectarian strife. The stage directions state that:

> *His reaction is one of horror. He raises a hand to quell the noise*
> *they're making but the hand falls to his side as they take no notice.*

The second act of the play is set in the present and as the previous one closed with expressionist ceremonial, so this opens in a similar fashion. The Eustace of the 1980s, son of the figure who appeared at the end of Act One, sleeps in a deckchair; an IRA group enters the auditorium, mounts the stage and faces the audience. They aim their guns directly as the people 'raking over the victims of this execution' (SA 28) before marching off slowly. This technique lifts the action out of the realms of tragi-comic realism and into tragic surrealism.

The soldiers disappear and the lights reveal Annie, Honoria, Eustace and Dotty who are expecting another visitor, Mr Mulcahy, engaged by Dotty to write a history of the family. The present Malcolmson heir, Dotty's son, is revealed as a harmless, ineffectual drunkard, generous to a fault, a striking contrast to the niggardly, humourless Mulcahy, a member of the Dublin Catholic bourgeoisie. From Honoria we learn that her brother Eustace, who had planned to restore tolerance to the area by re-employing Catholics on the estate:

> ... was drowned for his pains. In a hole in the marshlands.
> They held his head under.
>
> (SA 32)

The intervention of Mr Mulcahy allows for the discussion of the most important issues of the play. The sisters believe that the historian should record the family's guilt because they 'once assisted Orange William to a famous victory' and consequently they have a 'sentimental need to make amends'. (SA 38) Above all he should state that they were

> A noble family, a gracious family, English-sounding, yet
> more Irish than the Irish; fair and decent.   (SA 39)

Official history will not recount their amazing capacity to forgive, exemplified by Annie and Honoria's weekly visits to Rafferty, their brother's plan to re-employ Catholics, their nephew's reception of the senile assassin of his grandfather in the house and his condemnation of all factions in the current political strife – an action which has led to his isolation within the community. The Malcolmsons began in Ireland as history makers; they have become its casualties, some of them wiped out by the violence they brought with them, others scarcely more fortunate – ridiculous, impotent survivors.

The play ends on an ambivalent note. Even as the clouds of impending violence gather again and the sounds of war begin to drown out the music of civilisation, Eustace expresses hope for the future. 'Tomorrow might be different,' he says and his final words are a prayer:

> Oh God, tomorrow let the monster we brought with us be gone.
>
> (SA 40)

The book about the Malcolmson family will not be written, because the full story will never be told. The past as it is recorded in history books is best forgotten.

Considered as theatre, *Scenes from an Album* lacks dramatic impact. Its episodic plot carries about it the aura of narrative fiction. While the dialogue excellently illustrates the eccentric natures of the characters, at times it seems burdened by the message it bears. The play is most effective in the expressionist sequences which convey the author's personal vision of Irish history: terrible events have taken place and guilt must be accepted, but amends can be made and forgiveness is the only way forward.

The play was respectfully received by Dublin critics, who praised it for its sweep through history, but there were occasional quibbles about some of the characterisation, particularly of the two sisters, who were considered by some as too eccentric to be credible.[4]

*

Just as an idea occurring in a novel is reshaped in a short story, the latter may also grow into a novel. In January 1981 the *Atlantic*

Monthly published Trevor's short story 'Saints', which proved to be the embryonic form of his novel *Fools of Fortune* (1983). The narrator of the story, who becomes Willie Quinton in the novel, is a sixty-nine year old Irish exile, scion of an Anglo-Irish family, who has lived in the Italian town of Sansepolcro for the last forty years. The name of the town carries its own significance since the man has, in a sense, become entombed in the world of art, cut off from his past, an exile not only from his country but also from life. Reluctantly he returns to Ireland to visit Josephine, at one time a servant in his parents' house and now dying in a Cork hospital.

The journey home allows the narrator to dredge up memories which eventually account for his self-imposed exile. Aided by the consumption of alcohol, 'half dreaming, half remembering' (AM 30) his mind returns to events during the Irish War of Independence and the past is filled in with impressionistic brush strokes. Jumbled remarks of the dying woman spark off further memories until the whole picture emerges. Kilneagh, the man's home, had been burned down during the Troubles of the early 1920s, the only survivors being the narrator, his mother and Josephine. Later, when his mother committed suicide, the narrator moved to Italy where he has since lived a lonely existence, endeavouring to comfort himself with wine, women and art. Meanwhile Josephine has led a completely different life; after the narrator's departure she became insane and has been incarcerated ever since in St Fina's Lunatic Asylum. There she has developed a reputation as a saint and miracle worker. Although confused in her mind she has never ceased to pray for the comfort of all survivors of tragedy.

Josephine dies and the narrator instinctively rationalises the miracles and mysteries with which she has been associated. On his return to Italy, however, he sees things differently and is convinced of her saintliness. He compares his own useless self-indulgence with her altruistic caring for others and asks himself 'Of the three survivors, had I myself been damaged most?' (AM 36) He has rejected his humanity and sacrificed warmth and life for the aridity of art. Yet Josephine's dying wish to see him has revived that humanity to the extent that through a drunken haze he acknowledges the effect as a miracle:

> She had moved that embittered man to find pleasure in the
> wisp that remained of a human relationship.

(AM 36)

He recalls that on her deathbed she had prayed:

> ... that Ireland's murders might be forgiven, that all the
> survivors be granted consolation, and rescued from the
> damage wrought by horror.

(AM 36)

This prayer reverberates through all Trevor's work which touches on the Irish Troubles, past or present, carrying with it an expectation of the regeneration of the human spirit and consequently hope for the future.

Most of the incidents of 'Saints' are preserved within *Fools of Fortune*, but there are some important differences. The novel is above all a love story which spans sixty-five years and three generations. An extended narrative is required to dramatise the passing of time and the attrition of events on an expanded action and cast of characters. The two lovers, Willie and Marianne, address each other in a diary or letter form, while their daughter Imelda's thoughts are narrated in the third person. The novel fleshes out the background and history of the Quinton family, who are named for the first time. New characters are added, the most important of whom is Father Kilgarrif, a defrocked priest, who voices the book's pacifist message.

The Quintons are established as a liberal Anglo-Irish family. Willie's father is a Home-Ruler. His mother, although English, favours Irish Nationalist aspirations. The revolutionary Michael Collins is entertained in the house and Willie's father contributes financially to the Nationalist cause, but refuses to allow troops to drill on his grounds. The Quinton family had always been sympathetic to the oppressed tenantry; an ancestor, Anna Quinton, had died of famine fever, infected as she ministered to the starving people in the 1840s.

The picture of life in the Quinton family is idyllic: Willie is surrounded by loving parents, eccentric aunts, giggling younger sisters and loyal servants. But the tutor Father Kilgarrif strikes an ominous note when he asks his charge 'Will we tackle a bit of

Title: William Trevor: The Writer and His Work
Locator Code: HSAN02-00398
ISBN: 187459774X
Location: Kennys Bookshop
Special Comments: 250pp
Condition: Used - Like New

history?' (FF 13) The complicated subject of Irish history is raised and once again the author traces its effects in terms of individual lives rather than of political movements.

The relationship between Ireland and England is mirrored in the relationship between the two families, the Irish Quintons and the English Woodcombes. In three generations a Quinton son has fallen in love with a Woodcombe daughter, but each union ends in catastrophe. Although the book is a love story, it shows a world in which violence supersedes love. Its most striking image occurs when Marianne remarks that on the map 'Ireland and England seemed like lovers'. She asks 'Does the map remind you curiously of an embrace?' and goes on to comment, 'A most extraordinary embrace to throw up all this'. (FF 203) As the story unfolds the intimacy proves to have about it more of a death-grip than a love union.

An act of generosity by Mr Quinton in employing Doyle, an ex-British soldier, in his mill leads to the first disruption of this halcyon world. Doyle is hanged from a tree on the estate, his tongue cut out because he is suspected of being an informer. Doyle's death is avenged by Sergeant Rudkin and the Black-and-Tans, Kilneagh is burned to the ground and Willie's father and sisters, together with most of the servants, are murdered. Willie's mother is left an emotional cripple, and never recovers from the tragedy. The boy is sent away to school where he discovers a camaraderie which counters the distress he witnesses at home. Josephine sacrifices her own happiness to look after Mrs Quinton who eventually takes her own life.

The story up to this point is narrated by Willie, but it is continued by Marianne, his English cousin with whom he has fallen in love. After Mrs Quinton's funeral Marianne and Willie spend one night together before they part. Later, finding she is pregnant, she returns to Cork to seek out Willie, but he has disappeared and no one will tell her why. She is given refuge by his old aunts and settles down in the only intact wing of the gutted house to wait hopelessly for the return of her lover and to bring up his child.

Years pass and the events which precipitated Willie's exile are gradually pieced together. His mother's death had prompted him to exact revenge upon Sergeant Rudkin, the author of her sufferings. The barbarity of Willie's actions does not become clear until about ten years after the event when Imelda, Willie's daughter, finds a newspaper cutting. Although hints about the crime have been given, the details when revealed, even in the dispassionate manner of a newspaper report, are macabre:

> It is considered that a butcher's knife was most likely to have been the type of weapon employed ... The head was partially hacked from the neck, the body stabbed in seventeen places.

(FF 216)

The author stresses that Willie had been 'the most ordinary little boy' (FF199) as Sergeant Rudkin had been just an average soldier. On one level the book can be seen as a story of revenge: a father is murdered and a son, at the instigation of his embittered and unstable mother, avenges his father's death and by that act isolates himself from all he loves. As a result a family is destroyed. The saintly but mad Imelda is the last issue of the Quinton family. She shares the role of Josephine in 'Saints'. Beneath the family saga, however, is the relentless momentum of history, pushing forward the events as inexorably as fate.

The predominance of memory gives the book a nostalgic air which leaves the reader off guard when scenes of horror arise. Framed by the present of the opening and closing chapters, the past is recalled in order to clarify current events in the light of history. As happens in the short story 'Saints' a taximan chats to Willie of the 'trouble up in the North' (FF 224) as he returns to visit the dying Josephine. The old man on his way to visit a hospital seems an unlikely murderer; he appears to be a Fool of Fortune deserving sympathy, rather than a vicious killer eliciting condemnation. The fact that the killing of Rudkin took place off-stage serves to lessen the personal aspect of the horror. In addition the passage of time has allowed his deed to become glorified:

> the nuns at the convent spoke of him as a hero, even as somebody from a legend.

(FF 197)

We recall Mr Quinton's comment that the Irish are intrigued 'by stories with a degree of unreality in them'. (FF 87) But the reality behind what the writer John Millington Synge called 'a gallous story' is frequently 'a dirty deed'.[5]

A novel which spans such a long period of time and uses three narrative voices calls for innovative techniques. Events separated by time and place are recalled in impressionistic form, the gaps frequently filled in by the characters' imaginations. Willie's account of the fire at Kilneagh is purely subjective:

> There were stars in the sky. An orange glow crept over the edges of my vision. The noise there'd been had changed, becoming a kind of crackling, with crashes that sounded like thunder. I couldn't move. I thought: we are all like this, Geraldine and Deirdre, my mother and father, Josephine and Mrs Flynn, we are all lying on wet grass in pain.
>
> (FF 51-2)

Twenty years later Imelda, on the brink of madness, recalls the same events as she learned them from her mother and creates in her mind the details which she could not have known:

> Imelda closed her eyes. Pictures slipped out. The flames devoured the flesh of the children's faces and the flesh of their arms and legs, of their stomachs and their backs. Trapped in her bedroom, fat Mrs Flynn wept in panic; smoke filled her lungs, her eyes streamed. The man in the teddy-bear dressing-gown carried his wife down the burning stairs and went in search of his children. Frightened in case they'd been recognised, the soldiers returned. In the yard the gardeners who had come from the gate-lodge quickly died, and then the labradors died and then the stray dogs. The empty gate-lodge became a furnace also. The sound of the motor-car engine died away ...
>
> (FF 199)

This method of selective focusing, against a background of day-to-day reality to lend it credibility, allows the reader to piece together the complete narrative.

Although the plot of the book is sombre, comic scenes are strategically interspersed to lighten the mood. The vendetta theme is beautifully reworked in a humorous vein. The episode takes place in the boarding-school which Willie attends in the Dublin mountains. A dismissed geography teacher returns in the night to urinate through an open window on a sleeping colleague whom he holds responsible for his dismissal. He is aided in his scheme by Willie and his friends. Later, the boys are called to give an account of the incident by the Headmaster, who doesn't wish to acknowledge that anything so indelicate could have occurred. He remarks that they had all had a lucky escape:

> 'It is fortunate that we weren't burnt in our beds.'
>
> 'Burnt, sir?' Ring repeated in a startled voice. 'Burnt?' he said again ...
>
> Ring essayed a slow smile ... 'And maybe,' he chattily added, 'if he was intoxicated, sir, he could have imagined he'd started up a fire already. Maybe what he got up to, sir, was an effort to quench it.'
>
> 'That's a disgusting suggestion, Ring. We have agreed between us that nothing of that nature took place.'
>
> (FF 103-4)

Although the author's touch is light, the effect of this passage is gripping, as recollection of the earlier fire runs beneath the surface comedy like a chill current under a sparkling sea.

The novel ends on a peaceful note as images of her parent's love pass through the mute Imelda's head. An idyll has returned to Kilneagh, but it is now in the mind of a mad woman whose happiness is 'like a shroud miraculously about her'. (FF 238) Imelda's happiness is wrapped in the garment of death: Kilneagh has become a Holy Sepulchre.

In 'The News from Ireland' (1986) which as an historical short story is a literary rarity, Trevor builds on an idea which first occurs in *Fools of Fortune*. The story also shares the novel's technique of stereoscopic vision as events are seen from several different points of view. The story is set in the period of the Irish famine of the 1840s. In the novel Anna Quinton wrote to her English family of wholescale starvation and death as she witnessed it; in 'The News from Ireland' the English governess, Anna Maria Heddoe, confides her observations of the same events to her diary:

> There is a yellow-greyness in the flesh of their faces, they are themselves like obedient animals. Their babies die when they feed them grass and roots: in their arms at the gate-lodge the babies who survive are silent also ... (CS 900)

Once again there are close connections between Ireland and England. The Pulvertafts of Ipswich have inherited an Irish estate from a distant relative. Consequently they are in the same position as the later generation of Malcolmsons and 'though they are not themselves invaders ... they perpetrate theft without being thieves'. (CS 881) Members of the family and their employees react to the famine according to their sensibilities. Mr Pulvertaft creates employment for the starving populace by having a road built to encircle the estate. It leads nowhere and indicates the harmless and useless philanthropic gestures of people like the Pulvertafts. The huge wall which runs along by the road is equally symbolic: it serves to exclude the unseemly distress which happens beyond and protects those within from the rigours of reality. Outside the walls the last surviving child of a destitute couple is found to bear the marks of the stigmata. Whether the marks are supernatural in origin or are the desperate attempt of deranged parents to seek attention for their infant is never revealed, but this child-symbol of a people crucified by hunger and disease is allowed to die and her death is rationalised and forgotten.

The central consciousness of the story is that of Anna Maria Heddoe, a rather worthy English girl, governess to the Pulvertafts' son, George Arthur. The family gathering, as she perceives it, has itself the quality of a scene from an album:

> They made a handsome family picture – Emily beautiful, Charlotte petite and pretty, the plump motherliness of Mrs Pulvertaft, her husband's ruddy presence ... Only Adelaide, bespectacled and seeming heavy for her age, does not share the family's gift of grace.
> (CS 883)

As an outsider Anna Maria, 'a young woman of principle and sensibility' (CS 881) records events and impressions. Her perspective is one which the reader may share at the outset. But the metamorphosis which takes place in her consciousness illustrates the point at issue in the story: the people become inured to others' suffering and habituation is quickly followed by acceptance. The edge of Anna Maria's sensibility is dulled by contact with people with lesser sentience, particularly by her relationship with Mr Erskine, the estate manager whose proposal of marriage she eventually accepts. The woman who once felt moved to write passionately about the deaths of peasants succumbs to the temptations of status and security offered by a man of whom it is said:

> His temper is short, his disposition unsentimental, his soldier's manner abrupt; nor is there beneath that vigorous exterior, a gentler core.
>
> (CS 891)

Other characters find their own ways of coping with the tragedy at their gates. While Mr Pulvertaft instigates employment schemes, his wife discharges her conscience through alms-giving and prayer. Avoiding the burden of guilt she reflects that 'No one can be blamed' (CS 893) and takes refuge from both postprandial indigestion and uncomfortable thoughts of starvation in sleep. Only one of the Pulvertaft siblings, Emily, has sufficient imagination to be aware of what is happening about her and even she is more concerned with aesthetic considerations than with humanitarian principles. Preoccupied with the romantic past and with her own longings for intellectual experience, Emily too learns to ignore events which she finds too difficult to admit.

The famine progresses while the family continues its social round. Details of food and drink prepared and consumed underline the author's ironic intent. The butler, Fogarty, also an outsider as a Protestant member of the servant class, has all the marks of a certain type of Trevor character – sly and cunning – he is nevertheless a truth-teller whose insight into the contemporary scene and vision of the future are chilling. He voices the question which the author raises and which the other characters choose to ignore:

> ... what use a few spoonfuls of soup, and a road that leads nowhere and only insults the pride of the men who built it?
>
> (CS 903)

Like the sisters in *Scenes from an Album* he wishes to see the estate crumble away because it had its origins in confiscation and exploitation. His dream of the future strikes a prophetic note:

> The descendants of the people who had been hungry were in the dream, and the son of George Arthur Pulvertaft was shot in the hall of the house, and no Pulvertaft lived in the

place again. The road that had been laid in charity was
overgrown through neglect, and the gardens were as they
had been at the time of old Hugh Pulvertaft, their beauty
strangled as they returned to wildness ... The house of the
estate manager was burnt to the ground, and people burnt
with it. The stone walls of the estate were broken down,
pulled apart in places by the ivy that was let grow.

(CS 905)

This thrust into the future gives dimension to the events and places
them in an historical context. Anna Maria Heddoe notes in her
diary that 'families and events are often seen historically in Ireland'
(CS 884) and her legend of the True Cross broadens this view. The
past does not wither away as Fogarty would wish it to; instead it is
perpetuated and becomes part of the future.

The novel *The Silence in the Garden* (1988) brings Trevor's cycle
of work dealing with the members of the Anglo-Irish class to a
close. The Rollestons of Carriglas live on an island off the coast of
County Cork. The family came to Ireland in the wake of
Cromwell, colonising the land and expelling the natives in the
traditional way. Later they became caring landlords, known as 'the
Famine Rollestons' because of their kindness to their tenants
during the 1840s when they waived rents and as a result lost the
titles to some of their lands and thereby impoverished themselves.
Colonel Rolleston, a widower, was killed in the Great War. His
sons, John James and Lionel, and his daughter, Villana, live with
their grandmother at Carriglas. Also in the household is Sarah
Pollexfen, poor relation, governess and housekeeper. Below stairs
is Brigid whose husband-to-be, Linchy, the butler, was murdered a
week before their planned wedding by a Republican booby-trap
bomb intended for the Rollestons during the Troubles of the 1920s.
After her financé's death Brigid gives birth to an illegitimate son,
Tom, with whom she lives in the gatehouse.

The Rolleston family, like the house in which they live, is in
decline. The Colonel had been an exemplary man and his mother
personifies the virtues of decency and compassion, but the younger
members of the family, mirroring their counterparts in the
Malcolmson family of *Scenes from an Album* and the Quintons of
Fools of Fortune lead lives of ineffectualness and despair. John
James who was wounded in the war which killed his father spends

his time with his mistress, the voluptuous Mrs Moledy, the owner of a boarding-house who is determined to marry him. Lionel lives like a farm-hand, ploughing his fields and failing to communicate with Sarah Pollexfen who loves him. Villana who mysteriously broke off her engagement to her childhood sweetheart, Hugh Pollexfen, marries an elderly solicitor, Finnamore Balt, whom she does not love but who agrees to her stipulation that they have no children.

Like *Fools of Fortune* the novel spans more than sixty years. There are glimpses of the family in the period before the Great War, and although events are framed from the vantage point of 1971, most of the action takes place in 1931. As outsiders Sarah and Tom are important figures in the book. Through their eyes the reader is guided into the mysteries which haunt the Rollestons and render them impotent. The book begins with an excerpt from Sarah's diary and further entries punctuate the narrative at intervals. Many of these demonstrate the futility and purposelessness of life in the Big House:

> Carriglas, April 6th, 1931. It is the dead time of the afternoon between lunch and tea. Lionel is already back in the fields, his three sheepdogs keeping him company. Villana is out for her walk. Mrs Rolleston is resting, John James is visiting the woman he believes we do not know about.
>
> (SG 37)

The echo of Chekhovian axes can once again be heard 'in the orchard, where old trees are being felled'. (SG 169) At the same time the journals allow us to discover a happier time in the past when the family flourished and its members looked forward to the future with hope and confidence. The mystery of Villana's disappointed love is hinted at, but only at the close of the novel is the 'secret' which destroyed the family disclosed.

The greater part of the book is related in the third person as the author takes us into the minds of a variety of characters, in particular that of Tom, through whose consciousness we perceive the community beyond Carriglas. Tom crosses to the mainland every day to attend school – and to carry out errands for Mrs

Rolleston. As an illegitimate child he is regarded by many of the town's people as a pariah, quite literally an untouchable:

> A sin of that type, Holy Mullihan added, would afflict the child who came out of it. The sin would only go from a person after death, and then only if there'd been penance enough and sufficient Hail Marys said. 'There would be people who'd be frightened of the sin, Tom. They wouldn't mean harm to an afflicted person, only it's the way they'd see it. You might see them crossing a street if they saw you coming. Another thing is, they mightn't like to touch you.'
>
> (SG 87)

Both Sarah and Tom are innocents; they remain outside the circle of guilt which ultimately destroys the Rollestons. Once again it is a heritage of violence which brings about the family's downfall. The secret at the core of the book was an act of intimidation committed by the children of the house on a local boy, Cornelius Dowley: 'As of right, they hunted. They were the children of Carriglas.' (SG 184) Because of their treatment of the young Cornelius 'monstrousness was bred in him.' (SG 185) Consequently when he became an adult Dowley channelled his desire for revenge against the Rollestons into the Republican movement and during the War of Independence planted a bomb to kill his former tormentors. But instead of the Rollestons the victim of the explosion was their butler, Linchy, Tom's father. In his turn Dowley was gunned down by the Black-and-Tans and became a martyr for the Nationalist cause. Realising their responsibility in the affair, the Rollestons decide that the cycle of revenge must be ended by the dissolution of the family. After their deaths there will be no further generations of Rollestons at Carriglas. Villana will not marry her cousin, Hugh, the man she loves. Neither will her brothers provide heirs and Carriglas will become the property of Tom, a blameless victim of events, who will allow it to decay.

The demise of the Rolleston family, like that of the Quintons, the Malcolmsons and the Pulvertafts, symbolises the extinction of the Anglo-Irish class in Ireland. They came as conquerors and introduced a dissonance which reverberated through history. But violence ends in self-destruction and Carriglas which once represented an alien civilisation will eventually return 'to its clay'. (SG 203) The Big House will become a monument to the past, evoking another age in the way that the ruin of the island's abbey and its ancient burial mound already do. In 1931 a bridge is built to connect Carriglas to the mainland, its isolation from the mainstream of Irish life is set to end. The structure is ironically named after Cornelius Dowley and is built in the least convenient place for the Rollestons. A new order holds sway in Ireland and the epoch of the Big House is at an end. By 1971 the last vestiges of colonisation have disappeared; at Carriglas the death of Sarah Pollexfen brings the era to a close. Her diaries are read, their story noted, then they are burnt.

From a literary point of view *The Silence in the Garden* is a triumph of restraint. The plot is developed by subtle shading until the whole picture emerges perfect in detail. Characters are crafted with the same delicacy of touch. While some are but faint sketches – Villana with her 'strangely intense eyes ... her manner affected by a diffidence that stifled charm' (SG 12) remains a fey figure in the distance – others, particularly Sarah and Tom, appear in greater relief. Sarah is a worthy spinster whose 'story, of duty and unrequited love, was shaped by other people's greater claims' (SG 195), while Tom, the family's 'inheritor' (SG 173), a victim of the past and a link with the future, is a wonderful blend of innocence and resilience.

Mrs Rolleston comments that 'The past does not obligingly absorb what is not wanted.' (SG 185) Trevor's work demonstrates the truth of her observation. Responsibility must be taken for wrongs perpetrated but historical events cannot be used to justify further oppression. We are never in doubt as to how the author feels about history and its increment of violence, but his judgement is never offered as a moral or a lesson; he is too sophisticated a writer for that. Instead it is borne on the fabric of his narrative, in the interplay of characters and of past and present.

Chapter 5

'This pall of distress ...'

In 1977 William Trevor was made an honorary Commander of the British Empire, a distinction awarded to few Irish citizens and to no other contemporary Irish writer. This was in recognition of his standing as a world-class, prize-winning author who at this point had been an English resident for more than twenty years. Since he retains his Irish passport and citizenship, permission had to be sought from the Irish government in order for Trevor to be able to accept the award. Because the recipient was not a British subject, the Queen did not perform the ceremony; instead it was administered by the Minister for Arts, with the Irish ambassador in attendance.

Trevor is also a member of the Irish Academy of Letters, a body which had within its cohorts such illustrious figures as George Bernard Shaw, W.B. Yeats and Samuel Beckett and which for many years conferred both prestige and prizes on Irish writers. Although it has never officially ceased to exist, the Academy appears to have petered out and its functions have been effectively taken over by Aosdána, a government-sponsored association which elects its own membership, and to which Trevor has recently been elected.

Although he has been resident in England since 1954 and is acknowledged as a world-class writer, in Britain Trevor is nevertheless recognised as being a very 'Irish' writer. Terence DeVere White, who nominated him for membership of the Irish Academy of Letters and who was one of the first Irish critics of his work, believed that 'with six of his best short stories, Trevor could represent Ireland anywhere'.[1] When Trevor himself is asked if he considers himself an Irish writer, he replies rather disingenuously that of course he does, in that he is not a Russian or a Swede or an American. Pushed further he agrees that he sees himself as following in the tradition of people such as Frank O'Connor and Sean O'Faolain – both of whom hailed from the Irish Nationalist tradition rather than from the ranks of Anglo-Irish writers. By birth and upbringing, however, he straddles both the Nationalist and the Anglo-Irish traditions; his family background, early education and social status in small-town Ireland giving him insight into the former, while his religion and later education provide him with access to the latter.

Trevor has been described as 'The most English of Irishmen'[2], an epithet which could apply not only to the author's remarkable capacity to capture in his writings the essence of a particular kind of Englishness but also acknowledges Trevor's debt to English writers. He has always been an avid reader and admirer of Charles Dickens and the influences of that most English of writers can be seen in his early novels, which abound with an array of heterogeneous characters whose eccentricity and humour give them life and make them memorable. Even Trevor's most obvious influences, however, extend far beyond the English novel. Some of his books also resonate with a melancholic and eerie mood which recalls the writings of the great Russian authors, in particular those of Chekhov and Turgenev.

While acknowledging the eclectic nature of any writer's influences, it must be seen that Trevor's most obvious literary antecedent is James Joyce, in particular the James Joyce of *Dubliners*. In his non-fiction work *A Writer's Ireland* (1984) Trevor describes Joyce as setting out in his short stories to

> ... present the childhood, youth, middle age and public life of the city, to catch its citizens' varying moods and emotions, to expose their mundane predicaments and regrets, often simply to let them talk to one another.

(WI 127)

Like Joyce Trevor writes of human situations, in which characters move towards a revelation or epiphany which is moral, spiritual or social. The circumstances by which the characters reach this state of awareness are those of ordinary life. The process is admirably illustrated in the title story of his collection *After Rain*

(1996) in which Harriet, a woman holidaying in Italy in the aftermath of a failed love affair, gazes at a Renaissance painting of the Annunciation. She notices the details of the picture:

> There is blue as well as grey in the wings of the angel, little flecks of blue you don't notice when you look at first. The Virgin's slipper is a shade of brown, the empty vase is bulb-shaped with a slender stem, the Virgin's book had gold on it but only traces remain.

(AR 92)

In the midst of her examination of the masterpiece the woman has a sudden realisation, that she is

> Too slick and glib, to use her love affairs to restore her faith in love: the thought is there mysteriously. She has cheated in her love affairs: that comes from nowhere too.

(AR 92)

Harriet's instantaneous experience of self-knowledge is mirrored in the subject of the painting, in the Virgin's dawning awareness of her destiny. Equally the painting reflects Trevor's technique in writing a short story – the essence of a character or a situation is captured and illuminated, the details of the whole picture carefully distinguished, yet blended into the whole to produce a flawless effect.

Joyce described *Dubliners* as a 'chapter of moral history'[3] which would contribute towards 'the spiritual liberation'[4] of his country. He also wrote:

> the odour of ashpits and old weeds and offal hangs round my stories.[5]

The tang of corruption is equally perceptible in Trevor's work, but it also incorporates a sense of moral growth as his characters, like those of Joyce, come to a realisation of their condition, a process which is the basis of moral development.

When Joyce spoke of *Dubliners* he claimed that he named his series of short stories as such because he wished

> to betray the soul of that hemiplegia or paralysis which many consider a city.[6]

The citizens of Dublin as he portrays them are victims of this paralysis in mind, in body or in soul. Trevor's characters suffer likewise. Bridie in 'The Ballroom of Romance' is as helpless as Joyce's Eveline, while the guests who attend the parties in 'Angels at the Ritz' or 'Sunday Drinks' are as moribund as those at the Misses Morkan's annual dance in 'The Dead'. Other similarities abound: the 'queer old josser' of 'An Encounter' is the literary antecedent of Mr Lynch of 'An Evening with John Joe Dempsey' or Commander Abigail of *The Children of Dynmouth*, while the emotional paralysis which destroys the relationship between Mr Duffy and Mrs Sinico in 'A Painful Case' is the same as that which affects Mr McCarthy and Mavie in 'The Forty-seventh Saturday'.

Both Joyce and Trevor established their characters against backgrounds of detailed realism – using what Joyce called a 'nicely polished looking-glass'.[7] The Devlin kitchen in 'The Raising of Elvira Tremlett' is furnished with the same meticulous care as is Mr Duffy's uncarpeted room in Chapelizod and the city which Trevor creates in *Mrs Eckdorf in O'Neill's Hotel*, though a later version of the Dublin of *Ulysses*, is just as authentic.[8] Neither writer intervenes to any extent in his stories. In each case he avoids as much as possible the use of the authorial voice, preserving instead an air of benign impartiality. However sordid the actions of the characters, their humanity is acknowledged, while humour and irony are used to maintain a compassionate view of fallen man.

Trevor's 'Two More Gallants' is a direct allusion to Joyce's story in *Dubliners*. It is an occasional piece, written at the behest of Leeds University for the Joyce centenary celebrations of 1982. The story is a pastiche of the original and echoes its tone. Above all it is an acknowledgement of the influence which Trevor feels Joyce had on his work. Similar Joycean undertones are apparent in a story called 'Music' in which a boy's musical education is undertaken by a priest and his woman friend, so that they can further their own relationship. The boy's ambitions are unfulfilled and they end in disappointed failure.

It is equally interesting to trace in Trevor's work, the influence of another Irish writer, Flann O'Brien. Speaking of O'Brien, Trevor says:

You can't find somebody as funny and you can't be so sympathetically disposed towards him without being influenced by him ... I often find that there are lines of my dialogue which very much remind me of Flann O'Brien.[9]

A close look at passages from each writer's work shows that the speech patterns used by their characters are syntactically the same. In O'Brien's *The Dalkey Archive* Sergeant Fottrel and Mick Shaughnessy are in conversation:

> – Did you ever discover or hear tell of mollycules? He asked.
> – I did of course.
> – Would it surprise or collapse you to know that the Mollycule Theory is at work, in the parish of Dalkey?
> – Well ... yes and no.
> – It is doing terrible destruction, he continued, the half of the people is suffering from it, it is worse than the smallpox.

(p.80)

Morrissey, a character in *Mrs Eckdorf in O'Neill's Hotel* has an exchange with a young soldier:

> 'Are your parents alive?
> 'Ah, they are of course –'
> 'I'm parentless myself. I was brought up in an institution.'
> 'Is that a fact?'
> 'I was given no advantage. There was a time when I used to go down Henry Street and take the stuff off counters.

(MEON 112)

In each case the speaker responds to a direct question with the typical Hiberno-English repetition of the verb used in the interrogative. The affirmative statement is then followed by 'of course', a phrase which lends emphasis and suggests that agreement is a foregone conclusion. The instigator of the conversation now builds on the original statement, in one case by question and in the other by a further declaration. Each involves the addition of another item of information relating to the original topic. A non-committal rejoinder is made (is that a fact? – Well ...

yes and no) and the interlocutor continues to elaborate in each case by making three further points.

Since the characters come from roughly the same social class, perhaps these resemblances are not surprising. There are, however, other points of comparison. Both writers present their readers with worlds of obsession, madness and ludicrous deaths. Yet these worlds are not unrelentingly grim. Malign undercurrents may be at work, but humour – often the absurd kind – softens the sense of doom.

In his early writings, Trevor's relationship with his native country was ambiguous. The setting of his first novel *A Standard of Behaviour* (1958) is uncertain and largely irrelevant to the plot and characterisation. The action might be taking place in either Ireland or England although, as earlier noted, occasional topographical details evoke elements of Irish life and there is a peculiarly Irish quality about some of the dialogue. Trevor's first short stories, published in the early 1960s, give no indication that the writer is Irish, while the paperback edition of *The Old Boys* published in 1966 carries on its cover an extract from a *Times* review which describes its author as 'one of Britain's finest novelists', an understandable error on the part of the reviewer since the book focuses on that most English of institutions – the public school. The epithet was rectified, however, in later versions.

The first developed Irish character appears in *The Boarding House* (1965). We are told that Mr Studdy was:

> a red-haired man of fifty-three. He was tall and heavy, and he wore, winter and summer alike, a thick, black, double-breasted overcoat with a large grip on its belt. Stuck into the left lapel was a small religious badge, the emblem of the Sacred Heart.
>
> (BH 38)

A con man who escapes the status of villain because of his ineptitude, he is recognisably a modern 'stage' Irishman. Although *Mrs Eckdorf in O'Neill's Hotel* (1969) is set exclusively in Dublin, the city is seen primarily through the eyes of outsiders, London born Ivy Eckdorf and the Liverpudlian Mr Smedley. While its depiction is meticulous in detail it serves only as a background to the main pursuits of the book. With *Miss Gomez and the Brethren* (1971)

Trevor again returns to an English setting, but includes two Irish characters in the book: the brawling navvy, Atlas Flynn, another 'stage' Irishman, and Alban Roche, who is another stereotype – a young man whose psycho-sexual problems emanate from a puritanical upbringing at the hands of a repressive religion and an emotionally domineering mother – a phenomenon which is arguably more typical of the 1950s than of the 1970s.

As the previous chapter has shown, the outbreak of the Troubles in Northern Ireland concentrated Trevor's attention on his native country and the legacy of its post-colonial history. Other aspects of Irish life, however, had also begun to preoccupy him. In *The Ballroom of Romance* (1972), a collection of short stories, a view of what might be called 'Trevor's Ireland' begins to emerge. This is rural and small town Ireland, a bleak place where people endure life rather than live it; a place of loneliness, frustration and undramatic suffering. Timeless, except in its details, its moral climate remains constant whether its people live in the 1940s or the 1990s. Public events have little impact upon the inhabitants of the isolated farms, drab small towns, or, less often, dreary suburbs where individuals exist in states of unarticulated desperation. The title story of *The Ballroom of Romance* remains to this day Trevor's best-known work in his native country, mainly because of the extremely successful television adaptation which won several film awards in the early 1980s. Such was the film's success that, ironically, it evokes a nostalgia for a period of Irish life which had been exceptionally grim. In spite of the sordidness of its realism, the rural ballroom – its clientele arriving on bicycles from remote farms in search of love, or at least in an effort to ward off loneliness – becomes romanticised in the blur of distance.

The character at the centre of 'The Ballroom of Romance' is one of the author's typically marginalised people. Bridie, a thirty-six year old spinster, lives on a small Irish farm, with her crippled father for company. The only bright spot in her humdrum existence is the weekly dance held in the local Ballroom of Romance. The unmarried people of the area – the young and those like Bridie nearing middle-age – congregate there every Saturday night, in search of marriage partners. The ballroom from which the story takes it title:

> ... was miles from anywhere, a lone building by the
> roadside with treeless boglands all around and a gravel
> expanse in front of it.
>
> (CS 190)

The facade of the building is painted pink and decorated with
coloured lights, but the other walls are 'a more ordinary grey' (CS
191). The story was inspired by just such a ballroom which Trevor
spotted as he drove through rural Ireland.

Music at the Ballroom of Romance is provided by The
Romantic Jazz Band, who, ironically, never play jazz. The ersatz
quality of the entire occasion is established by the author's
frequent, if surreptitious, use of irony. Not only is The Romantic
Jazz Band a misnomer in the musical sense but its romantic
associations are completely undermined by the description of its
members:

> They were three middle-aged men who drove out from the
> town in Mr Maloney's car, amateur performers who were
> employed otherwise by the tinned-meat factory, the
> Electricity Supply Board, and the County Council.
>
> (CS 191)

In this world romance is superficial and romantic illusions fragile.

Towards the end of one evening in the ballroom Bridie
experiences an epiphany – a moment when she recognises what her
future holds. Dano Ryan, a member of the band whom she had
hoped might marry her, will instead wed his landlady. Bridie
reflects that he 'would have done' (CS 194) even though she had
only ever considered him as a substitute for Patrick Grady, the love
of her youth who emigrated to England and married there. Once
she had dreamt of a future with Grady:

> ... she believed then that he would lead her one day from
> the dim romantic ballroom, from its blueness and its
> pinkness and its crystal bowl of light and its music. She
> believed he would lead her into sunshine, to the town and
> the Church of Our Lady Queen of Heaven, to marriage and
> smiling faces.
>
> (CS 196)

Now if she is to marry at all her husband will be Bowser Egan, one
of three middle-aged bachelors who arrive drunk at the dance every

week and who are '... wedded already, to stout and whiskey and laziness, to three old mothers somewhere up in the hills'. (CS 194)

Bowser Egan will have her because he will need a home when his mother dies and she will marry him because 'it would be lonesome being by herself in the farmhouse'. (CS 204) As the band plays 'The Destiny Waltz' and 'The Bells are Ringing' Bridie's romantic illusions are exposed in the light of reality, their flimsiness revealed like the tawdriness of the ballroom itself when the full lights are switched on at the end of the evening:

> In the glare the blue walls of the ballroom seemed tatty, marked with hair-oil where men had leaned against them, inscribed with names and initials and hearts with arrows through them. The crystal bowl gave out a light that was ineffective in the glare; the bowl was broken here and there, which wasn't noticeable when the other lights weren't on.
>
> (CS 203)

As she leaves the dancehall Bridie meets Patty Byrne, a young girl whom the reader recognises as a younger version of herself, before she lost her belief in romance. Here Trevor uses one of his favourite devices for encapsulating past, present and future. Characters appear as mirror-images of each other, the reflection at times distorted to reinforce and give depth to the central character. Bridie too makes the connection as she wonders if a day will come when the younger girl will also decide to leave because she has become 'a figure of fun in a wayside ballroom'. (CS 202)

Bridie's life allows for neither weakness nor self-indulgence. Her decision on the way home to enter a field with Bowser Egan marks her acceptance of him and of her fate. She has no illusions about her future. Acknowledging the fact that there is no place for tears in her life, she looks beyond herself and remembers her father who, she says

> ... had more right to weep, having lost a leg. He suffered in a greater way, yet he remained kind and concerned for her.
>
> (CS 201)

In spite of her courage, Bridie is, in Trevor's words:

> ... beaten by the land and by the neighbourhood. There is no real way that she could rescue herself. [9]

Similar fates befall other Trevor heroines in rural Ireland. The eponymous heroine of 'Kathleen's Field' and Maura Brigid of 'A Husband's Return' are also defeated, not just by the land and the neighbourhood, but by moral pressures which deprive them of the ability to fight against their circumstances. To enable her impoverished parents to buy a much needed extra field for their farm, Kathleen is forced into domestic service in a household where she is both exploited and sexually abused. Maura Brigid, for her part, has to live with the shame she brought on her family by marrying a man who allowed himself to be seduced by her sister. Acting against her own will, but in accordance with the dictates of her family, she refuses to acknowledge his gesture of repentance and consequently denies herself all hopes of happiness.

The desperate plight of lonely people such as these is a universal theme, but Trevor conjures up, in a particular way, life in the remotest parts of rural Ireland before the advent of easy communication, when people lived isolated lives, bedevilled by material and spiritual poverty. Faced with such circumstances many of the characters develop insight and consequently rise above their roles as victims and attain the status of tragic heroines. There are, however, no dramatic events in their lives, just small disappointments and betrayals as described by Patrick Kavanagh in his poem 'The Great Hunger':

> No crash,
> No drama ...
> No mad hooves galloping in the sky,
> But the weak, washy way of true tragedy.[10]

'The Ballroom of Romance' deals with the circumstances which lead to Bridie's acceptance of her fate but 'The Property of Colette Nervi' takes the reader beyond that point and dwells on its heroine's ability to survive the compromise of her ideals. The setting of the story is again a remote area of rural Ireland. Dolores Mullally is cut off from what little social life obtains in Drumgawnie. Because her leg is 'shrivelled to the bone as a result of infantile paralysis' (CS 951), she is set apart from her peers and prevented from joining the other young people in outings to the dancehall or the cinema in the nearest town. Her world is confined almost entirely to her mother's crossroads huckster's shop, which is frequented by local people and by the occasional tourist on a visit to Drumgawnie Rath – 'a ring of standing stones that predated history'. (CS 949)

In the summer of 1968, when Dolores is twenty-two years old, a smart young French couple visits the Rath. The woman's handbag is mislaid and she leaves her name, Colette Nervi, and her address at Mullally's shop, in case the bag should be discovered. Dolores had witnessed the couple's embrace and starved of romance herself, she fantasises about them, feeding her imagination on the diet of Wild West novels which are her only source of romance:

> Perhaps when the lovers returned to the car there had been another embrace, which had driven everything from their minds – like in *Travellin' Saddles* when Big Daunty found his Indian love and both of them went into a swoon, lost to the world.

(CS 955)

Realising that her choices in life are severely limited Dolores agrees to become the wife of Henry Garvey, a man nearly twenty years her senior, who uses his intelligence to avoid work and whose motives for marrying her are mercenary and selfish. On her wedding day the young woman wears concealed under her dress a necklace which her bridegroom has given to her as a gift. She knows it to be part of the property of Colette Nervi which had been stolen by Garvey. In spite of the method of its acquisition, however, the jewellery is a secret comfort to the wearer, a treasured talisman which symbolises the romance which, fostered by her reading of novels, is hidden in the bride's heart. It provides her with a strength of purpose which will sustain her in her marriage to a mean-spirited and insensitive man.

In 'Teresa's Wedding' the woman trapped in a loveless marriage is moved a step farther beyond the point reached in the previous stories. It focuses on the moment during the wedding festivities when the bride becomes starkly aware of what she may expect of her marriage. In the course of the evening Artie Cornish, Teresa's bridegroom, enquires of her if it is true that his friend, Screw Doyle, has 'had a great bloody ride of her'. (CS 433) Calmly, Teresa reflects that

> ... it was only to be expected that a man you didn't love
> and who didn't love you would ask a question like that at
> your wedding celebration.
>
> (CS 437)

Artie is no worse than any of the other men Teresa knows. She
admits to herself that she could 'hardly tell the difference' (CS 435)
between any of them.

Teresa is already pregnant on the day of her wedding to Artie
Cornish. The local priest, Father Hogan, had 'persuaded Artie of
his duty when Artie had hesitated'. (CS 433) As the story unfolds
the subject of marriage is examined from a variety of angles, each
of which to some extent reflects Teresa's predicament. All of the
women in the story had at one time dreamed of a romantic union:

> Only the bridegroom had been mysterious, some faceless,
> bodiless presence, beyond the imagination.
>
> (CS 435)

In spite of their romantic notions the women settle eventually
for husbands who provide them with the means of escape from
humdrum existences and a status in the community. For many
marriage brings disappointment and bitterness, but Teresa, like
Dolores Mullally, accurately appraises her situation and even finds
comfort in it:

> ... she and Artie might make some kind of marriage
> together because there was nothing that could be destroyed,
> no magic or anything else.
>
> (CS 437-8)

The women in these stories may ask, like Mary Anne Maguire
in Kavanagh's 'The Great Hunger':

> Who bent the coin of my destiny
> That it stuck in the slot ...?[11]

as they stoically accept what they cannot alter. Some of the
protagonists, however, find release by manipulating events even
within the confines of fate. While characters like Bridie and
Dolores are forced to accommodate themselves to the
circumstances of their lives, others fight back and take a hand in
shaping their own destinies. Even when they remain victims of

environment or events they manage to rescue themselves after a fashion. Dervla, the girl at the centre of 'The Wedding in the Garden' is also faced with intractable circumstances in a story which finely delineates the class divisions of a small town. The owners of the Royal Hotel, the Congreves, are Protestants who are believed to 'have good breeding in them'. (CS 922) Their son Christopher attends a boarding-school in Dublin and has no knowledge of places like Thomas MacDonagh Street where Catholic working-class families like Dervla's live. There are rather more social than political implications in the names of the hotel and the street, the former recalling the British regime, the latter commemorating an Irish patriot.

The writer allows the two characters from these disparate backgrounds to meet in their teens, when the girl is employed as a maid in the hotel. The young people fall in love and plan to marry. Eventually, however, in her son's absence, Mrs Congreve pressures Dervla into terminating their relationship. In return for her acquiescence she promises the girl permanent employment in the hotel. With the passage of time Christopher obliterates all memory of the relationship from his mind. By contrast Dervla remains devoted to him, consoling herself that 'only reality had been lost'. (CS 934) In due course Christopher finds a socially acceptable girl, an Archdeacon's daughter, while Dervla meanwhile rejects the advances of several men from her own milieu. On Christopher's wedding day, however, it becomes obvious that Dervla will have her 'undramatic revenge'. (CS 937) She will remain in the hotel, a living reminder of the past they shared, her presence subtly creating a chasm between Christopher and his wife. Her constancy will follow him as inexorably as the town's dogs once did during the solitary ramblings of his adolescence. His destiny is determined by a woman who has 'kept faith' (CS 937) and who will exercise her will to the limits which are available to her.

Similarly Fina, the heroine of 'Big Bucks'[12], takes control of her life by choosing not to marry. When her fiancé, John Michael, rejects the chance of a frugal living in Ireland and decides instead to emigrate to the United States in search of better things, the girl at first agrees to follow him. The young people's knowledge of America is based on some hazy facts remembered from schooldays, combined with images gleaned from the television screen:

> They watched America, they heard its voices. Its ballgame
> heroes battled, rigid in their padding and their helmets.
> Steam swirled above the night-time gratings of its city
> streets. Legs wide, eyes dead, gangsters splayed their
> fingers on precinct walls.
>
> (NY 70)

Egged on by an elderly bachelor, Bat Quinn, who advises others to seize the opportunities he had lacked the courage to take himself, John Michael plans to make his fortune.

The day-to-day existence of an illegal immigrant, the reality of which is conveyed to Fina through brief letters from John Michael – and more eloquently through his silences – brings the young woman to the realisation that she does not wish to leave the life she knows – with all its shortcomings – for the uncertainty of exile. Of more significance, however, is Fina's discovery that she does not love John Michael, that the distance between them had allowed her to develop a sense of herself as an individual:

> Close to one another, she and John Michael had sometimes
> hardly seemed two different people. Apart, they were
> aware of the insistence that they were.
>
> (NY 73)

The unused material for her wedding dress is returned to the shop to be sold as a remnant – a relic of her romance, but while others might pity her plight, Fina fully appreciates 'the fragility of love' (NY 73) and is consoled by the fact that in ending her relationship 'destruction had been averted' (NY 73).

Although she lives in Ireland of the 1990s, Fina's choices are seen to be as limited as those of her counterparts from earlier decades. Poverty still cripples the inhabitants of fishing villages and hill farms. In spite of the advent of televisions and telephones, people still fail to communicate at any important level, writing instead 'lines to be read between' (NY 73), circling each other without meeting. Once again, however, the woman has sufficient self-awareness to survive the situation and to find comfort in her own resoluteness.

While these women are forced to relinquish their dreams and to accept instead a very different and inferior reality, they are sustained by the courage with which they bear their various reversals. Bridie casts aside self pity, Dolores treasures her secret symbol of romance, Teresa determines to see her loss as a gain, Dervla imposes a silent retribution on the man who has wronged her and Fina experiences insight and self-determination. All of the women take comfort from the fact that in being deprived of their illusions they have nothing else of value to lose. This brings its own consolation and with it a kind of salvation. Dervla has a certain revenge on her former lover, but her greatest triumph occurs in her mind. This is true of the other women also. On the surface they appear as victims, but in the seclusion of their own hearts they have their small victories.

Other Trevor characters too escape from repression in the isolation of their imaginations. This is the experience of the boy at the centre of 'An Evening with John Joe Dempsey', a story about an adolescent's dawning sexuality. John Joe is celebrating his fifteenth birthday on the day on which the events unfold. The only child of a widow, he is an odd boy, friendless apart from a strange relationship with Quigley 'an old, simple-minded dwarf' (CS 258)

In the small Irish town in which John Joe grows up in the 1950s, entertainment is to be found only in the pub or the cinema. On the evening of his birthday John Joe is sent by his mother to buy some groceries at Keogh's, a public house which 'as well as refreshments and stimulants ... sold a variety of groceries' (CS 255). While he waits for the return from confession of the proprietor, Mrs Keogh, the boy falls into conversation with a regular customer of the place, Mr Lynch, an ageing bachelor who lives with his elderly mother. As John Joe samples his first bottle of stout, Mr Lynch seizes the opportunity to talk to the boy about sex, telling him of his own experiences while a soldier in the British army during the Second World War. Ostensibly he is telling a cautionary tale against casual sex, but his sordid story serves only to titillate both himself and his listener. The highlight of his narrative is the story of his encounter with the Piccadilly 'glory girls' (CS 256), an escapade which came to an abrupt end when Mr Lynch claimed he had a vision of a statue of the Virgin Mary which his mother had given him as a First Communion gift. Mr

Lynch maintains that he never married because of his shame about the incident. Once he has aroused John Joe's prurient curiosity, the man catechises the boy about his own sexual habits. Even as John Joe protests his innocence, his mind is filled with images of female bodies:

> All the women of the town – and most especially Mrs Taggart, the wife of the postman – John Joe had kept company with in his imagination.

(CS 260)

He also recalls the stories told to him by Quigley, whose improbable accounts of voyeurism supplement his own jejune imaginings. Quigley articulates the fantasies which are the stuff of John Joe's day-dreams:

> There was hardly a man and his wife in the town whom he didn't claim to have observed in intimate circumstances.

(CS 262)

Mr Lynch's warnings against John Joe's association with the dwarf echo a similar admonition delivered by Brother Leahy, one of the boy's teachers.

The second part of the story focuses on the relationship between John Joe and his mother. When, on his return home, John Joe mentions his meeting with Mr Lynch, the subsequent conversation about Mr Lynch and his mother underlines the stifling quality of John Joe's relationship with Mrs Dempsey. In the light of this other mother/son relationship the reader reaches a fuller understanding of John Joe and is allowed a glimpse of his probable future. Mr Lynch's war career was undertaken in an effort to escape from his mother, but she had 'reached out to him from a dream' (CS 269). Mrs Dempsey displays the same possessiveness with regard to her son and it becomes obvious that John Joe is trapped in a course which is parallel to Mr Lynch's. Perhaps in these women we can see Bridie, Dolores and Teresa, embittered by their own lack of passionate relationships, refusing to allow their sons to develop what they themselves have been to obliged to forego.

Even as John Joe submits to his future, however, he experiences a moment of insight in which he realises that:

> Only Quigley told the truth ... Only Quigley was honest
> and straightforward and said what was in his mind. Other
> people told Quigley to keep that kind of talk to himself
> because they knew it was the truth, because they knew they
> wanted to think the thoughts that Quigley thought.
>
> (CS 270)

John Joe recognises Quigley's voice as his own:

> Even though it was only Quigley who talked, there was an
> understanding between them: being with Quigley was like
> being alone.
>
> (CS 272)

All the other characters reject the primitive instincts which are embodied in the town's misshapen outcast. Mr Lynch's inclinations are thwarted and rebound upon him, distorting his view of women and sexuality. There are suggestions that other characters suffer likewise. Brother Leahy's implied sadism in the classroom is simply the outward projection of a similar frustration, while the two mother-figures, Mrs Lynch and Mrs Dempsey, effectively castrate their sons by their possessiveness. John Joe detects the real reason for Mr Lynch's celibacy:

> Mr Lynch was not an honest man. It was a lie when he said
> that shame had kept him from marrying. It was his mother
> who prevented that, with her dreams of legs on fire and her
> First Communion statues.
>
> (CS 271)

As he finds comfort in the solitude of his bed that night, John Joe indulges in his own sexual fantasies: 'In his bed he entered a paradise: it was grand being alone.' (CS 273). His retreat into masturbation is itself a symptom of the solipsistic outlook which unhealthy sexual attitudes have forced upon him and which the story implies will govern his adult life. He has seen through the hypocrisy of the world about him and realised that only in his dreams can he be ever truly himself.

Another adolescent boy is at the centre of Trevor's novella *Nights at the Alexandra*. Harry is also a loner who grows up in a small provincial town and feels the need to break out of the mould in which his family confines him. His future is to be in the family business, a fate from which he recoils, as did his older sister before him; her protests, however, went unheeded. Like John Joe Dempsey, Harry is drawn to an adult outsider who represents a way of life which is at variance with his upbringing. But while John Joe's influences can be seen as negative, Harry's appear to offer him both glamour and romance.

The events of the story are recalled by Harry in his late middle-age – a vantage point from which people tend to review their lives in the light of an increasing awareness of the constraints of time and the shadow of mortality. The opening of the novella immediately presents the reader with an intertwining of past and present, of memory and event, while at the same time it juxtaposes the lives and experiences of the two main protagonists:

> I am a fifty-eight-year-old provincial. I have two children. I have never married.
> 'Harry, I have the happiest marriage in the world! Please, when you think of me, remember that.'
>
> (NA 1)

The voice is that of Frau Messinger, as Harry remembers it from a distance of more than forty years. With her German husband, the English woman has sought refuge in neutral Ireland for the duration of the Second World War, because neither would have been safe in the other's country.

Harry begins his acquaintance with Frau Messinger when she enlists him to do errands for her:

> ... her tone of voice was not one normally employed when making a request. With a gentle imperiousness, she commanded what she wished ...
>
> (NA 3)

The boy is immediately smitten by her beauty and her lifestyle which appears exotic when compared with his own drab existence. He comes from a Protestant family 'of the servant class which had come up in the world' (NI 3), the father an uncouth proprietor of a timberyard, his wife an overworked mother of four children, who in addition copes with two grandmothers who share the same house but live in silent enmity with each other. In spite of his mother's disapproval, Harry becomes a regular visitor at Cloverhill House, the Messingers' home, and listens while the young English woman tells her story, becoming enthralled by her memories. Her girlhood was spent as a poor relation, staying with her mother, 'a very foolish little person' (NA 11) in other people's houses. A proposal of marriage from a man she had loved was rejected by her, but later in Germany she married Herr Messinger, a widower thirty-five years her senior, with three sons serving in Hitler's army. Her husband now surrounds her with the beautiful objects she had always admired but had never owned. His devotion is further shown in his determination to reclaim a garden for her to enjoy. As always in Trevor's work this is a symbol of hope.

Away at school Harry continues to be infatuated by Frau Messinger and fantasises about becoming a servant in her house. His preoccupation with her attracts the attention of his teachers, one of whom like Mr Lynch in 'An Evening with John Joe Dempsey' uses the pretext of warning the boy against the evils of sex to satisfy his own lustful curiosity.

During the holidays Harry learns that Herr Messinger is to build a cinema in the town as a marriage gift for his wife. The cinema, to be called the Alexandra in honour of Frau Messinger, represents all the splendour and fascination with which the boy associates the woman. Technically too it works like memory, framing still pictures that evolve into a sequence which appears to have life. Before it opens, however, he hears from Herr Messinger that his wife is dying. Her languor, her feverish colouring, her refusal to marry her first love and her childlessness are all explained by the tuberculosis from which she is suffering. Her husband clarifies the situation:

> 'An old man marries for the time that is left, Harry. Both of us seemed not to have much time.'
>
> (NA 57)

As the end approaches, the focus of Frau Messinger's conversations with the boy moves from the story of her life to the question of an afterlife:

> 'That may be what heaven is, Harry: dreaming through times that have been.'
>
> (NA 55)

In articulating her notions of life beyond the grave she is at the same time describing her conversations with Harry, in which she uses her memories to recreate her own past and to bequeath to her listener 'memories that are theirs, not mine' (NA 44) to the point where they completely engross him, absorbing his identity in hers, and thus, in a sense, ensuring the continuity of her life after death.

Harry eventually inherits the Alexandra, rejecting his place in his father's timberyard as he rejects all aspects of life outside his obsession, becoming, in his own words, 'the ghost of an interlude' (NA 71). With the passage of time cinema audiences decline and the building closes. Cloverhill House too falls into decay. In the final chapter of the novella the framework of the narrative is completed as Harry 'A fifty-eight-year-old cinema proprietor without a cinema', reflecting again on his life, insists that 'memory is enough' (NA 71).

Memory and survival are also at the heart of one of Trevor's most acclaimed novels, *Reading Turgenev*, which was published jointly with *My House in Umbria* in a volume entitled *Two Lives* (1991). The book focuses on the 'shrinking community' (RT 14) of Protestant families in a 1950s' provincial town. Like the nineteenth century Russian gentry about whom Turgenev writes, the Irish Protestants, an ever-decreasing minority in an increasingly Catholic Ireland, have lost their direction and purpose. There are other characteristics which Trevor shares with the Russian master. Both writers have a remarkable gift for observation and are meticulous craftsmen who mould their stories with fastidious elegance.

The feeling which Mary Louise Dallon, the heroine of *Reading Turgenev*, has for her cousin Robert is the kind of emotion which the Russian writer also centres on – a passionate love experienced within the confines of provincial life. Trevor's novel deals with the strategies used to ensure the survival of this sentiment amidst alien circumstances. The structure of the novel, with every other chapter alternating between past and present, not only allows the reader to see each of these time shifts in terms of the other but also underscores the opposition between an idealised love and an implacable reality.

As the story opens the reader is introduced to Mary Louise, a woman 'not yet fifty-seven, slight and seeming frail' (RT 1) who is about to be released from a mental institution in which she has been incarcerated for thirty years. Her return to the community is in accordance with the social and fiscal policies of the late 1980s which are to shut down such places, now deemed to be relics of a less enlightened age. Deftly the author shifts between Mary Louise's present position and earlier periods of her life. As a young girl growing up on her parents' remote farm in Culleen, she has the modest aspirations of other Trevor heroines – she longs to work as an assistant in the pharmacy of the nearby town. When no such opportunity presents itself, the girl becomes fearful that she will never be able to escape from her humdrum life and agrees to marry Elmer Quarry, a draper and 'the only well-to-do Protestant for miles around' (RT 5). Elmer is 'decent and reliable' (RT 30). He is also fourteen years older than Mary Louise and 'as square-looking as the origins of his name suggested' (RT 7). The marriage, however, will allow Mary Louise to escape:

> ... the long, slow days at Cullen, the kitchen, the yard, the fowl houses, for weeks on end not seeing anyone outside the family except at church or at the egg-packing station.
>
> (RT 26)

Elmer equally recognises that it is a marriage of convenience. Like his forbears he marries to provide an heir to the family business.

From the outset the relationship, into which they have entered in both innocence and ignorance, seems doomed. Neither of their families approves of the match and as Mary Louise's brother and sister warn her:

> Elmer Quarry was a man who never laughed and rarely smiled.
>
> (RT 9)

Further opposition comes from Matilda and Rose, Elmer's spinster sisters, who regard Mary Louise as an intruder into their lives. Even Miss Mullover who had taught both Elmer and Mary Louise in the Protestant school is uneasy. The old teacher's insights, in keeping with her name, serve as a choric commentary on the events.

The nature of the courtship further brings the relationship into question. Only after he has proposed marriage to her does Elmer attempt to kiss his bride-to-be. The details of the events are ominous:

> He had passed his tongue over his lips, dried them with a handkerchief and announced that he was going to kiss her ... he had found the experience a little disappointing.
>
> (RT 31-2)

The failure of the marriage is charted through a series of tragi-comic events. An uneasy wedding reception is the prelude to an abortive honeymoon during which it is revealed that Elmer is impotent. The ensuing embarrassment and guilt drive the formerly abstemious draper to seek comfort in alcohol, while his young wife becomes increasingly lonely and withdrawn.

In her isolation Mary Louise turns to her invalid cousin, Robert, whom she had known in childhood. Under the pretence of visiting her parents at Culleen, she has regular meetings with him – rather appropriately in a graveyard. There he reads aloud to her from three Turgenev novels: *On the Eve, First Love* and *Fathers and Sons*,[13] stories of idealism and passion which become more real to the young people than the illness and stifling repression which dog their own lives. When Robert dies, shortly after declaring his love for her, Mary Louise takes refuge from her drunken husband and his bullying sisters in an attic in the Quarrys' house. Here she creates for herself a shrine to the memory of her dead love, surrounding herself with mementoes of his life – including his books – and moving inexorably by means of Turgenev's fiction into the realms of fantasy:

> When they married they travelled in Italy and France. They sat outside a café by the sea, watching the people strolling by, Robert in a pale suit and a hat that matched it. He leaned across the table to kiss her, as he had the first time in the graveyard.
>
> (RT 141)

Brief excerpts from the Russian novels surface through the young woman's consciousness becoming an integral part of her imagined life and crowding out reality.

As a child when Mary Louise had shown a particular interest in Joan of Arc, Miss Mullover had wondered if she possessed 'an imagination that would one day bear fruit'. (RT 4) Its yield is a romantic dream which protects her from the boredom of her loveless marriage and gives her strength to withstand the machinations of her vindictive sisters-in-law. A well-laid plan to convince Matilda and Rose that she is attempting to poison them calls into question her supposed insanity. She may be crazy and dangerous or she may be merely exerting her independence, amusing herself at their expense and even manipulating their reactions for her own purposes. Her activities result in her confinement in a mental asylum and consequently it would appear that the sisters have triumphed over her. Yet it is in this institution that Mary Louise finds for herself a refuge in which 'her love affair could spread itself' (RT 221) and the shelter of which she is loath to leave.

The penultimate chapter of the novel draws together the past and present as Mary Louise returns home with her husband. The structure of the narrative which recalls episodes from the woman's life in an apparently random manner reinforces the philosophy which over the years she has come to accept:

> A person's life isn't orderly ... it runs all over the place, in and out through time. The present's hardly there; the future doesn't exist. Only love matters in the bits and pieces of a person's life.
>
> (RT 161)

The love which has sustained her for more than thirty years and which has given a meaning to the details of Mary Louise's life now provides her with a new purpose – to have Robert's body exhumed and reinterred in the graveyard in which they had conducted their romance and where she too intends to be buried. She confides her wishes to a young clergyman who is impressed by 'her innocence and her boundless love' (RT 220) and as the book ends it becomes apparent that in due course he will carry out the arrangement.

Whether Mary Louise's insanity is real or just a ruse which provides her with a means of escape from an impossible situation is never completely resolved within the book. Other Trevor characters find refuge from their quotidian difficulties in the alternative worlds they create in their minds, but Mary Louise's mischievous sense of humour and her extraordinary determination suggest that she is less helpless than characters such as Mrs Acland in 'Mrs Acland's Ghosts' or Imelda in *Fools of Fortune*, as she deliberately manipulates events so that she will be removed to a place where she can more tranquilly indulge her obsession. The reading of Turgenev's books had been 'the act of love' (RT 187) between Robert and herself and it is fiction which empowers her to rise above a sordid reality and to create her own happiness.

There is even an element of triumph in her eventual return to the town, where old age has rendered her sisters-in-law harmless, their loss of vigour and status mirroring the decline of their class in contemporary Ireland. For the Irish Protestant community in the 1950s had 'no reserves of strength' (RT 14) and the fortunes of the Quarry and Dallon families in the following decades reflect its fate and serve as a metaphor for the diminution of its power and influence. Mary Louise's marriage to Elmer is childless. The Dallon farm at Culleen is no longer economically viable and will soon pass into other hands. Mary Louise's sister, Letty, has married a Catholic and 'the priest will want the children' (RT 121). The names given to Letty's first born, Kevin Aloysius, are more typically Catholic than Protestant and indicate the change of religion. Mary Louise's own preoccupation is with the past. The few happy encounters which she had with her sickly cousin took place among tombstones and it is in death that she will have her greatest victory – when she shares a grave with Robert. Like the lovers, the Irish Protestant community is shown to live in the shadow of death.

In his 1994 novel *Felicia's Journey* Trevor chooses to take the eponymous heroine from her home in rural Ireland on a voyage of self-discovery to industrial England. The theme of the novel will be dealt with elsewhere in this work, but it is worth examining rural Ireland of the 1990s as it appears in Trevor's book. Felicia might be a younger version of Bridie in 'The Ballroom of Romance'. She too is motherless and lives a cheerless existence in her family home where she is an unpaid housekeeper. In all its essentials Felicia's life is as materially and spiritually poor as that of Trevor's other Irish heroines from earlier decades. Felicia's father is less sympathetic than Bridie's and with her in the house are her uncommunicative brothers and her great-grandmother who is almost a hundred years old and with whom she shares a bedroom. There are outward signs of the late twentieth century in the small Irish town in which Felicia lives. The girl shops at the Centra foodstore and the town boasts a Two-Screen Ritz and Dancetime Disco. But when Felicia falls in love with and becomes pregnant by Johnny Lysaght, a young man who has returned from England to visit his widowed mother, she finds herself as isolated as any unmarried mother of the 1950s. The values which obtain in 1990s' rural Ireland, as Trevor depicts them in this book, have not changed in over half a century. Felicia's great-grandmother with whom the girl is forced to live intimately, represents traditional Ireland. The old woman in her youth had lost her husband in the struggle for Irish freedom and had subsequently endured a life of hardship, believing it to have been ennobled by her young husband's bloodshed. She has outlived two generations and has also 'outlived her own rational thought' (FJ 25). In a scrapbook she keeps memorabilia of Ireland's history – photographs, newspapers clippings and copies of documents. Amongst these are 'the hallowed sentiments of Eamon deValera' (FJ 26-7). The document is a copy of deValera's famous radio broadcast made on 17 March 1943 on Radio Eireann. It tells of his dreams of a people who would value:

> ... material wealth only as a basis of right living, of a people who were satisfied with frugal comfort and devoted their leisure to the things of the spirit ... a land with cosy homesteads ... sturdy children ... athletic youths ... the laughter of comely maidens ... the home of a people living the life that God desires men should live.
>
> (FJ 26-27)

This is the Ireland which did not tolerate lapses from what deValera called 'right living'. Felicia has herself been named after 'A woman who'd manned the barricades in 1916' (FJ 62) – a woman who had given her life for her country. When Felicia discovers that she is pregnant, she does what countless others in her position have done – she takes the boat to England and eventually has an abortion. The ethical code which forces her to take this decision – her father calls her 'a hooer' when he realises what has happened – has not changed greatly in fifty years. Just as

'The Ballroom of Romance' more appropriately fitted into the 1950s rather than the 1970s, so even in this book set in the 1990s, it is the moral climate of the 1950s and earlier in which Trevor's characters live. This is the Ireland which Trevor left in 1954. In his work the outward details may have altered but essentially things have remained the same. This is Trevor's Ireland – a bleaker landscape perhaps than the Ireland familiar to people who live there today – a place viewed from a backward glance but one which is nevertheless recognisable.

William Trevor is a product of a declining class – that sliver of a people he so often talks about. In moving from Ireland himself he joined a cosmopolitan and more urbane society and seemed at first in his writings to have cast aside his Irishness. When he first looked back at his native country it was to see the quirks and foibles of his countrymen. But with the passage of time he entered into a closer relationship with the place of his birth. Now when he turned his writer's attention to his own country he brought to his work the objectivity of an outsider, combined with a close knowledge of the country and its people. This mixture of objectivity and subjectivity manifested itself in a tremendous compassion towards his characters as they struggle against the undramatic but unrelenting vicissitudes of fortune. Trevor's Ireland is a unique and very special place in which are chronicled the small victories and failures of little lives.

Chapter 6

'Goodness is a greater mystery than ... evil'

Evil fascinates William Trevor. He is particularly interested in its ordinariness, the way in which its perpetrators are largely indistinguishable from the rest of mankind until the moment when they are responsible for some heinous act which propels them into the limelight. Once this has happened they are no longer of concern to the writer. It is not the dramatic events which attract him, instead it is the process by which the ordinary becomes extraordinary that claims his attention.

Several of Trevor's early short stories, we have seen, featured children who early in their lives lose the innocence we associate with infancy. In his novel *The Children of Dynmouth* (1976), the author in placing such a child at the centre of the book creates an admirable opportunity to explore the nature of evil as it manifests itself among the inhabitants of a small English seaside resort. Dynmouth, the author tells us, has a population of 4,139, half of whom are children. The odd digit might alert the reader to expect a similar peculiarity or unbalance in the lives of the characters, the most interesting of whom is Timothy Gedge. The fifteen-year-old boy lives with his mother and sister, both of whom largely ignore him. He is a typical latch-key child who spends hours alone in an empty flat, eating junk food and watching comedy programmes on television. His great ambition is to be a popular entertainer and with this end in view he is determined to compete in a talent contest which will be held during the Easter fête at Dynmouth. His contribution is to be a one-man show which re-enacts the infamous Brides-in-the-Bath murders. His plan to reconcile death and comedy in a theatrical piece reveals not only a macabre imagination but an unwholesome preoccupation with both transvestism and sadism. Since he needs stage props for his performance, Timothy finds it necessary to blackmail a number of Dynmouth citizens into providing them, by threatening to reveal unsavoury details of their private lives.

Timothy has plenty of material with which to practise extortion since he spends a great deal of time spying on the adult population of the town. He has discovered the promiscuity of both his mother and his sister. He knows about Commander Abigail's penchant for playing 'Find the Penny' with cub scouts and he uses that information to acquire the Commander's dog-tooth suit for his performance. He intimidates an elderly couple, the Dasses, into providing stage curtains by threatening to reveal details of a bitter quarrel with their only son. Even the pugnacious Mr Plant, a publican, agrees to provide Timothy with a tin bath when the boy threatens to disclose the man's extramarital exploits to his wife 'a big Welshwoman ... with a temper like a cat's' (CD 66). The core of the story involves the acquisition of a wedding-dress for Timothy's impersonation of the brides. In order to obtain it he menaces two twelve-year-olds, Kate and Stephen, whose parents have recently married, by insinuating that Stephen's father pushed his first wife over a cliff in order to be free to marry his mistress, Kate's mother. The dead woman's wedding-dress must be given to him if the 'murder' is not to be exposed.

Initially Timothy's victims refuse to co-operate, but all of them eventually capitulate as he plays on their fears and weaknesses. The boy's real strength lies in the fact that there is a large element of truth in the discreditable stories he threatens to reveal. He is a ruthless manipulator and as amoral as any megalomaniac in history. Trevor is not just presenting the reader with a delinquent teenager who is the product of parental neglect; he is also examining the nature of lost innocence and the book is essentially a lament for its demise. It shows corruption stalking childhood, a bogeyman who is all too real.

Timothy becomes the catalyst of Dynmouth as the lives of all those around him change while he remains obdurate. Commander Abigail is reduced to a blubbering parody of an authority figure as both he and his wife acknowledge that:

> ... only the truth had passed from Timothy Gedge, the
> unarguable strength of it, the power and the glory of it.
>
> (CD 107)

Timothy's disclosure is as inexorable as the biblical phrase it
echoes. The Dasses too have to live with the truth about their
relationship with their son and even Plant has to acknowledge to
himself, and to Timothy, that he is afraid of his wife.

Timothy's encounters with genuinely innocent characters are,
however, even more interesting. We first see the boy through the
eyes of the rector, Mr Featherston. It is a day in early April, the
feast of St Pancras who is, ironically, the patron saint of children.
Encounters with Timothy make the vicar uneasy. The boy's
vacuous good humour, together with his ceaseless string of
wisecracks gleaned from *One Thousand Jokes for Kids of All Ages* and
his frightening single-mindedness, strike a chill note. Mr
Featherston realises that:

> ... of all the people of Dynmouth this boy in his
> adolescence was the single exception. He could feel no
> Christian love for him.
>
> (CD 121)

Kate and Stephen, the children whose parents have recently
married are the other innocents whom Timothy menaces. The
symbolism is clear as he comes as an intruder into their garden,
bringing with him intimations of evil. Mrs Blakey, the
housekeeper, notes that:

> He didn't belong in gardens, any more than he belonged in
> the company of two small children.
>
> (CD 140)

The twelve-year-olds are easy targets for Timothy. When he
informs them that their parents had been lovers while Stephen's
mother was still alive, they lose their faith in the adult world. The
implication that Stephen's father may have murdered his mother
becomes increasingly credible and even when the story is proven to
be a fabrication, there remains for the children the awareness that
their parents were not entirely blameless in the matter. Stephen's
mother had killed herself in despair:

> They would never see their parents in quite the same way again, and ironically it was apt that they should not, because Timothy Gedge had not told lies entirely.
>
> (CD 207)

Kate, who has faith in a personal God, had promised that if Stephen's father were exonerated, she would have Timothy exorcised. The vicar, however, can only respond by explaining his own purely rational view of religion:

> There were good people and people who were not good: that had nothing to do with devils. He tried to explain that possession by devils was just a form of words.
>
> (CD 194)

Through the minds of the vicar and his wife, Lavinia, the question of Timothy's evil is debated. While Mr Featherston cannot accept Kate's belief that there is an exterior force of evil at work, neither can he accept his wife's view that Timothy is just the product of social and environmental factors – 'circumstances created by other people' (CD 211-2). The rector echoes Joseph Conrad when he speaks of the boy's existence as a 'horror' (CD 208)[1] He believes that Timothy, like many other unfortunates, is battered by existence in a world where 'God permits chance' (CD 210). As a clergyman he feels helpless in the face of this random suffering. He can pray for Timothy, but his personal belief is that 'prayer wasn't enough in a chancy world' (CD 210).

In spite of his feelings of inadequacy, Mr Featherston is sustained by his faith. At the same time, it is his wife Lavinia's hope and charity which help her to come to an understanding of life. She hopes that one day she may pierce the shell which Timothy has grown about himself for protection. She even sees him at some future time taking the place of her unborn son. The reader, however, may find it difficult to share her aspirations as the book concludes with Timothy's retreat into a new fantasy.

The vicar's view of evil as the outcome of 'chance' or fortune is a notion which recurs in Trevor's work. All people, it appears – to a greater or lesser extent – are capable of perpetrating wickedness; it is precisely its everydayness which makes it interesting. Moreover, the impulse and habituation to evil are as much the result of happenstance as of circumstance. To look for any more logical explanation would be fatuous in an illogical world. Ultimately one is confronted by the possibility that we are all 'fools of fortune'.

While the study of evil emerges again as a theme in Trevor's novel *Other People's Worlds* (1980), this time a connection between wickedness and madness is made. The book also examines more fully evil's opposite state, goodness. Underpinning each and forming the main focus of the work is the imagination which inspires each of these conditions. 'Make-belief is all we have' (OPW 68), Francis Tyte, the villain of the book remarks, but Julia Ferndale, who represents the force of goodness, calls it 'poisonous make-belief' (OPW 195). As the issues of evil, madness and goodness are explored through the narrative, the writer's skill ensures that these essentially metaphysical themes are played out in a world which is instantly recognisable to the reader. The principal characters are each given equal prominence and the structure of the novel depends on techniques of mirroring and contrasting – particularly apt devices since *Other People's Worlds* deals with a variety of realities and illusions which are distinct yet interconnected. Much of the book's interest comes from the collision of these disparate worlds and the circumstances through which they relate to each other.

To illustrate his belief in the banality of evil, Trevor has created Francis Tyte as a superficially common-place character. Gradually more sinister aspects of his psyche are revealed. A small-time actor, he is a fantasist who is weak, warped and untrustworthy. He exploits others and is genuinely baffled when his victims removes him. He readily admits his transgressions and then expects his victims to enjoy vicariously his excitement when he reveals the details of his actions and his fantasies. Underlying his amorality is a consuming rage which allows him to blame all those who do not succumb to his charm when his wrong-doing is revealed.

As the novel opens, Francis is about to be married to Julia Ferndale, a well-to-do, attractive widow – who at forty-seven years of age is fourteen years his senior. Up until her remarriage, Julia's life has been one of untested virtue in comfortable surroundings. A devout Catholic, her God has remained the 'bearded cloudy God' (OPW 196) of her childhood.

Her sedate faith has ill-prepared her for an encounter with the weird imagination of her 'husband'. Julia's world is one of bourgeois 'niceness' (OPW 243) and it is shaken to the foundations of its faith when it collides with 'other people's worlds': Francis's seamy, promiscuous world of half-truths, Doris's vulgar, foolish alcohol-soaked world and Joy's world of child neglect and drug abuse. In *The Children of Dynmouth* the author allowed Timothy Gedge to have access to well-ordered lives. In *Other People's Worlds* Francis Tyte – a grown-up version of Timothy – is in a position to wreak the same kind of havoc in the lives of those about him, and in each case readers are left to draw their own conclusions from the results.

Before her marriage Julia lives with her elderly mother, Mrs Anstey, in Stone St Martin, a small town in Gloucestershire. Her life is comfortable and conventional. From his demeanour Francis Tyte appears to be the perfect fiancé for Julia, yet early on in the book there are small hints which imply that all is not what is seems. The most disquieting thing about Francis is his fascination with Constance Kent and 'the nature of her crime' (OPW 32). Trevor uses the case of the Victorian child murderer to give resonance to his theme. It is a leitmotif which runs through the novel, binding together different elements as both Francis and his mistress, Doris, identify with the murderess. As such it advances the theme of environmental determinism which the book underlines. The author suggests reasons why Francis is evil: he was born to ageing parents and was sexually abused by a lodger in his parents' home. One can feel compassion for the child, Francis, who was unable to cope when:

> Among the marching soldiers the deception and the treachery increased.

(OPW 89)

These circumstances also lend credence to the predicament of Francis's daughter, Joy. Above all they preclude the possibility of making facile moral judgements.

From the first mention of the Constance Kent case one revelation after another adds to the reader's mounting unease. It is disclosed that Francis is not only homosexual, but promiscuous; that he has an elderly wife who is a dressmaker in Folkestone; that his parents did not die in a railway accident as he claims, but are instead lonely inmates of an old people's home; that his ex-mistress, Doris, had borne him a daughter, Joy, who is now a twelve-year-old illiterate drug abuser. The seedy world to which these characters belong takes shape almost casually. It exudes menace and the reader can only wonder in what form and from what quarter terror will eventually come. Francis is undoubtedly a psychopath, but his madness is such that it is virtually undetectable by people who live outside his world. He uses his acting talents to play out his fantasies and occasionally those who are victims of his make-belief realise the truth:

> 'You're a nutter, Francis,' a girl he'd thought to be sympathetic had pronounced six months ago in Cleethorpes. 'You're sick the way you cry, old boy,' a man once said in Dieppe.
>
> (OPW 91)

In 'Stone St Martin' only Julia's mother, Mrs Anstey, is suspicious of the prospective bridegroom, but her fears remain 'formless, like a fragment from a dream' (OPW 25) and she willingly stifles them.

As the chapter titles indicate, the first half of the book glides smoothly from the world of one main character to that of another: from the safety of Stone St Martin – where the only ripples beneath the calm surface of life are made by Fr Lavin's chaste tenderness for Julia and Nevil Clapp's tendency to petty crime – to the squalid, shabby London underworld, on the fringes of which Francis moves. Meanwhile in the background there reverberates the gruesome case of Constance Kent.

Although Timothy Gedge in *The Children of Dynmouth* was mainly preoccupied with George Joseph Smith and the Brides-in-the-bath murders, he was also attracted to the case of Constance Kent.[2] In *Other People's Worlds* Trevor cleverly draws the reader into the pathos of Constance Kent's story as it is to be presented on television, only to undermine our sympathy by revealing that what we are involved with is fiction – and fiction which is artistically questionable. Francis Tyte has a small part in a television dramatisation of the notorious case. The actor develops a sentimental attachment not only for Constance Kent, the character, but also for the actress who plays her part. In Constance Kent's life he finds a sentimentalised version of himself:

> All her life she'd been let down; other people had destroyed her.
>
> (OPW 131)

So successful is Francis in evoking the pathos of Constance Kent's life that Doris too is drawn to the girl and she also begins to identify with the young murderess. Francis fantasises about killing his wife, the Folkstone dressmaker from whom he had hoped to inherit money, and very late in the novel Doris actually kills her, illustrating a point which is made in the television play and which Trevor makes very strongly – that ordinary people can do terrible things.

The first close-up study of Francis's illegitimate daughter, Joy, is made, significantly, in the chapter dealing with Constance Kent's world. The comparisons are obvious. The inappropriately named Joy is another casualty of other people's relationships. She was born to satisfy her father's whim to experience paternity. At twelve years of age she is already marginalised by his indifference and by her mother's alcoholism. Her world centres on Tite Street Comprehensive School where she seeks integration by following the fashions set by the school bullies, whether it be using paint-guns, indulging in arson or experimenting with drugs. Her mother claims that she has already lost her virginity, yet for all the depravity by which she is surrounded, she is still a child in search of paternal love. When she catches sight of her father in the street:

> Her heart-beat quickened, the way it always did when she saw him. She felt warm all over, and for a moment she couldn't believe her eyes.
>
> (OPW 65)

In spite of all the evidence there is to the contrary, the girl shares her mother's faith that one day Francis will settle down to family life with them. Just as Francis focuses on his own fantasies so others make him the centre of their dreams.

Julia Ferndale's wedding is related through the eyes of Francis's best man, the same person who plays the part of Constance Kent's father in the television play. His actor's perception and his position as an outsider allow him to sense the strangeness of the occasion. For the reader, there is no feeling of shock when the marriage comes to an abrupt and immediate end. It is only of importance in the novel in that it signals the departure of Francis from the action. In one of the 'confessions' to which he feels obliged to subject his victims, Francis on their wedding night reveals his true position to Julia. This is the action of a deeply tormented being, himself a victim, who tries to regain innocence through confession, but without either a real sense of guilt or a purpose of amendment. Once he has gained possession of Julia's jewellery – trinkets of little value – he is content to depart, ready to construct further fantasies and to evade all responsibility.

In the absence of Francis, the book changes course and concentrates on Julia. Goodness is now put under the microscope and is revealed as an even more fascinating quality than is evil. If the latter is ordinary then the former is extraordinary and much more difficult to explain. There are no easy solutions offered to the problems of the world in which the author situates his heroine. Life continues after tragedy and Julia must learn to survive. Faced with the full force of suffering, she does not seek to anaesthetise it with alcohol as Doris does, nor does she resort to neurotic fantasies as does Francis. In an exchange with Fr Lavin she finds her faith tested for the first time. She claims that God has failed her as He failed other good people in their hour of need. She cites the case of missionaries whom He allowed to die in torment. The priest upbraids her for 'making connections that are not there' (OPW 196) but Julia counters with the argument that 'surely God's creatures are all connected'. (OPW 196) She reminds the priest that just as the world contains the contrary forces of goodness and evil side by side, so it allows goodness and suffering to be intrinsically linked. She reminds him:

> 'You cannot think of St Catherine without her wheel, or St Sebastian without the agony of the arrows.'
> (OPW 198)

In her unhappiness Julia feels remote from Christ's compassion. She sees Calvary as 'just another distant act of violence'. (OPW 198) The limbo which she first experienced on a hot day in Pisa when Francis deserted her, developed into a dark night of the soul when she returned to England and she has now entered her own particular hell. Only through the awakening in herself of compassion for others can Julia rediscover the comforts of religion. She had wanted a miracle to remove her pain, but like the eponymous heroine of *Elizabeth Alone* she finds that when it comes, the miracle has a human character and is contingent on her involvement with other people's worlds.

Francis's departure does not bring to an end Julia's participation in his life. The unremitting consequences of his actions draw her into encounters with the other people with whom he is associated and these connections give the second half of the novel its intensity. Through Doris, Julia is introduced to the world which Francis told her about on their wedding night and which she now finds to be more real than her own genteel society. She writes in her diary 'my life has been less real than other people's'. (OPW 190) Her new experiences lend purpose to her hitherto limited and conventional sphere, which she realises is no longer safe from invasion by people from other backgrounds and with different mores. As her safe, staid existence crumbles about her, at first she is paralysed by despair. Eventually, however, she is drawn from her introspection and self-pity by the plight of Joy, the child she is in a position to save, when in a drunken frenzy Doris murders the Folkestone dressmaker, whom she blames for all Francis's problems. The crime in which the victim is beaten to death with a teapot is grotesquely comic and parodies the gruesome Constance Kent murder. It takes place off-stage, its horror consequently mitigated as it is conveyed to the reader amongst other items in a newspaper:

> A cricketer had made a hundred and eighty-three runs. Two men disguised as house-painters had been chased and caught by the police. In London Zoo an elephant was ill. In Folkestone an elderly dressmaker had been battered to death with a tea-pot.
>
> (OPW 237)

This is Trevor's humour at its blackest, its comedy manifesting itself as the underdeveloped side of tragedy.

Julia's spiritual adoption of Joy and her realisation that 'she couldn't pack God and Francis Tyte away' (OPW 243) ensure that the book ends on an optimistic note. The miracle of humanity is part of a world which acknowledges both good and evil. Julia's goodness had made her the victim of other people. Tested in the fire of experience, however, it emerges reinforced by the twin graces of conscience and compassion. It provides for a future in which her 'niceness'(OPW 243) can have both scope and purpose.

Even in his early work, as we have already seen, Trevor used elements of the gothic convention to examine themes which have traditionally preoccupied writers of that literary mode – evil, guilt, madness and their possible connection with each other. These themes continue to exercise his mind. In common with other contemporary writers in the post-existentialist world, the author finds himself faced with the task of depicting an absurd universe in which characters experience alienation and personal crises. Many of them – victims of loneliness and pain – view the 'real' world as a hostile place and as a result withdraw into their imaginations and create in their minds alternative versions of existence in which they are happy. In their private worlds they experience a higher state of consciousness and a greater ability to perceive the truth of a situation than do those who live in a so-called rational state. At some point, however, there is a clash between these personal worlds and reality and inevitably those characters who have already found sanctuary in their imaginations are deemed to be insane and are forced to seek refuge in mental asylums.

This is what happens to the central characters in three stories, 'Mrs Acland's Ghosts', 'The Raising of Elvira Tremlett' and 'Lost Ground' – the first two dating from the 1970s and the last written in the 1990s. In each case the creation of imaginary worlds peopled by 'ghosts' necessitates their creators' withdrawal from the real world whose hostility led to the need for alternative versions of reality. In 'Mrs Acland's Ghosts' Trevor uses the same device as does Henry James in 'The Turn of the Screw' – a letter which recounts strange happenings, written by a woman who, while at the centre of events, might yet be regarded as an unreliable witness. As in 'The Turn of the Screw' part of the story's effectiveness lies in its unresolved ambiguities. The conventional limits of the 'real' world are questioned and the author draws the reader into accepting a wider range of possibilities.

The opening paragraph of the story succinctly outlines the uneventful life of Mr Mockler, a man chosen arbitrarily from the telephone book by Mrs Acland, the inmate of a psychiatric institution, to be the recipient of her confidence about her life and her experiences of 'ghosts'. The letter begins unceremoniously with Mrs Acland's comments on the doctors and inmates of the asylum. Dr Friendman, as his name implies, is a humane man, while Miss Acheson, an elderly inmate, has been forgotten by the world outside, but still experiences her visions of St Olaf of Norway. She it is who recommends that Mrs Acland should write her account of the events to some unknown person.

Mrs Acland tells of her idyllic childhood with loving parents, a brother and two sisters, until her family is killed in a motor accident. Significantly Mrs Acland reveals neither any details of the deaths nor of her feelings at the time, stating only that 'after that the silence began'. (CS 503) Seven years later she marries a prosperous man, many years her senior, who has a fondness for food. It is during his absence from home on an extended business trip that Mrs Acland is first visited by the ghosts of her dead brother and sisters. Alone in the house with only two servants, Mr and Mrs Rachels, for company, inexplicable happenings occur. A radio seems to turn itself on in the middle of the night, a bath shows signs of having been used, the breakfast table is mysteriously laid for four people. Mrs Acland believes that these events are caused by the ghosts of her dead siblings and shortly afterwards she catches glimpses of the ghosts themselves. While she welcomes the apparitions and is happy again, the Rachels are frightened and leave the house for good. With their departure the ghosts also vanish and Mrs Acland retires into her loneliness.

Woven into the accounts of her strange experience are hints that Mrs Acland is already psychologically unbalanced and that the mysterious incidents are the products of her confused mind. Subtly the author suggests that her anxieties are those of an obsessive personality. In addition there is the implication that the poor lighting on the first-floor landing may have caused her to imagine that she had seen her dead brother, and it is conceivable that the tune which the radio was playing when her first bizarre experience occurred, 'Looking for Henry Lee', may simply have evoked Mrs Acland's childhood and thereby sparked off subsequent developments.

After the departure of the Rachels, Trevor has Mrs Acland move everything she needs into one room and attempt to attract back the ghosts with friendly messages scrawled on the wallpaper and childish tit-bits scattered throughout the house. On his return her husband is angered and appalled to find her living in such conditions and when she tells him the story of her family and makes an impassioned declaration that her loneliness was 'like a shroud' (CS 508), he replies by informing her that she is insane.

This is the story as it unfolds in the letter to Mr Mockler, a compassionate man, who resolves to visit Mrs Acland. From this point the events of the story are seen as he experiences them, the narrative voice adopting his pattern of speech. When he is offered a glass of sherry by Dr Friendman he is 'surprised at this line of talk'. (CS 510) As he listens to the doctor's account of the circumstances which led to his patient's committal to the asylum, he finds that they are completely at variance with hers. According to the doctor, Mrs Acland was the only child of embittered parents 'who did not speak to one another'. (CS 511) Mr Mockler, however, remains unconvinced by Dr Friendman's explanation. He believes that the ghosts are part of Mrs Acland's reality:

> he felt it in his bones and it felt like a truth ... They'd been real to her, and they'd been real to the Rachels because she'd made them so. Shadows had slipped out of her mind because in her loneliness she'd wished them to. (CS 512)

Mr Mockler acknowledges that the ghosts are artificial but at the same time he believes that they exist as an alternative to the ordinary experience of reality and this is precisely what the author is demonstrating. Just as there is no absolute truth, neither is there a single concept of reality. The world is as we perceive it. There is also the suggestion that Mrs Acland's reality, however insubstantial its basis, is somehow superior to the more circumscribed world of Dr Friendman and his colleagues, about whom Mrs Acland confides in her letter:

> They're so sure of themselves, Mr Mockler: beyond the limits of their white-coated world they can accept nothing.
> (CS 501)

When Mrs Acland tries to explain to her uncomprehending husband her experience of loneliness and alienation, she says:

> 'People were only shadows ... when you had loneliness and silence like that, like a shroud around you.'

(CS 508)

The Irish boy who is the central character in 'The Raising of Elvira Tremlett' uses the same moribund simile when he tries to explain why he raised the ghost of a long-dead English girl:

> I wanted to be listened to, to be released from the shame that I felt like a shroud around me.

(CS 658)

As in the former story, the protagonist does not address the reader directly. The boy, who remains nameless throughout, articulates only in his imagination. He is prevented from speaking aloud by the fear he senses in those around him, those who do not wish to hear his version of reality. His story is told, he reveals in a kind of epilogue, by a weekly visitor to the institution in which he lives. This anonymous person, who does not have any other function in the story, has placed him at the centre of the story:

> ... because that, of course, is where I belong.

(CS 658)

Serving the same purpose as Mrs Acland's letter in the previous story, this device of second-hand narration distances the reader from the events and consequently allows him to enjoy the mysterious aspect of the story, while at the same time he can enter the boy's consciousness and view the events from a second perspective. Because of this dual vision he can fully appreciate the boy's final statement that:

> ... the story as it happened wasn't a mystery in the least.

(CS 659)

Early in his life, we learn, the boy feels alienated from the other members of the family, the Devlins, who treat him as though he were mentally deficient. His siblings find their niches in the family business, but he finds the carelessly run garage a frightening place:

... a kind of hell, its awful earth floor made black with sump oil, its huge indelicate vices, the chill of cast iron, the grunting of my father and my uncle as they heaved an engine out of a tractor, the astringent smell of petrol. It was there that my silence, my dumbness almost, must have begun.

(CS 649)

To avoid the tension in his home caused by his father's drinking and his uncle's bouts of womanising, the boy creates in his mind the character of Elvira Tremlett, based on some very scanty information which he reads on a memorial stone in the local Protestant church. An eighteen-year-old English girl had died in the town in 1873. The girl's voice is introduced abruptly into the story at a point when the boy feels he can no longer visit the Protestant church as he has drawn the unwelcome attention of the sexton:

'Well, it doesn't matter,' she said. 'You don't have to go back. There's nothing to go back for ...'
    'It's curiosity that sends you there,' she said. 'You're much too curious.'

(CS 652)

The boy recognises that it is this curiosity which distinguishes him from the rest of his family; it also makes him accepting of an alternative world.

Elvira Tremlett, as she comes alive in the boy's consciousness, is the very antithesis of his real-life experience. She is English and in his family this implies a certain superiority. She is Protestant; his home is oppressively Catholic with garish religious emblems in every corner. Elvira's physical appearance reflects the stereotype heroine of the films which the boy watches at the town's Electric cinema. She reminds him of Myrna Loy except that her voice was nicer. What he most liked about her was her 'quietness' (CS 651). All this contrasts sharply with the loud, quarrelsome, gossiping Devlin family, just as Elvira's home, Tremlett Hall in Dorset, a place constructed by an imagination nurtured on romantic films, stands in complete opposition to the shabby untidiness of the Devlin home in a small Munster town, the detailed authenticity of the latter acting as a foil to the romantic ideal which emanates from his imagination.

The girl articulates the thoughts which the boy is unable to communicate. She is the voice of his silence. She is also his consolation:

> When Brother Cahey hit me one day she cheered me up.
> When my father came back from Macklin's in time for his Saturday tea her presence made it easier.

(CS 653)

In time he adds details to her dress and person and with the onset of puberty he responds to her sexually. It is Elvira who finally articulates his fear and shame – that he is the child of an illicit union between his mother and Uncle Jack

> born of his weakness and my mother's anger as she waited for the red bleariness of my father to return, footless in the middle of the night. It was why my father called my uncle a hypocrite ...
> 'They have made you,' Elvira said. 'The three of them have made you what you are.'

(CS 654)

The boy loses command over his ghost when he inadvertently addresses her aloud during a family meal. His imaginative powers are no longer under his control. Elvira's physique changes. At first she loses her demureness; later she takes on the appearance of an old woman. Now she is the one who does not speak. Instead she looks accusingly at him. He has projected the guilt he feels about his parentage into his imagined world, and has thus distorted the ideal. The imagination which at first had been consoling is now shown to be a darker, more threatening force. Terrifying nightmares follow for the boy and eventually he is immured within a mental institution. There he achieves tranquillity and ceases to be haunted by his self-created ghost, comforted by the conviction that through her intercession he is living in the room in which she stayed on her visit from Dorset.

Like Mrs Acland the boy must ultimately withdraw from the real world into the sanctuary of a mental institution. There, ironically, neither of them is visited by the ghosts of their loneliness. Removed from the alien, real world they no longer need an alternative reality.

In 'Lost Ground', the ghost which visits Milton Leeson, a Protestant boy living in Northern Ireland during the Troubles, is that of the Catholic St Rosa, who urges him to preach against the mutual fear which keeps the two communities – Protestant and Catholic – at enmity and brings suffering to all. As with the figure of Alvira Tremlett, there are sexual undertones in the boy's relationship with his visitant:

> When she's kissed him her lips hadn't been moist like his mother's. They'd been dry as a bone, the touch of them so light he had scarcely felt it.

(AR 148-149)

The 'saint' may emanate from the adolescent fantasies of a sensitive youngster, who cannot acquiesce in the religious and political division in his community, but the message he preaches disturbs those who listen. Embarrassed by Milton's actions and unable to accept the truth of his message, the other members of the Leeson family first imprison him and eventually collude in his death.

These stories leave the reader with uneasy feelings of ambivalence. Speaking the truth can be dangerous. Truth is also seen to be relative, the perceptive characters realise that there is no single explanation of events. They can be rationalised and accepted as merely manifestations of loneliness – we are given ample evidence for this interpretation. Yet this is to view the world from a very narrow angle and to ignore the complexity of the human spirit.

Mrs Emily Delahunty, the narrator of the novel *My House in Umbria* (1991), is another character whose imagination provides her with a unique view of the events she witnesses and subsequently interprets according to her own vision. Structurally the book is one of Trevor's most ambitious works; a narrator of doubtful credibility tells her story in a disjointed manner intermingling fragments of memories, dreams and statement together with snippets of romantic fiction, whose characters mouth a philosophical commentary. Out of this apparent rigmarole, however, there emerges once again a message of the ordinariness of evil, the necessity for its forgiveness and the healing power of love.

The novel is set in Italy but the main characters are all ex-
patriate English-speaking people; only the very minor ones are
Italian. Yet the country is more than a mere backdrop against
which the events are played out. In several of Trevor's short stories
with the same setting, Italian towns and cities, their churches
containing magnificent artistic treasures, frequently provide
sanctuary for characters fleeing from unhappiness. Among the
Raphaels and the Peruginos many of them gain self-knowledge and
with it emotional freedom. For the others the country provides at
least a temporary refuge from the pain of living.

Mrs Delahunty is a middle-aged Englishwoman, her name
chosen at random from the many pseudonyms she has used during
the course of a variegated life. Some date from a time when she
worked on board an ocean liner and in an African café – in each
case her duties are dubious but unspecified. Others belong to her
later career as a writer of Mills and Boon style novels, with titles
such as *Flight to Enchantment, Precious September* and *Behold my
Heart*.

In spite of her success as a novelist Mrs Delahunty's life, like
that of Mrs Acland and of the boy in 'The Raising of Elvira
Tremlett' has been one of loneliness and pain. As a child she had
been abandoned by her parents – motorcyclists who rode the Wall
of Death. Abused by her foster father who told her that 'good girls
don't tell' (MHU 246), she ran away from home only to continue
the pattern of exploitation and betrayal which had begun with Mr
Trice. Now fifty-six years of age, she lives in Italy, the proprietor of
a pensione which is run by Quinty, an eccentric Irishman of
equally doubtful background and morals 'Half a child and half a
rogue he is'. (MHU 228) For Mrs Delahunty it is the stories she
writes which allow her to blot out the reality of her sordid past and
to create instead life as she would have wished it:

> The girls of my romances were never left by lovers who
> took from them what they would. Mothers did not turn
> their backs on little children. Wives did not pitifully plead
> or in bitterness cuckold their husbands. The sombre side of
> things did not appeal to me; in my works I dealt in
> happiness ever after.

(MHU 227-8)

In the summer of 1987, however, Mrs Delahunty finds that she has writer's block. On a shopping trip to Milan she shares a railway carriage with a number of tourists: an English general accompanying his daughter and son-in-law, an American couple with two children, a young German man and his girlfriend. As she muses on the title for a new book, *Ceaseless Tears*, the compartment is bombed. The only survivors among the group are the General, one of the American children – a little girl called Aimée, the German whose name is Otmar and Mrs Delahunty herself.

As she lies recovering in hospital, memories of her past prevent Mrs Delahunty from developing the plot of her new novel. While she has been deprived of her escape route through fiction, the others have suffered even greater losses. The General is alone in the world, the child is orphaned and suffering from traumatic aphasia, Otmar has had an arm amputated and is mourning the death of his fiancée. The police search for those guilty of the outrage but no terrorist group claims responsibility. Since none of them appears to have anywhere else to go Mrs Delahunty invites her fellow survivors to her house in Umbria where they form an ad hoc family unit, helping each other towards recovery.

Because she finds herself unable to continue writing the ominously titled *Ceaseless Tears*, Mrs Delahunty begins to weave a plot around her guests. She needs to tell stories as a way of coping with reality, just as the child Aimée needs to express the horror of her experience through paintings. Having gleaned some information about the lives of her companions, Mrs Delahunty imposes her own design on the facts. Like Timothy Gedge in *The Children of Dynmouth* she uses scraps of information acquired from her guests as the rather fragile foundations on which to build her narrative. 'Fragments make up a life' (MHU 280) Mrs Delahunty had written in one of her novels and using this philosophy the romantic novelist begins to reconstruct the biographies of her residents. The minds and bodies of the survivors have been decimated by what has happened to them and while they gather the pieces together again, their hostess fashions the shards into a whole. There is, however, no guarantee that the segments will fit together properly.

Most of what Mrs Delahunty hears and imagines is typical of many lives: the General disliked his son-in-law and tried unsuccessfully to disguise his unhappiness about his daughter's marriage; Aimée's parents had quarrelled with her uncle because of his divorce and remarriage. As she insists:

> The child was an ordinary child, and I believe the others were ordinary too.

(MHU 236)

The tale which she relates about Otmar, however, is both extraordinary and dramatic. The young German planted the bomb, she believes, because his father had been executed as an ex-Nazi and his mother had subsequently committed suicide. His motive is revenge:

> ... the children of the fathers locked in another turn of the wheel, a fresh fraternity of vengeance.

(MHU 347)

His Jewish girlfriend, Madeleine, has been deliberately chosen so that she can unwittingly carry the bomb on board a plane bound for Tel Aviv. Ironically the youth discovers his love for the girl even as he attempts to kill her. While this story does not have the happy ending which Mrs Delahunty doles out in her books, it has all the melodramatic content which one might expect from a writer who may have invented her own life or, even if what she says is true, one who has experienced more than her share of drama.

As readers we are never sure of what truth, if any, lies behind the scenarios Mrs Delahunty describes. She is the epitome of the unreliable narrator whose perceptions – a mixture of dreams, speculation and intuition – render her a distorting centre of consciousness in the book. As she states herself:

> Everything in storytelling, romantic or otherwise, is hit and miss, and the fact that reality was involved didn't appear to make much difference.

(MHU 297)

Her obvious alcoholism adds to the problem and whether she is revealing what is true or creating fiction remains a mystery to the end. The question is not of any great significance. The author as always allows enough evidence to emerge to suggest that what she is saying might be fact, but what is important is that from different perspectives the world may appear in different shadows and lights.

Even if Otmar is a terrorist, he can be redeemed by love. He too has been a victim. His devotion to Aimee and his wish to help the General in creating a garden for Mrs Delahunty are part of what she sees as the miracle of forgiveness, an echo of the generosity shown by Italians who erected a cross to a nameless American soldier remembered for the compassion he had shown to his enemies during the Second World War:

> When evil was made good it was as though the evil had never existed.
>
> (MHU 361)

Once again Trevor uses the garden as a symbol of hope. Through effort and goodwill, plants can be generated, even from the barren soil of Umbria.

With the advent of Aimée's uncle, Thomas Riversmith, from the United States, the chill of reality is introduced into what was becoming a cosy Umbrian menage. The American resists both Mrs Delahunty's postulations about the bombing and her sexual advances. He is as incapable of understanding her 'illusion and mystery and pretence' (MHU 340) as she is of making sense of his esoteric entomological research. Mr Riversmith sees what Mrs Delahunty calls her 'vision' (MHU 366) as 'grotesque' (MHU 345), a mere 'drunken fantasy' (MHU 345), in which case her claims about Otmar's guilt are evil. But the American's cynical detachment, the book suggests, has no greater credibility than any other truth. In fact Riversmith's demeanour implies that in spite of his assurances Mrs Delahunty's fears for Aimée's future in his care may be all too justified. The child might seem to have regained her normal self – as evidenced by her response to the *Sano di Pietro* painting in the Cathedral of Siena – but almost immediately her mental health is shown to be precarious and her uncle's reaction is not promising.

Mrs Delahunty has survived by turning the heartbreak of her life into stories. As the texture of her fiction emerges, it is the pattern of the woman's own life which is most clearly revealed and which becomes the greatest source of pathos in the book. Breaking through her rather chatty and apparently imperturbable voice is a tone of anguish, as we learn of her attempts to find love and of the betrayals which inevitably followed.

What Trevor as author is presenting us with in *My House in Umbria* is several versions of reality. In the background, but very important to the events, is an historical fact – the terrorist bombing of a railway station in Bologna. In addition there is Mrs Delahunty's own life story for which there is little verification beyond the presence of Quinty. Then there are her theories about her guests, in particular concerning Otmar's terrorist involvement, a cocktail of dream, supposition, instinct, alcohol and imagination. It is always possible, however, that there are elements of truth in what she alleges, just as there is a fraction of factual basis even in her romantic fiction. Her former Sunday-school teacher – the only person who seems to have shown her genuine kindness and whom she loved as a child – serves as the model for one of her characters. She recounts how she explained her creative process to Riversmith:

> 'Lady Daysmith had her origins in a Sunday-school teacher.' I described the humility of Miss Alzapiedi, her gangling height, the hair that should have been her crowning glory. 'Flat as a table up front. I turned her into an attractive woman, Tom.'
>
> (MHU 339)

Ultimately it appears that there is no true reality anymore than there is any real fiction.

In spite of the events of the novel *My House in Umbria* is not primarily an investigation of evil; instead it focuses on understanding and forgiveness. In a similar fashion *Felicia's Journey* (1994), Trevor's subsequent novel, is to some extent a morality drama in which good and evil are played out against each other, but it also goes beyond this to explore the process by which understanding gives rise to forgiveness – no matter how heinous the crime. According to her girlfriends Felicia has 'the face for a nun'. (FJ 21) Like so many Trevor characters she has been 'allocated a life' by others – one of loneliness, poverty and dependence. The small town Irish world which the girl inhabits has been examined elsewhere in this book. From there she sets out in pursuit of Johnny Lysaght, the father of the baby she is carrying, whom she believes to be working in a lawnmower factory in an English Midlands town. The journey to which the novel's title refers takes Felicia not only away from her home but from her own private world to a place of shared hardships and dangers in which she has to grow morally and psychologically.

Felicia is singularly ill-equipped to negotiate a successful search for her erstwhile lover. The guilelessness which allowed her to succumb to Johnny Lysaght's charm and to his equivocations would make her an easy victim for someone much less practised in evil than is Joseph Ambrose Hilditch. Using the form of the thriller Trevor pits Felicia's innocence against Hilditch's wickedness. Early in the novel the reader senses the girl's danger, yet the exact nature of her peril remains vague for a time. In keeping with the technique of the genre, information is scarce, is given in part or is withheld altogether so as to build up an atmosphere of uneasiness. Even after we have guessed Hilditch's intentions there remains the question of whether or not he will be able to carry them out and how he will achieve his goal.

Mr Hilditch is one of Trevor's most sinister creations. Perhaps only the character of Gilbert in the short story 'Gilbert's Mother' is his equal as a monster. The focus of the story is of necessity narrower than the novel; it concentrates on the mother's dawning realisation of her son's tendencies and does not attempt to explore the mind of a psychological deviant. In *Felicia's Journey*, however, the reader is gradually drawn into the inner life of a character with a serious personality disorder, the full extent of which is revealed as the novel progresses, until a full conception of a distorted mentality is reached.

Felicia is completely artless while Mr Hilditch is both artful and self-deceiving. She encounters him when she asks him for directions. He is the fifty-four-year-old catering manager of a factory and does not immediately appear sinister to the naive girl; if he is not attractive, neither does he seen to be particularly threatening:

> Mr Hilditch wears spectacles that have a pebbly look, keeps his pigeon-coloured hair short, dresses always in a suit with a waistcoat, ties his striped tie into a tight little knot,

> polishes his shoes twice a day, and is given to smiling
> pleasantly. Regularly the fat that bulges about his features
> is rolled back and well-kept teeth appear, while a twinkle
> livens the blurred pupils behind his spectacles. His voice is
> faintly high-pitched.
>
> (FJ 6)

From the beginning, however, the reader is alerted to Mr
Hilditch's little oddities. Since his mother's death he has lived
alone. Because of his friendly manner he is popular at his work
place, yet nobody ever visits him at home. He is obsessed with food
and is inordinately greedy. His peculiarities at first seem innocuous
if somewhat curious – he plays only 78 RPM records, he has lined
the walls of his house with portraits of people who are not his
relations and he has an extraordinary preoccupation with privacy.
But as his peculiarities accumulate they become more strange,
revealing him as a typical paranoid personality with delusions. He
has never been married, yet he talks to Felicia of his ailing wife
Ada. In his mind he dwells on his relationships with a number of
young women, but they never appear and live only in what he
refers to as 'Memory Lane'. (FJ 42)

Mr Hilditch is a lonely figure, but Felicia is also isolated in a
completely alien environment. Both suffer from romantic dreams
and disappointed hopes, although the catering manager's, for the
moment, remain vague. He is always present when the girl finds
herself in a crisis, offering to help her find lodgings or to make
telephone calls for her and driving her to a nearby town where
there may be a lawnmower factory. As he draws her increasingly
into his net, the girl grows dependent upon him and unknown to
her he continues to sabotage her efforts to find Johnny Lysaght.
Felicia's father had suspected that the young man was a member of
the British army and Mr Hilditch soon discovers that this is so.
Ironically, a military career was one of Mr Hilditch's own most
cherished ambitions, his frustrated plans a painful regret.

There are other people whom Felicia encounters on her journey
who give her refuge – down-and-outs such as an elderly bag-lady
from County Clare and the skeletal Lena, recently released from
prison. She tells the girl how she was once persuaded:

... to have snow-capped mountains tattooed on her back.
They're there forever now; act on an impulse and you have
a landscape all over you for the rest of your days.

(FJ 105)

Accompanying Lena is a gentle young man called George who
sends birthday cards to bishops because he believes they are lonely.
In his cultured accent George recites a rhyme which he encloses
with the birthday cards:

> 'Of all the trees that grow so fair,
> Old England to adorn,
> Greater are none beneath the sun
> Than Oak, and Ash, and Thorn.'

(FJ 110)

These lines evoke a country of natural beauty which has been lost
in the desiccated, urban sprawl that greets Felicia:

> Now, there is plain, similar architecture everywhere, shops
> and office blocks laid out in a grid of straight lines,
> intersections at right angles. Wide pedestrian walkways
> were planted in the 1950s with shrubs and flowers in long,
> raised central beds; and the new town's architects included
> burgeoning arcades, and hanging baskets on the street
> lights. Since then the soil has soured in the long raised
> beds; heathers have died there, leaving only browned
> strands behind, among which beer cans and discarded
> containers of instant food provide whatever splashes of
> colour there are.

(FJ 8)

These minor characters, with their harmless eccentricities,
provide some welcome comic relief to lighten the growing tension
of the novel. So too do the inhabitants of the 'Gathering House',
the head-quarters of an evangelical cult which offers solace and
salvation through the mysterious notion of 'paradise earth' (FJ 84)
– a 'heavenly picture of fruit and flamingos and well-behaved
rabbits' (FJ 85). Playing a more important role, however, is one
member of the religious community, a Jamaican woman called
Miss Calligary. Just as Mr Hilditch may be seen to have had his
origins in Timothy Gedge from *The Children of Dynmouth*, so Miss
Calligary is a literary descendant of Miss Gomez, the Jamaican
evangelist of the Church of the Brethren of the Way in *Miss Gomez*

and the Brethren. Miss Calligary offers the same easy comfort with the same hard-nosed persistence to those whom she hopes to convert. Felicia stays a few days at the Gathering House, but leaves after a dispute which follows her discovery that her money has been stolen.

Mr Hilditch had taken Felicia's carefully-hidden nest-egg so that it would be impossible for her to return to Ireland. Now that she is once more in his power he persuades her to have an abortion, paying himself for the operation and enjoying the notion – however incongruously – that people in the clinic will conclude he is the girl's partner:

> It is then that the excitement begins, creeping through him, like something in his blood. He is the father of an unborn child, no doubt in any of their minds. The girl they have all seen, who was here not ten minutes ago, whey-faced and anxious, is at this very moment being separated from their indiscretions. A relationship has occurred, no way you can gainsay it.
>
> (FJ 136)

Later he entices her into his home, claiming that his wife had died only days earlier. As we witness these deceitful strategies, suspicion begins to increase about the fate of the other girls Mr Hilditch has befriended. It becomes obvious that Sharon, Bobbi, Jakki, Gaye, Beth and Elsie Covington have all perished, but whatever violence they suffered is hidden from the reader as it is concealed from its perpetrator who wipes it all from his consciousness:

> It is usual, when a friendship finishes, for Mr Hilditch to suffer in this manner. He is mistily aware that something may be missing and attributes the aberration in his memory to the intensity of his loss – the moment of each departure having been so painful that an unconscious part of him has erased the surrounding details.
>
> (FJ 159)

Just when she is at her most vulnerable Felicia becomes aware of her danger and with all the odds against her makes a bid for escape. The author skilfully sets up the reader's expectation of a dramatic confrontation, only to subvert it completely by turning away from the scene so that we do not know what has become of the girl. By the time her fate is revealed the focus of the book has trained more steadily on Mr Hilditch and the thriller aspect has evaporated, giving way instead to an investigation of a psychotic personality and raising the question of whether the evil deeds of such a person can be forgiven.

Mr Hilditch has attracted the attention of Miss Calligary whose missionary zeal constitutes a real persecution. Unhinged by her persistence, memories of past failures and hurts begin to haunt him. The only child of a single mother, he had been the victim of incest. When the succession of casual lovers was no longer available to her – including Uncle Wilf who had inspired his interest in the army – Mr Hilditch's mother had turned for comfort to her son:

> His blue-striped pyjamas, a shred of tobacco on her teeth when she smiled down at him, her ginny breath: in his private life the occasion had always been there, never lost – not for a moment – in the oblivion that kindly claimed the other. Like a tattoo, she said, the lipstick on his shoulder. Her face was different then.
>
> (FJ 195)

None of the main characters in the novel has a satisfactory relationships with his/her mother. Felicia's dies when she is very young, Johnny Lysaght's who is 'Bitter as a sloe' (FJ 45) because her husband abandoned her, is over-possessive of her son. The other mother figure, Felicia's great-grandmother representing Mother Ireland, is preoccupied by the past and has little to offer her great-grand-daughter.

Mr Hilditch's aspirations in life had at one time been very ordinary:

> Manoeuvres on Salisbury Plain; a house in Wiltshire that had been a rectory once, a garden, and a family growing up.
>
> (FJ 194)

The abuse he suffers as a child and his consequent loss of innocence, however, prevent him from forming any normal relationships. The young women whom he lures into his orbit soon guess his secret. Some even exploit his loneliness; none of them ever considers him as a possible partner. When Felicia comes downstairs in his house wearing her nightdress he realises that she too:

> ... doesn't care how she appears to him because she sees him in a certain light.

(FJ 151)

As one after the other the girls prepare to leave him, he kills them in order to prevent them from going, burying their bodies in the shrubbery in his garden. He then obliterates the murder from his mind and converts his victims into companions who live on for him in 'Memory Lane'. (FJ 158). The details of the girls' deaths are withheld from the reader as they are from Mr Hilditch's own consciousness. By this means it is possible to continue to focus on his humanity, to see him as a grotesque figure for whom it is possible to feel a degree of sympathy, in spite of his evil deeds. For as Felicia realises:

> Lost within a man who murdered, there was a soul like any other soul, purity itself it surely once had been.

(FJ 212)

The actions and decisions of others are seen to have played a large part in corrupting that innocence.

Felicia manages to escape from Mr Hilditch and he is the one who dies. Driven demented by Miss Calligary's unflagging pursuit and by his own guilt, he commits suicide. Once the possible explanations of Mr Hilditch's perverse nature have been revealed, the final part of the novel brings Felicia again to the foreground of the story. She has abandoned her search for Johnny Lysaght and has become a beggar on the streets, lost in a subculture which appears desolate but which is also redemptive. In this society the girl experiences the mystery of human goodness. While it is possible to understand why Mr Hilditch had become an evil man as it is to imagine why Mrs Lysaght had become a bitter woman, it is more difficult to explain the blessing of human benevolence. In her life among the flotsam and jetsam of society, Felicia discovers the goodness which is also at the heart of man. Just as there had been people who were kind to her as a motherless child, there are now those who bring soup to the hungry and look after their needs.

Of a woman dentist who tends the homeless without expecting any payment, the girl reflects:

> Her goodness is a greater mystery than the evil that distorted a man's every spoken word, his every movement made.
>
> (FJ 213)

This is the truth which Felicia learns on the streets. With it comes the grace of 'negative capability' – acceptance without need for explanation. Her journey continues even though it no longer has purpose. It is a 'muddle of time and people' (FJ 212) but she has survived, she has retained her innocence and she is happy. As the novel concludes Felicia:

> ... turns her hands so that the sun may catch them differently, and slightly lifts her head to warm the other side of her face.
>
> (FJ 213)

The demimonde of the homeless and disadvantaged into which Felicia retreats comes into sharper focus in Trevor's next novel *Death in Summer* (1998). Once again the corruption of innocence is explored, but essentially it is the pathos of the unloved and the mystery of goodness which are at heart of the book.

The novel opens in a country house in Essex, the home of the Davenant family for a century, its name – Quincunx House – deriving from the five cherry trees originally planted in its garden. Over the years the family fortunes declined, but were rescued by the marriage of the house's present owner, Thaddeus, to Letitia Iveson, a woman of wealth and 'a person of almost wayward generosity'. (DS 2) It is Letitia's death – the first of three that occur in the course of the book, set in a hot summer of the mid 1990s, which sparks off the events that follow. When she is killed in a road accident, Thaddeus is moved by guilt rather than by grief, because in spite of her obvious goodness, he had never loved his wife. His inability to love anyone other than his baby daughter is, he believes, the result of 'an unusual childhood'. (DS 2)

Shortly after Letitia's funeral, Thaddeus's mother-in-law, Mrs Iveson, advises him to advertise for a nanny to look after the four-month old Georgina. None of the girls who reply to Thaddeus's advertisement is deemed suitable to be Georgina's nurse-maid and Mrs Iveson decides to undertake the responsibility herself. Pettie, 'just into her twenties but seeming younger' (DS 28) is one of the rejected applicants. She had formerly been an inmate of the Morning Star, a London orphanage where children were systematically abused by Sunday visitors called 'uncles', one of whom had given her the name Pettie. Because of these experiences, the girl tends to become obsessed by older men. Her visit to Quincunx House for the interview is sufficient to leave her enthralled by the place and in particular by its owner, Thaddeus Davenant. When she realises that she will not be employed there, she begins to stalk her quarry – the baby Georgina – partly in order to exact revenge for what she feels was the wrong done to her by Mrs Iveson, but more particularly because of the imaginary passion for Thaddeus which has begun to grow in her mind and which drives her to invent any scheme which will gain his attention and, as she crazily believes, his love. Her intention is to kidnap Georgina and then pretend to have rescued her. Her plans, however, go awry and she abandons the child in the rat-infested ruins of the Morning Star, notifying her friend, Albert, of the baby's whereabouts. Later Pettie dies in the derelict remains of the same building.

Structurally the book moves back and forth between two worlds – from the genteel if rather dispiritingly reticent society of Quincunx House, where 'melancholy is Thaddeus's natural state' (DS 15) to the squalid, less controlled milieu in which the former inhabitants of the Morning Star wrestle with the problems of unemployment, poverty and disadvantage. The search for a suitable person to take care of the infant, Georgina, opens the doors of the Essex mansion to Pettie and from that point onwards each world impinges on the other.

Just as he does in *Felicia's Journey*, the author uses components of the thriller to create tension in the book. Shifting scenes and interrupted sequences excite the imagination, while innuendo in place of information encourages the reader to fear the worst. All of the dramatic events which occur in the novel are revealed obliquely: the particulars of Letitia's death are recounted in retrospect; so also are the details of Thaddeus's affair with Mrs Ferry – a hotel keeper's wife who entertained guests in a spare bedroom during her husband's absence. Later, tidings of the woman's demise come in a telephone call. Even the kidnapping of Georgina is disclosed indirectly, the report of her disappearance all the more sensational for its lack of detail – tension built up and sustained by the very lack of information and by glancing references to books of crime fiction and to the historic case of the Lindbergh baby. When she is found safe and well in the ruins of the Morning Star, surrounded by scraps of bread and a butterfly made of cellophane, it is the poignancy of Pettie's futile attempts to comfort her victim which strikes the reader and recalls how the innocence of her own childhood was destroyed in the same place, the evil deed also camouflaged by gifts.

Echoing the fractured nature of the plot's disclosure is the fragmented dialogue in which the socially disadvantaged characters engage. Stripped of all superfluities their communications are elementary and apparently disconnected, the hiatus in understanding supplemented by the author's account of the inner workings of each character's mind. A conversation between Albert and Mrs Biddle, his elderly landlady, serves as an illustration:

> 'Make us a bit of toast?' she calls out, and he says he will.
>
> Extraordinary, that he'd be mixed up with a girl who'd sweet-talk her way into a bed-ridden woman's house. All you have is your house, the view from the window, folk going by. You can't be expected to take in all and sundry. 'Lovely animals,' was what the girl said when she was caught with the camel.
>
> 'All right then, Albert?'
>
> He calls back, saying he is. She tries the television, but all that happens is snow coming down. She turns it off and watches a woman across the street sweeping the pavement in front of her door. He's far from all right, with that girl affecting him, that Joey Ells coming up the way she always does. The last few weeks he's not been himself by a long chalk.
>
> (DS 104)

These marginalised characters have only the most tenuous associations with the mainstream of society and their speech patterns resonate the disjointed rhythms of their lives, occasionally disconcerting the reader, who must construe meaning from what seems like incoherence.

The inhabitants of Quincunx House lead comfortable, if arid, lives. But they are not immune from pain. As a child Thaddeus was aware of being an 'unwanted presence' (DS 68), isolated by his parents' exclusive relationship, with the result that in adulthood he is unable to love women. While his wife, Letitia, loved him unconditionally, even before her death he was aware of his own lack of feeling for her. Polite and agreeable, but given to 'mild prevarication' (DS 4), he is a benign character who lacks passion. Aptly named after 'the obscure apostle' (DS 19) Thaddeus remains a shadowy figure until the final section of the book, when his heart is stirred by real compassion for Pettie and her companions of the Morning Star.

Mrs Iveson, Thaddeus's mother-in-law, realising his monetary motives for marrying her daughter, distrusts him. Her own life also has its share of suffering: her husband is confined to a nursing home, no longer aware of the existence of his family; her only child married against her better judgement and then lost her life in a road accident. When her grand-daughter is snatched by Pettie, who wants to demonstrate that the old woman is not capable of looking after her properly, she refuses at first to listen to any explanation of the girl's twisted logic. 'We're not concerned with these people,' (DS 208) she declares, but as the author demonstrates through the structure of the book one person's story is always interwoven with another's so that connections are made and the concern of one is ultimately the concern of all.

It is Trevor's representation of the inner worlds of Pettie and her friend, Albert, which lends the novel its pathos. Abused as a child and never loved by anyone apart from Albert, the girl is easy prey to a number of unscrupulous older men. When inevitably they later shun her, the revenge she wreaks on one man and his wife reveals a dangerously warped personality:

> But nothing was reported. And nothing was when she asked Joe Minching where the house was and cut the woman's clothes with a razor-blade, when she poured away her powder and marked the television screen with her lipstick. She cut the sheets on her bed and on her children's beds, and dumped stuff in the dustbins, and smashed the

light-bulbs in the rooms: nothing was said, there was no
complaint.
(DS 123)

Like many Trevor characters who cannot cope with an
unacceptable reality – Mrs Acland in 'Mrs Acland's Ghosts', the
boy in 'The Raising of Elvira Tremlett' among others – Pettie
becomes a fantasist. But even as she engages in lies and deceit, her
guilt is mitigated by the reader's growing awareness of the extent to
which she herself is a victim, and by some typical Trevor touches
which reveal her simplicity and her artlessness: she makes
butterflies out of cigarette-pack cellophane and tries to better
herself by following advice gleaned from a newspaper column on
etiquette.

Pettie's only friend is Albert Luffe, who once helped her to run
away from the Morning Star and who now works in the
Underground at night, cleaning graffiti from railway station walls.
With an 'ovoid countenance' (DS 27), Albert is simple-minded and
mildly obsessive. The nature of his character is subtly captured in
his speech which is basic and clipped, cliché ridden and frequently
confined to the present tense:

'I come in for a place,' he passed on to Pettie. 'There's an
old lady give me a room.'
(DS 47)

Albert is, however, a saintly innocent whose disposition is to
help any afflicted person with whom he comes into contact. He
befriends the vulnerable and never seeks 'to cultivate a relationship
for profit'. (DS 45) Just as he quietly removes the obscenities from
the walls of the Underground, so unobtrusively he ministers to the
sick and elderly, helping to erase the evil of gratuitous suffering.
His unqualified charity towards all his fellow human beings
contrasts sharply with Thaddeus's inability to love even those who
are most lovable.

Albert is one of Trevor's finest creations, finely drawn and
whole. Although his manner is shambling and awkward and the
expression of his consciousness is limited, his sensitivity and
concern for others reveal an inner wisdom:

> Keeping company is the heart of looking after people, as
> Albert first experienced in his Morning Star days. 'Stay by
> me, Albert,' they used to say, a catchphrase it became. The
> time the youths laughed when the man with elephantiasis
> sat down to rest himself on the edge of the pavement he
> stayed with him until the youths went away, even though
> the man said he was used to abuse on the streets.
>
> (DS 48-9)

He acts as Pettie's protector, first helping her to escape from the
Morning Star, then finding her accommodation, advising her,
always concerned that she may end up as a prostitute 'up
Wharfdale' (DS 99) like her friends Marti Spinks, Ange or Bev, the
latter of whom seems to have disappeared without trace.

While the world in which Albert and Pettie live is sordid and
mean, the young man's innocence survives, sustained by his
selfless love of others and by the spiritual support he receives from
the members of the Salvation Army, who eventually allow him to
join their ranks.

Death in Summer is peopled by a plethora of characters, even the
most minor of whom is distinct and with his/her own narrative,
reminding the reader that the author is primarily a short story
writer. These include the former children of the Morning Star, and
the retainers, Maidment and his wife, Zenobia, who work at
Quincunx House. Maidment is a figure familiar from detective
stories, a snooping presence, who listens at doors and reads other
people's letters and whose suspicions frequently echo those of the
reader. Zenobia, on the other hand, is a good and rather proper
woman, who believes in the power of prayer, attending a service of
worship each Sunday, always in a different church, unconcerned
about its denomination.

Although Pettie had paid a number of visits to Quincunx
House, it is only the appearance of Albert there in the final chapter
of the book which allows any interconnections between the two
worlds of the novel to take place, Until her kidnapping of
Georgina, the girl had never made any impact on either Thaddeus
or Mrs Iveson. Only Maidment had taken any notice of her. Now
Albert in his attempt to set things right by recounting Pettie's story
forces them to take her into account. At first his explanations are
treated with indifference and then with anger. Only the revelation

of the ghastly details of the girl's death move them from indignation to compassion. In the process Thaddeus and Mrs Iveson, who had never been close, are drawn together by Pettie's ghost.

In *Death in Summer* Trevor is once again examining the question of evil. Its nature has already been debated in earlier novels, notably in *The Children of Dynmouth* and in *Other People's Worlds*. Most recently in *Felicia's Journey* and in *Death in Summer* he demonstrates how evil often emanates from circumstances in which the human need for love has been either unfulfilled or violated. Conversely the writer illustrates how love can survive and even grow in the most unlikely situations. Thaddeus was emotionally crippled by parents who were totally absorbed in each other and as a result he remains impervious to his wife's love, but the birth of his daughter, Georgina, inspires in him feelings which have never before been aroused. Mrs Iveson, understanding her son-in-law's nature, neither liked nor trusted him, yet the two are united, firstly in their concern for the missing child and then in their pity for the baby's abductor. For although Pettie is a frightening figure, she too evokes compassion. Even though her moral sense has been almost entirely extinguished through a lifetime of maltreatment, her small gestures of generosity show that the spark of benevolence still glows, as she places flowers on Letitia's grave or leaves bread and cellophane butterflies for the kidnapped child. Her humanity is acknowledged by the dignity with which her body is treated by the crane man who discovers it among the rubble of the Morning Star.

The writer visits the darker aspects of the human psyche and dwells on the dangers which beset the innocent, but he also meditates on the triumph of goodness even in the midst of evil. The spirit of love remains 'Immortal, Invisible' (DS 189), in the words of the hymn which echoes through Albert's mind as, in the final chapter of the novel, he trudges through the rain-soaked countryside on his journey to Quincunx House. It is embodied in Albert himself who, in the closing paragraphs, is pursuing his efforts to save his fellow-creatures. The reappearance of the missing Bev suggests that this time he may succeed and offers hope for the future.

The deliberately ambiguous nature of Pettie's death, however, indicates that the struggle between good and evil continues and remains unresolved. A certain randomness is to be found in the division between those who are redeemed and those who fall victim to evil. This is a notion explored by Trevor in many of these works. Timothy Gedge, Francis Tyte, Mr Hilditch and Pettie were all born innocent, but abuse at the hands of others, it would seem, brought them to perdition. But many characters suffer similarly and yet their goodness survives. Mr Featherston and Julia Ferndale are shaken in their faith, but they do not succumb and they emerge from their trials with new insight and wisdom, while Albert achieves a kind of sainthood although surrounded by evil. Not all characters are sustained by faith in either God or man. Some seek sanctuary in their dreams or fantasies and these support them. But the imagination has its own dangers – fostering guilt and sometimes turning a refuge into a place of incarceration – as it does for the boy in 'The Raising of Elvira Tremlett' or encouraging mild sexual deviance as it manifests itself in Mr Lynch or John Joe Dempsey. If the perversions of the mind are sufficiently twisted and are turned outwards to other members of the community, then they can result in the criminal actions of characters such as Pettie or Mr Hilditch.

Ultimately, Trevor's work demonstrates the Post-modernist idea that the world is as we perceive it, constructed in the mind to suit the needs of the individual. Like Mrs Delahunty each one tells his or her own story and this is the only valid reality for the teller.

Chapter 7

'In a manner of speaking, we represent the media'

Though well known as a novelist and short story writer, William Trevor has also been a prolific writer for radio and television. From very early in his career his plays for both media have ensured that his work has reached a wider audience than that enjoyed by many other writers of fiction. Of the more than fifty plays which have been broadcast, all but a few were written originally as short stories or novels and an even smaller number were adapted by writers other than Trevor himself.[1]

Radio is a medium very close to the author's heart. He considers writing for it as an art form: a similar relationship exists between the writer of a radio play and the listener, as does between the writer of a short story or novel and the reader:

> It seems to me that there is as much left to the imagination with radio as there is with the novel or a short story, and that's a feeling which is right for the writer because you have to have this relationship with your opposite number – the person who's receiving you. You have to have that contact even though you can't visualise these mysterious people. You have to have the feeling that there's a kind of thread, as it were, between you.[2]

Like the written word, radio reaches out to a mass audience and yet is received as a private, solitary experience. In each case the author relies on words to bring characters to life and to create imaginary worlds, whether it to be to convey a quotidian reality or to explore the inner recesses and complexities of an individual's psyche. A writer in either medium is as free to enter the consciousness of a character and disclose his/her thoughts as he is to inhabit whatever time and space he chooses – bounded only by the imaginations of listener and reader. Sound is the added ingredient which radio utilises to enhance the text. While the reader must depend entirely on the imagination, the listener has the advantage of voice and sound effects to enrich the mental picture, and the judicial use of silence can be one of the medium's most effective tools.

Although Trevor's radio plays retain the literary quality which marks the short story writer, they are also successful in the aural medium. *Marriages*, written originally for live television, was also performed on stage before being broadcast on radio. The piece involves only two characters – Mrs Landsdowne, whose husband of twenty-four years has just died of a heart attack and Mrs Swingland, the deceased's former mistress. The two women meet on the afternoon of the funeral at the invitation of Mrs Landsdowne, in the room in which her husband and Mrs Swingland had carried on a romantic liaison, twice a week, for the previous six months. There are few sound effects – merely the ringing of a doorbell and the creaking of a door as it opens and closes, the clinking of glasses and the pouring of drinks. Music too is used sparingly, serving very occasionally to enhance remembered moments of idyllic happiness.

The greater part of the play involves two virtual monologues as both women reveal not only the details of their own relationships with their respective spouses, but also of the marriages of a number of other couples. At first Mrs Landsdowne, the wronged wife, dominates the conversation, with infrequent interjections from Mrs Swingland. In long speeches she describes her own situation:

> **Mrs Landsdowne:** Like the sisters, the parents never cared much for me either. 'Not good enough,' they said, 'not nearly good enough'. His mother said it to my face – six weeks before he married me. 'Now look, my dear,' his mother said, 'let's just be frank, shall we?' And on she went to say that all the family – father and sisters too – had had a chat about the matter and decided that I wasn't right. They knew him better. Well, they'd known him all his life! She was a woman all in blue, all soft. Angora wool she looked like. 'My dear, he needs a forceful wife,' she announced – with a kind of finality, as though that was simply that. 'A quick, no-nonsense sort, a help-mate, dear'. And I could

see in her eyes all that they'd said about me – 'So disappointing,' she'd said to herself – the blue angora pussycat. 'So somehow small,' the father said, 'such nondescript hair'. And the sisters – big girls themselves – had added that you could hardly call her pretty.

My own parents too – running a bankrupt hotel in Gloucestershire – 'He's not your type,' my father said. 'He'll never hold a job down'. Poor Daddy, who had a problem with holding down jobs himself. And poor Mummy, who'd made the best of poor Daddy for so very long. 'For God's sake marry money,' she whispered. 'Don't end like me – four nights a week in the Smokers' Lounge of the Musgrove Arms, behind the bar'.

None of them wanted us to have anything to do with one another. Do you know why that was, Mrs Swingland? Can you guess now that twenty-four years have passed?

Mrs Swingland: I'm afraid I've really no idea. It's none of my business, you know. Look – I – I think I'd better go.

Mrs Landsdowne: They didn't want us to have anything to do with one another, because they were jealous, because there was something about us, about him and me, which made them think that we were going to be happier than ever they could be. The Musgrove Arms was too much in the end for poor Mummy and poor Daddy – as everything else had been.

And his own parents quarrelled like cat and dog, you know. The only thing they ever agreed on was that I wouldn't make a wife for their son.

His sisters – God help them – married the two dullest men that God ever allowed to walk a pavement.

As she recalls her first meeting with her husband, music swells – augmenting her words and transporting the audience to a scene of romance. The mood changes abruptly, however, as Mrs Landsdowne describes how, through some love letters, she had discovered her husband's infidelity and consequently has come to the conclusion that what she had considered for twenty-four years to have been a happy marriage for him had been 'a load of rubbish' and 'pure hypocrisy'. As she speaks bitterly of her shattered dream, Mrs Swingland accuses the widow of self-pity and insists that she listens to her own story.

In another series of long speeches, again with occasional interjections from the second character, Mrs Swingland explains how she and Mrs Landsdowne's husband had met on an aeroplane and when their flight had been delayed had spent one night together in a hotel bedroom. Mrs Swingland's own childless marriage had always lacked passion and she and her husband had ceased to communicate. It is a marriage, she says in which 'nobody listens':

> 'I wish you wouldn't,' my husband says 'go on so'.
> All chat is dead. I – I'm just as much to blame – chatting on to him beyond my time.

Following their one occasion of intimacy, Mrs Swingland had begged him to continue the relationship, realising that at last she had found a man she could love, even if he did not reciprocate her feelings:

> I pleaded with him the way no woman should ever plead – without pride or dignity or self respect. I made him feel ungenerous – dry, mean and empty of humanity. I wanted to do that until he said at last that yes we'd meet again.
>
> I trapped your husband, Mrs Landsdowne, like an animal is trapped. You're wrong when you think that the words in those letters were inspired by any words of his. I rented this room myself – hopelessly thinking that if only we met often enough he'd turn one day to me and say 'I love you' as he did to you, Mrs Landsdowne, in your Musgrove Arms.
>
> And you're wrong about this room. A love nest, you think? An interesting, romantic place? It wasn't quite like that. It is a place a man came to perform an act of charity ...

Finally the women go their ways – each having told her own story and listened to the other's. Emotionally their positions have been reversed. The wronged woman is no longer the victim; it is the wrong-doer who has become the object of pity. Things are not what they seem to be and we accept Mrs Swingland's statement that 'Marriage has nothing to do with perfection, nor perfection with marriage.'

Since the play consists largely of story telling and uses so few of the devices of radio, its success lies in the management of its narrative. The plot focuses on the states of mind and motivations of the two characters. The only action is an encounter and conversation between the women. Events begin close to the climax and prior circumstances are sketched in by choosing significant details. A few sentences tell of each courtship and marriage, but these are chosen carefully to portray one passionate relationship which prospers in spite of obstacles and another which is merely a union of convenience. These are all features of the literary short story, as is a denouement in which there is a revelation – in this case not the salacious minutiae of an *affaire* the listener might have expected – but instead the wretchedness and pitiable state of the seducer. Although *Marriages* retains many of the essentials of the short story, however, the addition of voices and even the minimal sound effects used contribute a dimension of realism which lifts the play above the level of what might otherwise be little more than a short story read aloud. By placing the two characters face-to-face in the same room the dialogue plays out the moment of insight in dramatic form as each woman expands her awareness of the real situation while she listens to the other's version of events.

The acting out of the dialogue also dispels the occasional literary phrasing to be found in the long speeches, lending them a more natural effect and interjecting on occasion a note of wry humour:

> **Mrs Swingland:** Can you see him, Mrs Landsdowne, this bulky figure now, his moustache still neat on the redness of his face? He's clumsier than he was. He knocks the salt and pepper over. He's not so nimble on the putting greens. Can you see him?
>
> **Mrs Landsdowne:** *(Angrily)* Of course I can't see him!

The spoken dialogue guides the emotional response of the listener in a more direct way than the written word.

William Trevor's fiction lends itself to adaptation to radio. While most of it has its origin in the short story, frequently the author's working of a piece for radio takes place alongside its development as a narrative. In using the medium of radio he chooses to rely on traditional techniques in which the narrative remains central to the work and the idioms of radio are explored only in so far as they enhance the power of words. There is no requirement to use particularly advanced recording techniques or to utilise sophisticated sound effects.

As has been seen already, there are several elements of the author's writing which facilitate the transition from one medium to the other. As a writer Trevor's own voice is so unobtrusive in his stories that he is spared the trouble of eliminating it; the perspective of his characters always dominates. Many of his stories are narrated by people who are part of the action. All drama includes a certain amount of narrative, and radio drama is particularly suited to the soliloquy; the seclusion of the audience allows it to play the part of confidant quite naturally. As a master of short fiction, Trevor tends to concentrate on a small number of characters. This too is advantageous for the writer of a radio play, since a host of different voices may lead to confusion for the listener. Furthermore, although he occasionally includes sensational incidents in his plots – acts of atrocity are not unknown – the main focus of the plot is on the interior worlds which the characters inhabit in their minds.

The transition of 'The Blue Dress' from short story to radio is facilitated by the fact that the narrative voice of a character called Terris carries a great deal of the burden of the story in the form of a monologue. A middle-aged foreign correspondent, Terris has a passion for the truth in both his private and his professional life. The story reveals that as a child he had disturbed his parents with his desire to unearth unpleasant secrets. Later his wife questions his sanity as he strives relentlessly to uncover the real facts behind political stories. Reporting from Belfast he writes in one of his newspaper articles:

> Ruairi O Baoill is a sham ... And so, it would appear, is a man called Trubstall. Fantasy rules.
>
> (CS 775)

Attending the funeral of his now ex-wife's mother in Bath he remembers:

> She and I had shared the truth about her daughter, and it was that I'd honoured by making the journey ...
>
> (CS 774)

From the outset, the reader of the short story realises that Terris is the inmate of a mental institution and that he writes his version of what happened for its therapeutic value, on the instructions of his doctors:

> I must try, they tell me; it will help to write it down.
>
> (CS 772)

Because Terris is deemed to be of unsound mind, certain doubts must arise about the validity of his perceptions: his preoccupation with discovering what he regards as the truth may be obsessive; his own family life had been unhappy and this may lead him to suspect the contentment of others. Yet as he makes the connection with other deceptions – his former wife's adultery, the false claims of a church, political dishonesty – it is easy to accept his assertion that he knows that he is right. As the story unfolds a link is made between family life and the wider political scene. In each case a veneer of respectability is seen to camouflage a hidden horror.

On the day of his mother-in-law's funeral Terris meets a young girl called Dorothea Lysarth with whom he subsequently falls in love. Somewhat to his surprise he is welcomed as a prospective son-in-law by what seems to be an idyllic family. No objections are raised in spite of the couple's age difference and their plans to live abroad. Terris finds this remarkable because the Lysarth family – Dorothea, her parents and her two brothers – are exceptionally close:

> I formed the impression that the Lysarths invariably knew what was coming next, as though lines had been learnt.
>
> (CS 778)

Shortly before the wedding is to take place, Dorothea tells her fiancé of an incident which had occurred when she was twelve. As she and another child, Agnes Kemp, had raced each other to the top of a tree, her companion had fallen and been killed. With his unerring instinct for the truth Terris realises that Agnes, an infuriating child, had been pushed from a branch and that Dorothea had been responsible for her death. He visualises the scene as the Lysarth boys must have witnessed it:

> Their sister's hand reaches out, pulling at the blue dress, at the child who had been such a nuisance all summer ...
>
> (CS 781)

A conspiracy of silence has shielded the family from the consequences of what Terris recognises had been murder.

In the radio version of 'The Blue Dress', the actor's voice fleshes out the narrator's character, making the monologue more effective on radio than on the page, denoting immediately the man's age and social class. As the drama opens a collage of sound effects, interspersed with snippets of dialogue at the beginning, establishes Terris's preoccupations as well as his present position in an asylum for the mentally deranged.

The second movement of the story – Terris's meeting with Dorothea in the Pump Room at Bath – translates almost directly from the page, the realistic dialogue necessitating only the occasional assistance of narrative asides:

> **Dorothea:** ... What about you? What was your wife like?
> **Terris:** Fond of clothes. Fine tweeds, a certain shade of scarlet, scarves of every possible variation. She hated trailing after me, abroad.
> **Terris:** *(As narrator)* I didn't add that Charlotte had been unfaithful with anyone she had a fancy for; I didn't even want to think about that. *(Pause)* The waiter brought Dorothea veal escalope and steak *au poivre* for me ...

This same technique is used to reveal the developing relationship between the couple, as well as Terris's introduction to the Lysarth family. It is, however, the dramatisation of a croquet match, an episode which merits only a few lines in the story, which provides the first extended clue to the radio audience that all may not be as it seems in the Lysarth family. Mrs Lysarth has remarked that the game is a 'perfect training for life'. In an exchange between Dorothea and her brothers it is disclosed that Dorothea's father, a medical doctor by profession and an amateur archaeologist, is less than honest:

> **Jonathan:** I remember a great occasion when old Major Winthrope said someone else had cheated. We were no more than eight, Adam.
> **Adam:** It was Father, he said, who cheated.
> **Dorothea:** And he was right.
> **Adam:** Father has a way of taking two tiny shots to slither a ball through a hoop. The second one is well disguised.

Shortly after that we learn that Dorothea, herself, 'can't bear to lose'. The full significance of these revelations becomes clear in the light of the events surrounding the death of Agnes Kemp. Dorothea had killed the girl because she had beaten her in a race to the top of the tree and Dr Lysarth had then covered up the truth about his daughter's crime.

In the story the reconstruction of Agnes Kemp's death takes place only in Terris's head. The addition of the children's voices in the radio production accentuates the full horror of what happens. The whispered fury of Dorothea as she climbs through the branches is powerful in its frankness:

> **Dorothea:** I hate you. I hate you, Agnes Kemp. I hate your
> pig eyes and your ugly voice. I hate your awful smile.

while the subsequent merging of her voice with the rustling of leaves adds to the sinister effect. A moment before Dorothea touches Agnes Kemp, the child pleads with her:

> No, Dorothea! No, Dorothea, what are you doing?

As she falls to the ground Agnes gasps breathlessly, but does not scream. The reaction of the watching boys is equally muted:

> **Terris:** *(As narrator)* ... Adam says something, a rasp of
> words in his throat that does not make sense. Jonathan
> cries.

In an art form in which speech is the main component the effect of this voicelessness is particularly dramatic– the thump of the falling body as it hits the ground resonating through and accentuating the aphonia. There follows immediately Terris's account of Dorothea's descent from the tree. Since this is both 'swift and agile' it consequently serves to underline the contrast it makes with the lifeless 'sprawling figure' on the ground.

The sounds of breakfasting signal a change of scene and time as Terris joins the Lysarths for a family meal, during which their innocuous conversation of dreams and crossword puzzles is undermined by his voice, as he articulates the confusion he feels when he attempts to weigh his hopes against his suspicions. Radio is particularly effective in exploiting the dramatic effect of conveying simultaneously the narrator's subjective consciousness and an objective reality – in this case an apparently happy family occasion.

From this point on Terris's voice dominates, with brief inserts from the past intruding in echo fashion. The device of echoing allows the narrator to come to the fore, while at the same time it both distances the other characters and reduces them to ghost-like figures of sinister significance. Most disturbing is the sound of Dorothea's laughter, which reaches a crescendo and then stops abruptly, thus creating the most chilling moment of the play. This dramatic instance is then reinforced by a reprise of the final exchange between the two girls immediately prior to Agnes's fall.

Silence indicates a return to the room in which Terris is confined, thus preserving in the radio play the cyclical form of the short story. His opening statement 'I am calm now ...' emphasises the change of mood and pace as he reflects on the hypocrisies – personal and political – which he has uncovered. The special advantage which radio offers – of being able to move freely between reflection and reality – had indeed been fully exploited. The listener has entered the inner recesses of Terris's mind and through his consciousness has reviewed his world, while at the same time his encounter with the other characters has been augmented by the experience of dramatic realism.

The truth about the past and its effect on current events is also central to the short story 'Autumn Sunshine'. An elderly Irish clergyman, Canon Moran, is trying to come to terms with the death of his wife, Frances, when he is visited from England by his estranged daughter, Deirdre, and her working-class boyfriend, Harold. The young man is an anarchist and Irish Nationalism in the early 1980s provides a focus for his inclinations. His empty rhetoric about the Republican cause barely masks his hatred of England, his own country. The Canon fears that under his influence Deirdre may have become involved in terrorist activities. Although Canon Moran feels guilty about his uncharitable attitude to Harold, he cannot help disliking him. The young man's griminess, his lack of humour, his bad manners, his accent and even the birthmark on his face all offend the old man, who concludes:

there was something sinister about Harold, something
furtive about the way he looked at you, peering at you
cruelly out of his afflicted face, not meeting your eye.
(CS 845)

While the Canon is preoccupied by his personal past, Harold is
fascinated by Ireland's political history. The two men disagree
about an incident which happened in Ireland in 1798, when twelve
local people were burnt to death in a barn by an English soldier,
Captain James. Subsequently the innocent owner of the barn,
Kinsella, was murdered as a reprisal. The Canon sees Kinsella's
death as an unwarranted act of violence, while Harold maintains
that it as a justifiable part of what he calls 'The struggle of the Irish
people'. (CS 843) Canon Moran believes that forgiveness is the
only possible response to hatred and terror and this is the message
he preaches to his congregation, whose own lives, he realises,
reflect his feelings.

Returning to the rectory alone after the young people's
departure, the old man is depressed about his daughter and her
boyfriend, whom he suspects of having gone to Northern Ireland.
Overcome by despondency he conjures up his wife's ghost in the
autumn sunshine. She had always understood people better than
he did – including his own difficulty in accepting any of his
daughters' husbands. 'Harold's just a talker,' (CS 851) she assures
him and as he gratefully accepts this opinion, Frances's death now
becomes more real to him and her spirit brings him comfort. For
the Canon, the past – personal and historical – has receded, leaving
room and hope for the future.

The strong characterisation in the story made it very suitable for
adaptation to radio. Garvin McGrath who produced the play for
RTE, the Irish radio and television service, felt that all he had to do
was to flesh out the characters in the radio version of 'Autumn
Sunshine'. Canon Moran, Deirdre and Harold are each very
distinct and the dialogue reinforces their differences. The Canon's
age and his nervous diffidence are reflected in his short, repetitive
and frequently broken off sentences. Harold's arrogant
obsessiveness and Deirdre's compliance all become obvious in a
few lines:

Canon Moran: Well, then, what do you think of County Wexford?

Harold: Great, Mr Moran. Really great.

Deirdre: Harold's fascinated actually. By Ireland.

Harold: The struggle of the Irish people.

Canon Moran: I – I beg your pardon?

Deirdre: It's that that fascinated Harold.

Silence. Deirdre waits for Harold to say something. When he doesn't she continues herself.

Deirdre: I didn't know a thing about Irish history. I mean not anything that made sense. It was Harold who got me going.

Canon Moran: *(To Harold)* Well, that's most interesting. Actually, I've always found Irish history particularly intriguing myself. There's a good story to it, isn't there? Its tragedy's tidily uncomplicated.

This elicits no response. There's another silence.

Canon Moran: You've come at a particularly lovely time of year.

Deirdre: Actually Harold doesn't go in for anything like that.

Harold: I've begun to read up on it, Mr Moran: the struggle of the Irish people, 1069 and all that.

Canon Moran: I suppose it did all begin then.

Harold: No way it didn't, Mr Moran.

Canon Moran: I see …

The young man's single-mindedness suggests an intractable personality, which may be as dangerous as it is stubborn. His insistence on addressing the old man as 'Mr' Moran, thus denying him his church title, may be merely studied rudeness or it may be an indication of a deeper disregard for authority. Harold only once addresses Deirdre by name, referring to her otherwise as 'she' when talking about her to her father, while the girl, by contrast, quotes his opinions frequently. Her deference to his views shows not only her infatuation but her willingness to be led by him.

The Canon reveals his fears about the young people's involvement in terrorism in monologues through which he addresses his dead wife. Piano music is used as a sound sign for these confidences. Trevor chose Schubert's Impromptu No. 7 for what becomes Frances's theme in the play. The listener has already learned that the Canon's wife likes to play the instrument, so the repetition of the piece not only marks the dramatisation of the old man's consciousness, but it also alters the mood, at first evoking an atmosphere of nostalgia which comforts the lonely widower. When, however, the music gives way to silence Canon Moran's solitary state becomes all the more poignant:

> **Canon Moran:** ... Our daughter has brought him here to find inspiration in Kinsella's Barn. They have journeyed to it as journeys are made to holy places. *(Becoming agitated)* Isn't that the truth? Isn't it, Frances? Isn't it?
> *Silence.*

Even when he resumes more calmly, the frequent pauses in his heart-felt outpourings illustrate the dramatic effect of the absence of speech.

A complete change of tempo takes place as the sound effects tell us that we are in a church. While the Canon preaches on the themes of repentance and fear, the listener enters the clergyman's head. Robert Cooper, who produced the play for the BBC agrees with Garvin McGrath that this scene shows Trevor using the medium to its fullest potential. Technically the scene is complex as the sounds of conflagration merge with the neighing of horses, the music of a military band and the screams of those trapped in the fire at Kinsella's Barn. Snippets of the conversation of Harold and Deirdre are repeated over and over, becoming fragmented and jumbled and finally lost in the frightening din. The external world again dominates as Canon Moran falters in his sermon and, to his congregation's astonishment, refers inexplicably to the events of almost two hundred years earlier. The service ends and the banalities which the faithful exchange with their Pastor return the action to the present.

As Harold and Deirdre prepare to leave, the Canon's anxiety about the young couple's plans is palpable as he tries to persuade each of them in turn not to visit Northern Ireland. His worries are brushed aside carelessly:

> **Canon Moran:** I wouldn't take him up the North.
> **Deirdre:** *(Laughing)* Oh, you never know with Harold. He goes where the fancy takes him, you know. I'll give everything a good clean-over before we go. Keep you going for a bit.

> **Canon Moran:** Yes, I shouldn't go up to the North,
> Harold. It's not – It's different from down here.
> **Harold:** Oh well, we'll see. *(Pause)* She got up really early,
> you know. She had the vacuum going at six.

When the pair finally depart the Canon is left alone with his
fears. Through the use of sound effects the violent incident at
Kinsella's barn merges phonically in the old man's head with the
contemporary scene in Northern Ireland. Past and present are
dramatically interwoven:

> *Canon Moran hears again the burning of the barn, the uneasiness
> of the soldiers' horses, the screaming, the band, and then Harold's
> voice.*
> **Harold's Voice:** So the struggle continues.
> *Bring up the noise of burning, screaming, etc. It becomes confused,
> emerges into clarity again as the sound of explosions, sporadic
> gunfire, the whine of ambulances, the shouting on a Belfast street.*
> *It ceases abruptly.*
> **Deirdre's Voice:** Harold's fascinated actually.

Seated in his garden, the old man seeks reassurance from his dead
wife who has now become a ghost with whom he can
communicate. Although the Schubert music plays softly, there is
no comforting voice for either the Canon or the listener. Instead
there is a long pause during which the old man listens. What he
hears provokes him to make an anguished protest:

> No, please don't say anything else.

The Schubert piece which had formerly brought calm to the
Canon now seems menacing as it increases in volume and then
cuts abruptly. The voice of a newscaster tells of the death of some
children caught in crossfire during protest marches in Northern
Ireland. The music returns and with rising emotion the Canon in
the final speech of the play addresses Frances's ghost:

> **Canon Moran:** I wish you'd said Harold was just a talker
> and left it at that. What's the *good* of saying he's right? *(His
> voice rises agitatedly)* What comfort's there in it? Why did
> you always have to tell what you thought to be the truth?
> *(Becoming very emotional)* He's a horrible kind of person.
> You're not here, you didn't meet him. Can't you see he's a
> horrible kind of person? How could a person like that
> possibly be right?

As the play closes the music continues inexorably.

In the radio version of 'Autumn Sunshine' there is no easy comfort for either the old clergyman or the listener. While the short story ends on a hopeful note, the radio play is less auspicious. The opportunity which the medium offers to exploit the dramatic aspects of the events lends them such immediacy that the truth, as it is portrayed to the audience, is too complex to allow for facile solutions. Like the Canon, the audience has encountered Harold. The face of terrorism may be ugly and disfigured but it is nonetheless human and cannot be ignored.

Neither can the past be discounted. Through the Canon's consciousness the fusion of past and present has been dramatised. The clergyman might wish the former to recede but it is a part of current events. Significantly the radio version of the story concludes with a series of questions. The original story may have suggested answers, but in the dramatisation certainty has been removed and the questions remain paramount.

Thematically and technically Trevor's radio plays have become increasingly complex. For the audience the outcome of the plot is less important than the total experience of the medium, which not only portrays characters and ideas but also shapes the reaction to them. The author remains essentially a short story writer yet he exploits with ease the power of radio – to move in and out of consciousness, to pass from external to internal events, to use music, other sound effects and silence to evoke in his audience a sense that they are witnessing the enactment of significant events.

*

In the television version of William Trevor's short story 'Events at Drimaghleen' an elderly nun comments that an incident reported in a television documentary had never taken place. A younger sister replies 'They showed it; they showed it happening'. Her statement bears out the adage that a picture is worth a thousand words and its corollary that the cinemagraphic enactment of a sequence of events is the most credible means of approximating reality.

Trevor has adapted a number of his own works for television and because of the popularity of the medium these have reached a far wider audience than have his books. In spite of his acclaim as a writer of television plays, he makes light of the process by which he translates the written word to the screen:

> All one is trying to do is to get the short story onto the television screen. It's not a question of dramatising it. I don't think of myself as a dramatist or a playwright. I just simply think that I've been asked to produce a number of sheets of paper which will get that story onto the screen and turn it into a mainly visual commodity. The big thing about it, the extraordinary and odd thing to me about it is that if I write a short story it will be read by quite a small number of people. If it is translated for television it will be seen by a very, very large number of people and yet I don't make any changes. I make as few changes as I possibly can, and that seems to me to be the only really interesting thing about it.[3]

The formal elements of a novel or story remain substantially unaltered: character, plot and the atmosphere of the piece must retain their authenticity. Nevertheless, in adapting a work for the screen a writer transforms and develops it in order to exploit the full potential of the new form. Verbal concepts are presented in both visual and aural terms, a metaphor used in narrative must now be shown, and situations shaped and altered in order to give a sense of spectatorship. Through the camera, the viewer's focus may be directed to the most minute detail and a variety of angles used to guide his response as he is presented with a series of points of view. In this way discourse takes place between the screen and the viewer as the latter responds to both direct and indirect stimuli. Although sound remains central to film the verbal content of a work may be lessened. Trevor speaks without regret of turning his words into images:

> The more silences you have, the better TV it's going to be. You can't afford to be that fond of your lines, especially the funny ones, the ones that really work on the page.[4]

Early in his writing career Trevor began adapting his work for the small screen, with considerable success. To date he has been responsible for almost forty television productions of his stories, while the screen plays of four works have been adapted by other writers. The story which has made the biggest impact on television audiences to date is undoubtedly 'The Ballroom of Romance' broadcast in 1983. The story was originally set in 1971, but director

Pat O'Connor suggested that the television version should be placed back in the 1950s. Asked why he had chosen to set the story at such a comparatively late date Trevor explained:

> Time goes slowly in rural Ireland and the past lingers in the West of Ireland. A way of life was killed by the 1960s but some of the old ways remained in Ireland. The story was about the tail-end of something. The real end came at the beginning of the 1970s, so I set the story in 1971. The TV production quite rightly dated it in the 1950s. In a way it was about a way of life which was before the '50s – it goes back beyond to the '40s and '30s. But in Ireland things linger on from earlier times – for example people continued to use bicycles in the West of Ireland long after the car was in common use.[5]

Change comes slowly in Ireland, but by the 1960s there were many signs of modernisation in the country. The economy was improving, bringing relative prosperity to a state, which in the first four decades of independence had been bedevilled by the twin problems of unemployment and emigration. Now the population began to increase for the first time since the Great Famine of the 1840s as young people found jobs at home and many emigrants returned from abroad. In 1961 television came to rural Ireland and by the end of the decade free secondary education was available to all. In the popular perception, therefore, the problems which beset the characters in 'The Ballroom of Romance' – material and spiritual poverty – are more readily associated with the 1950s than with the early 1970s.

The artistic association between William Trevor and Pat O'Connor was particularly fortuitous. As well as 'The Ballroom of Romance', O'Connor directed 'One of Our Own' – the film version of the short story 'An Evening with John Joe Dempsey' and a full-length film of the novel *Fools of Fortune*. O'Connor admired Trevor's ability to present a profound view of human nature through character. While working in RTE, he saw the script of 'The Ballroom of Romance'. He subsequently talked to the author and a co-production with the BBC was arranged. Both men brought to the project their own perceptions of the country. O'Connor had grown up a Catholic in rural Ireland and had had first-hand experience of ballrooms, while Trevor had been long enough absent from the country to enable him to illuminate Irish life with the vision of an outsider.

O'Connor describes Trevor as 'a wonderfully atmospheric writer', a quality which is very important for television. The opening shots of 'The Ballroom of Romance' illustrate how the writer creates a mood which reflects the lives of the characters. A panoramic view shows a beautiful but barren landscape. Those who live there, however, remain oblivious of its beauty as they live bleak lives of frustrated hopes and lost opportunities.

In the first dozen scenes there are only a few lines of dialogue – a brief exchange between Mr Dwyer and his wife as they drive towards the ballroom of which he is the proprietor and a desultory conversation between Bridie and her crippled father as she prepares for her weekly outing to the ballroom. Instead the main thrust of the narrative is presented through images – a muddy farmyard, an exterior view of the ballroom on a remote hillside, its inauspicious interior where Mrs Dwyer prepares food for the dancers in a rough-and-ready manner, Bridie's red dress – her effort at glamour – and a complete contrast to the working clothes in which she first appears. Although there is little talk, sound is used to augment the visual messages. In these early scenes silence is filled by the playing of a radio which broadcasts patriotic ballads and features the voice of Eamon deValera speaking on agricultural matters. A news broadcast tells of a meeting between members of the Irish government and senior clergymen of the Roman Catholic church. Thus a picture of Ireland in the 1950s is created – a rural society, staunchly Catholic, a place in which church and state have a close relationship, a circumstance which is borne out by the icons to be seen in the interior of the ballroom, where a banner proclaims 'Happy Homes for Ireland and for God' and a portrait of the Irish patriot, Patrick Pearse, hangs on the wall.

The camera cuts to the interior of Carey's Bar and Grocery where three bachelors – Bowser Egan, Eyes Horgan and Tim Daly – are silently drinking pints of stout. Their demeanour is morose. For the most part they stare straight ahead. One, with an air of deliberation, removes wax from his ear and examines it with interest. These are men who are crude in their habits and lack any social graces. Meanwhile people begin to arrive at the ballroom, among them the fancifully named Romantic Jazz Band, which consists, ironically, of three middle-aged men whose musical instruments are a saxophone, a piano accordion and a set of drums, and who throughout the evening play a selection of Irish and American tunes, almost exclusively in slow waltz tempo.

As Bridie enters the ballroom, the camera angle surveys the scene from her point of view. A number of girls are dancing together; other women sit along the walls; a few men stand in a group but do not speak; a single man – the man with the long arms – stands alone; a young girl sits apart looking slightly apprehensive. She walks down the hall exchanging greetings, her gaze drawn to Dano Ryan, the drum player, and a bachelor in whom she has an interest.

The scene switches back to the bar where the three bachelors continue to drink as before. With masterful economy, the dialogue reveals the preoccupations and attitudes of the drinkers:

> **Tim:** I was wondering is there talent there tonight?
> **Eyes:** Well, there'll be the same talent there always is. What better could a man want?
> **Tim:** You could want for it to be obliging.
> **Eyes:** You're a holy bloody terror, Tim.
> **Tim:** If a man works seven days isn't he entitled to a bit of relaxation? Isn't that a fact, Willie?
> **Mr Carey:** That's right, Tim.
> **Tim:** All work and no play.

The camera cuts to the ballroom where dancing has begun.

> **Eyes:** I wonder will the Bolger one be there?
> **Tim:** Isn't she always?
> **Eyes:** She has great knees.

The men snigger and Bowser Egan appears to wake from a reverie. Suddenly he begins to sing 'Phil the Fluter's Ball' in a deliberate, unemotional manner – still staring straight ahead into space. The others join in and the song rises in the manner of a ritualistic incantation. This is necessary to stir the men from their torpor and excite them for the night ahead. The effect is dramatic – at once amusing and sinister. The women too have their ceremonials as they jockey for position in front of the cloakroom mirror, touching up their make-up and commenting on each other's appearance. The camera moves in for a close-up of Bridie examining her face and the viewer identifies with her concern as she silently notes the signs of ageing.

The rather sedate strains of 'Galway Bay' issuing from the ballroom are replaced by a raucous chorus of 'Ghost Riders in the Sky' as the three bachelors cycle unsteadily – one without a flashlight – towards the ballroom. The panoramic view of the mountains against the setting sun is breathtakingly beautiful – the West of Ireland in all its glory. It is the American Wild West, however, with which the trio are associated as they approach the dancehall in the manner of outlaws arriving at a saloon bar. The allusion is echoed sometime later when Eyes Horgan remarks that Cat Bolger has a great pair of legs – 'Oh, none better in the Wild West' Bowser Egan agrees. Mr Dwyer may claim that 'the old values' still pertain in his ballroom but they are being demonstratively challenged by outside influences. The altercation between the two is dramatised during the interval in the dance when the bachelors prevent Mr Dwyer from continuing with his speech by their singing of the Irish-American 'McNamara's Band' which deteriorates into a puerile, vulgar ditty.

The desperation of the ageing unmarried woman is conveyed through image alone as the camera focuses on the unattractive, middle-aged Madge Dowding – the woman Bridie may become in a few years. By sheer determination Madge manages to dance with the man with the long arms. Her reward is to be ignored by him. As they circle the ballroom, he looks over his shoulder as if oblivious of her and never utters a word. Later in the evening she offers him a cigarette which he accepts mutely and lights – leaving her to attend to her own. At the end of the dance she watches him ride away on his own. At no point, by even a look or a gesture, has he as much as acknowledged her presence. In this world there is little dignity for those who have neither youth nor beauty.

The theme of emigration is presented through the conversation between Bridie and a young man with whom she dances, and is pursued as Bridie chats to Patty Byrne, a young girl whose first visit it is to the ballroom. Patty asks Bridie 'Did one go on you, Bridie? Did one emigrate you were fond of?' Bridie replies 'You can't stop things happening', her mind drifting into the past. The full potential of television is used in the flashback scene which follows. The throb of the ballroom music gives way to a new tune, played by a full dance orchestra. The people's faces become blurred and are replaced by dancers of twenty years earlier. Dressed in fashions of the 1930s, they are in plush surroundings as they dance to the strains of 'Yours 'til the Stars Lose Their Glory'. A younger-looking Bridie is in the arms of a handsome youth. He is Patrick Grady who went to live in Wolverhampton and with whom she had been in love. The camera tracks in on the pair who talk and look into each other's eyes. As the focus pulls back the music comes to an end and there is applause. The thin voice of Dano Ryan intoning 'I'll see you in my dreams' brings Bridie back to the present and provides an ironic contrast. As she sits chatting with Patty Byrne the viewer sees Dano from Bridie's point of view: he is 'a decent man' – respectable, middle-aged and dull.

When dancers and musicians pause for refreshment, the bachelors repair to the Gents Lavatory to drink alcohol surreptitiously and the women gather around the band. Bridie seizes the opportunity to talk to Dano Ryan, only to discover that he intends to marry his landlady. She cannot disguise her disappointment but her friend Eenie Mackie, recognising the hand of fate, points out 'You can't change the way things are, Bridie'. Standing alone Bridie focuses on Dano Ryan. His listless face dissolves and is replaced by Patrick Grady's. In her memory Grady comes towards her. Again the sound of a dance orchestra swells over the music of the band. The fantasy disappears and from Bridie's point of view the camera focuses on a group of young girls chattering and giggling – reminders of her younger self. Through flashback and contrast the past and its lost opportunities have been visualised with double effect.

Towards the end of the evening, disappointed in her hopes of marrying Dano Ryan and repulsed by Bowser Egan's behaviour, Bridie decides she will never return to the ballroom. In direct language she rebuffs Bowser Egan:

> I don't like being kissed by you. I don't like the sweat on
> the sides of your face and the way your teeth stick into me.
> I don't like the way you take a swig of the bottle before you
> have a go at me.

This is a much stronger Bridie than the woman in the story. She is capable of verbalising emotions, which in the written version were confined to her thoughts. Bowser Egan is embarrassed by her words, but even more, as the camera frame shows, he is mortified by the fact that they have been said in the hearing of both the young man with whom Bridie had earlier danced and Eyes Horgan.

In the women's cloakroom Bridie once again looks closely at her face in the mirror. The grey overcoat, which she has donned for her bicycle journey home and which covers her red dress, drains her of colour and accentuates the grey in her hair. In the harsh light her face looks older. In spite of her outburst she is defeated. This is confirmed when on the journey home she enters a field with Bowser Egan. A close-up of the man as she considers his invitation shows his windswept face with an expression of apparent sincerity. He talks with candour of marrying after his mother's death. Without making any verbal agreement, Bridie turns her bicycle towards the field – a signal of her submission. A shot of the exterior of the ballroom, its illuminated name 'The Ballroom of Romance' still distinguishable in the gloom reminds the viewer of her romantic illusions, while its dilapidated interior – becoming more gloomy as the lights are extinguished one by one – indicates her quenched hopes. The lonely sound of the solo saxophone reprises the song used in the flash-backs recalling Bridie's lost love. This underlines the contrast with the sordid reality of her present situation. Later as she cycles home in the dawning light, Bowser Egan stands at the iron gate of the field, raises a whiskey bottle to his lips and finishes its contents. He tosses the empty bottle away and a cunning smile spreads over his face – he is well satisfied with his life. His gesture is a metaphor for his indifference, his facial expression a revelation of his true nature. Neither bodes well for Bridie's future.

The television version of 'The Ballroom of Romance' struck chords in the folk memory of its audience, some of whom remembered their youthful excursions to similar dancehalls with nostalgia, their hardships and humiliations forgiven by the mercy of time, their charms enhanced by the glow of distance. For those who have never trodden a ballroom floor the experience still rings true, the authenticity of its emotional power lending it universal significance.

Although Trevor's television work is associated in many people's minds with rural landscapes, urban settings are also featured in his screen plays. The short story 'Access to the Children' is set in London. Malcolmson, an Irishman, leaves his wife, Elizabeth, and his two young daughters, Deirdre and Susie, when he meets an American woman on a train and falls in love with her. The story opens as he makes one of his Sunday visits to his old home as part of an agreement that he should see his children every week. The television version made by RTE and directed by Tony Barry relocates the events to Dublin. The Ireland in which they take place is contemporary, urban and middle-class – as distinct from the world of the 'The Ballroom of Romance' as was the original setting of the story. Apart from some minor changes to accommodate the change of venue, in its essence the screenplay captures the spirit of the story.

A sudden beginning introduces Malcolmson in his grim inner-city apartment – hardly more than a bed-sitting-room. He carefully lays the table in anticipation of a visit by his daughters. An attempt to remove a stain from the table-cloth is abandoned and he covers it with a plate. His kitchen is small and untidy – open packets of food clutter the shelves; the bed-sitting-room has an array of shirts hanging from hooks on the walls. In a distracted way he shaves part of his face, but leaves off to tidy up the bed when it catches his eye. Apart from the noise of his electric razor, the only sound is of heavy traffic coming from outside.

In this adaptation for television the narrative is translated through a series of flashbacks which form patterns juxtaposing past and present. These recollections structure the story as it moves from the halcyon days of Malcolmson's marriage, through its breakdown caused by an extramarital affaire with an Englishwoman called Catherine, to the ending of that relationship and his attempted rapprochement with his wife and family. The plot unfolds through the use of similarities and contrasts. While this technique was used sparingly in 'The Ballroom of Romance', here it becomes the main vehicle for the development of the story.

An early morning scene in the bedroom which he shares with his wife before the affair begins captures the essence of their relationship and Elizabeth's doubts about the quality of their lives together. Malcolmson wakes to find that, because his wife has forgotten to set the alarm-clock, he is in danger of missing an aeroplane to London. She has also neglected to have his suit ready. Sleepily, Elizabeth suggests that he should abandon his job because of the travelling which it entails and instead open a market garden and live a more tranquil life. On the flight which he catches with only minutes to spare he meets Catherine – cool, sophisticated and as she tells him 'always hours early'. Later when he is living with her, another early morning scene mirrors the first. Now the interior is more luxurious – almost exotic, with a large brass bed; it is a room full of light and colour. Yet as he walks about the bedroom, Malcolmson covertly glances at a family photograph hidden under some neatly ironed shirts. His clothes remain in an open suitcase – indicating that he continues to travel and perhaps suggesting that this is his mistress's bedroom and he is a visitor.

The monotony of the Sunday visits by the children is evident from the close-up shots in which Malcolmson struggles to make conversation with them in his car – a beaten-up Mini which has replaced the family saloon of former days. While the older girl, Deirdre, pretends interest in the pointless activities which he suggest, Susie, the younger child is blunt in her rejection of his suggestions. The seediness of his life is underlined in a number of scenes: on a visit to an ice-cream parlour, Susie shares a gambling machine with a prostitute; while they listen heedlessly to a street preacher, she wanders off and gets involved with a drunk in a doorway; in a museum she misbehaves, but is found happily chatting to an attendant. Susie's perkiness and her self-absorption are vehicles for some of the understated comedy which occasionally lightens the film. Her father's carelessness in looking after her is the result of the vivid memories which flood his consciousness. Happy domestic scenes are interspersed with equally blissful times with his mistress. There are striking similarities between the two women: both are blonde and pretty; they each wear feminine, flowing clothes and favour the colour blue. These resemblances are emphasised by the dialogue when

Elizabeth enquires of her husband 'How is she different from me?' 'She's just a different person,' he replies, referring to Catherine.

Malcolmson's distraction continues and he has to be reminded by the children that they need to eat. Characteristically Deirdre asks 'Shall we – shall we go and have tea now?' while Susie declares 'We're starving actually'. As they leave the museum, a moment of poignant recollection further depresses Malcolmson. On a beach with Catherine he hears a child call 'Daddy!'. Turning he catches sight of a couple with two children playing by the shore. Catherine recognises his loneliness. In the car as the children talk of Richard – Elizabeth's new love – Malcolmson's preoccupation with his thoughts affects his concentration to the extent that a car horn blows furiously at him. His mind returns to the occasion on which he finally left his wife. The camera frames each character in turn underscoring the breach between them. The intensity of the emotional exchange heightens in a scene in which dialogue is central. Close-up shots of the two characters eliminate all background except for some whiskey bottles on a table behind Malcolmson. Almost subliminally the viewer notes the association of the character with alcohol and is prepared for his eventual decline into drunkenness. The yellow wall in the background makes a harsh contrast with Elizabeth's red dressing-gown. Her face blotchy from tears and her hair dishevelled, she looks forlorn and less attractive. In this dramatic encounter she gives vent to her passion, while her husband retains his composure. Framed in the doorway, their children witness the scene.

The opening of the second part of the film moves between Malcolmson's kitchen and his bed-sitting-room, where his daughters watch television. At intervals he repairs to the kitchen, secretly bracing himself with whiskey before returning to play the part of father with his children. In spite of his ineptitude he struggles to retain a happy mien as in further flashbacks he recalls his affair and its inevitable end. In a rural setting Catherine tells him of her decision to return to England. The scene recalls his happy times out-of-doors with his family. As he assures the children that he will rectify the 'mistake' he made in leaving their mother, voices from a television programme echo 'stupid, stupid, stupid' – like a chorus making commentary.

When he returns the children to their home, in a state of drunken optimism, Malcolmson begs for a reconciliation with his wife, promising that he will make a fresh start and even begin a market garden. The interior of the house is cosy. A fire burns brightly; his bed-sitting-room by contrast had a one-bar electric heater. In a scene which mirrors their earlier dramatic confrontation, Elizabeth now makes it clear to her husband that their relationship is over and announces her intention of marrying Richard, whose presence in her life has been revealed through Susie's chatter. This time it is Elizabeth who assumes control and points out the truth of their situation. During part of the scene Malcolmson is seated while Elizabeth stands looking down at him, obdurate in spite of his pleas. Like Bridie she articulates her pent-up emotion in a cathartic moment; unlike Bridie she does not later relent.

Stung by his wife's words, Malcolmson flees the house, overturning a bottle of whiskey in his drunken haste. The contents spill onto the floor – a metaphor for his lost hopes and dreams. The final sequences reveal a sad, drunken bore who persists in his delusions, wearying a barman with his foolish tales and evoking in the viewer feelings of both sympathy and disgust. It is this ability of Trevor's to deal simultaneously with the tragic and comic sides of life and to treat his characters equally with compassion and irony which most attracted director Tony Barry to the making of the film and which has the greatest impact on viewers.

In spite of its change of location, the television version of 'Access to the Children' remains very faithful to the short story. The film of 'Events at Drimaghleen', however, is a much more ambitious project, which deals not only with the business of investigative journalism, but with film making in particular – the process by which the visual medium not only tells a story but produces a version of events which masquerades as reality – the very art of creation.

The story involves three violent deaths which take place in the mid 1980s in a remote Irish townland called Drimaghleen. A young woman, Maureen O'Dowd, her boyfriend, Lancy Butler, and Lancy's widowed mother are found shot dead in the yard of the Butler's farm. Maureen O'Dowd's family – together with the people of the area, including the parish priest, Father Sallins, and Garda Superintendent O'Kelly – all come to the conclusion that Mrs Butler, in a fit of jealousy, shot Maureen, that in an ensuing struggle Lancy killed his mother and then turned the gun on himself. They base their opinions on their knowledge of the characters involved and on the available evidence. While still in the process of coming to terms with the tragedy, they are approached by reporters from an English tabloid newspaper, who offer the family cash in exchange for interviews and photographs. The newspaper article which follows interprets the happenings in an entirely different way, claiming that Maureen O'Dowd had murdered Mrs Butler because of the latter's opposition to her relationship with her son, and had then killed Lancy, before committing suicide. In the priest's opinion 'what had been printed was nearly as bad as the tragedy itself'. (CS 1098)

'Events at Drimaghleen' as a story by William Trevor is unusual in that it has no strong characters. Neither is the outline of the plot especially engrossing. Yet making a film of the story presented its director, Robert Cooper, with what he described as 'so many possibilities that it was almost difficult to handle'. Its style as a quasi-documentary, according to Cooper, meant that certain interpretations of the events were placed before the viewers who then had to come to their own conclusions about what had happened. It was necessary to film it in an open-ended way, so as to make it clear that there was no definitive version of what had occurred. This posed particular problems for the actors involved, who had to give performances which were credible irrespective of whichever construction might be accepted as the truth.

As the film opens the camera pans through a derelict landscape, focusing on a ruined house, bare trees, a broken cart, a barbed-wire fence – stark images against the horizon. A bicycle stands by an iron gate – the field beyond is lost in fog. A verbal commentary immediately translates the scene into a new medium – the poetic language of the voice-over reiterating the visual impression, while at the same time transforming it into a presentation for the viewer. A signpost at a desolate crossroads points to Drimaghleen. The picture shrinks and becomes a television screen. Augmenting the mood is the music, specially composed by Barrington Pheloung. A spare, plaintive melody played by a solo recorder, soon joined by a solo cello, moves in semitones to create a melancholic air.

A close-up shot reveals a sophisticated young woman editing tape in a television studio. With an air of authority she presses buttons and works machines – the mystery of the medium at her finger tips. The signpost appears again and the woman's voice directs the viewer's attention to the town of Kilmona. Focusing and editing, she is engaged in the process of fabrication – of creation. Through her exposition she evokes the past, linking a number of dramatic incidents – a runaway wife, an outbreak of revolution, a summary execution – to events which, she tells her viewers, happened on 2 November 1988. The date, which differs from that cited in the story, is All Souls Day – the Feast of the Dead – a day which has strong reverberations in the Irish consciousness. The winter season also allows for the filming of bleak, desolate scenes. Once again the music predicates the sombre, cheerless tones of the images, as a single deep bass note is held and then joined by low strings.

The situation shifts to early morning scenes in the McDowd household as Maureen's father attends the cows and her mother dresses and prepares for the day ahead. (In the film version the family name has been changed from O'Dowd to McDowd.) Mrs McDowd is viewed through a mirror – the first of many shots in which the subject is seen through a reflection – a reminder of the distortion which is a part of any representation. After the discovery of their daughter's disappearance the pair breakfast together, framed by the kitchen window – a setting which also recurs in the course of the film and which suggests a view bounded by limits.

The McDowds drive towards the Butler farm, expecting to hear news of their daughter, their conversation drawing on the story's narrative as they discuss the strong misgivings they share about Maureen's involvement with Lancy Butler. As the car approaches the farmyard the barking of a dog intrudes on the dialogue. The sound of the wind becomes part of a desolate melody played on the recorder, accompanied by broken chords on a keyboard. The camera focuses on the carcasses of two dead rabbits and some spent cartridges. A close-up of McDowd and his wife shows her eyes drawn to a fallen bicycle. Their gradual realisation of the extent of the carnage is portrayed through the camera work which reveals the full scene to the viewer in the same fragmented fashion. Mrs McDowd approaches the bicycle as the deep bass note is heard again and a wordless soprano voice enters in an ethereal high register, merging eventually into the mother's heartbroken screams.

Opening the second part of the film is the funeral liturgy as the dead are interred in the churchyard. On the vestry wall a picture of Christ being laid in the tomb repeats the theme as the priest disrobes while brooding on the events. Later Father Sallins, in conversation with Superintendent O'Kelly – the police officer in charge of the case – recounts the story of Mrs Butler's obsessive love of her son. A woman with the 'cunning of a vixen' she was 'strange in the head on the subject of Lancy'.

Intruding on the quiet talk of the two men is the commentary of the female television presenter who recalls the brevity of the media's interest in the case. The bleakness of the accompanying shot of the crossroads with its signpost is increased by the sound of the howling wind, amplified by the wordless soprano voice, creating an atmosphere both sinister and mysterious. The notion of the passage of time is reinforced by a change of season as the priest and his housekeeper are seen working together in the garden of the Parochial House. Once again in Trevor's work the garden is seen as a symbol of healing and regeneration. As she weeds, the housekeeper by accident pulls up pyrethrum plants. This action not only invokes the gospel story of the wheat and the chaff, but also prefaces the action to come – the process of unearthing disturbs innocent and wicked alike.

'A simple case of good and evil,' one of the researchers at the English television studios declares as the crew decides to further investigate the tragedy which has befallen the people they refer to as 'peasants'. Initially the reporters' approaches made to McDowd as he works in the fields are rebuffed. A visit to the family home, however, is more successful. In a shot of the couple at the kitchen window which echoes the earlier breakfast scene, the viewer first sees the arrival of the two men, followed shortly by the television presenter, Miss Hetty Fortune. The latter's name indicates the part she will play in the lives of the people of Drimaghleen. Promising relative riches she will deliver misfortune. While the men talk to the McDowds, Hetty remains outside and peers through the window. From her point of view the camera focuses on a picture of the Sacred Heart, an emblem commonly found in Irish Catholic homes. The 'angle' from which she will present the story has been signalled. Meanwhile her assurance to the McDowds that 'it's the truth that's the important thing' is undermined by the image of money being counted out for the poverty-stricken couple.

An eerie effect is created by what seems at first to be a reprise of the scene of the crime. As the camera pans across the bodies in the farmyard, however, the fluffy outline of the television microphone suddenly appears, and the viewer realises that a reconstruction of the events is in progress. The black humour which is never far below the surface of Trevor's work now manifests itself as an uncooperative dog delays the proceedings and a hen becomes the centre of attention. The ineptness of locals who wish to help adds to the confusion. Some lines of dialogue too lighten the gloom. McDowd has already warned the television crew of the dangers of hanging about his farm:

> 'And if those dogs eat the legs off you when we're out, don't say that it wasn't mentioned!'

Now the aptly named Mr Colley who is in charge of the uncooperative dog ruminates quietly 'Maybe she'd eat them'. Later when McDowd tells his wife of the film which is being made, his inclusion of the details has an incongruous effect:

> 'They'd bodies laid in the yard at Butler's. They'd hens brought into it. They got hold of a dog from the Widow Ryan –'

Almost imperceptibly the people of Drimaghleen are drawn into the film. Despite their reluctance Superintendent O'Kelly and Father Sallins are interviewed and the latter accepts a donation from the programme makers for a parish fund to build a shrine in honour of the Virgin Mary. Neighbours and friends become involved and to their bewilderment the McDowds find their home taken over by strangers to whom they serve refreshments. Although the couple are outraged when they discover the nature of the film being made about their daughter, like all the other participants they have compromised themselves. Their effort to return the fee they have received is futile. The irony of their situation becomes clear when they are asked by a well-meaning young man 'Are you in the film?' Grimly they indicate that they are. 'God, isn't it great really?' the youth remarks. The ironic tone is sustained and emphasised by the visual image of the angry couple's presence in the background of a camera frame.

As the reconstruction takes shape the screen shrinks and the narrative voice of Hetty Fortune is heard outlining a new version of what happened on 2 November 1988. The allegation is made that Maureen McDowd had been the killer. She is dubbed 'The Saint of Drimaghleen' and it is claimed that her 'saint's fervour' enabled her to carry out the murders. It is further suggested that Superintendent O'Kelly had colluded in covering up the facts of the case. As the voice-over continues, rapid montage shots are used to reconstruct the girl's life. Included is the dramatisation of a child supposedly experiencing supernatural visions in a field. The use of real photographs on the screen lends an air of authenticity to the film. The murder itself is reconstructed in slow motion with several close-ups of the shotgun in Maureen's possession. A female singing voice adds to the surreal atmosphere, the indistinct vocals eventually becoming distinguishable as *'Lux aeterna luceat eis'*. As she turns the gun on herself the words *'Lux aeterna'* are sung at a higher register. Interspersed with the commentary and dramatisations are snippets of interviews with a variety of people, including the priest, the policeman and the McDowd family. Edited and taken out of context, their words appear to bear out the programme's premises. The camera moves smoothly from film to audience and the participants in the programme are now seen watching its screening, witnessing the manipulation and distortion of their contributions. As Superintendent O'Kelly turns off the television in disgust, the soprano continues a wordless Requiem, ending in a perfect cadence. The music forms a link as the screen momentarily becomes blank and then, in an echo of the opening shots, is filled by images of the derelict Butler farm.

The concluding scenes constitute an epilogue as, in the aftermath of the television broadcast, Father Sallins and Maureen McDowd's parents endeavour to come to terms with what has happened. The priest plays the dominant role, sympathising with the couple and trying to explain why the television presenter had misconstrued the events in order 'to make it all more interesting'. Mrs McDowd questions him about Hetty Fortune's use of the word 'disadvantaged' to describe both the Butlers and the McDowds. The priest's reply that 'It's the way she had of talking' reminds the viewer of how rhetoric has been used by the programme makers to corrupt words like 'justice' and 'truth'. Several times Hetty Fortune had spoken about the importance of truth, but Mr McDowd states 'They call it the truth, only it's lies about Maureen'.

The people of Drimaghleen followed their instincts in constructing the story of what they believed had happened at Butler's farm. The television crew destroyed that version of events and substituted their own. Father Sallins asks the question 'What good did it do to separate us from our instincts?' A shot of Hetty Fortune, alone, watching the video-tapes of the programme, fades into a still of the actress who played the part of Maureen McDowd, while the priest's final words – 'Only God knows the truth' are heard in voice-over. The soprano voice sings *'Dona eis requiem'* and repeats *'luceat eis'* as the credits appear. But neither the dead nor the living have been allowed to rest; instead they have become material for 'infotainment'.

Although the film ends on a sombre note, there are details which indicate hope and recovery. Birdsong is heard in the Butlers' farmyard and the priest sits in his garden in the early summer – signs of new growth about him. As always in Trevor's work the human spirit triumphs in spite of suffering and desolation. The viewer is left to ponder the events and to consider which interpretation of the facts – if either – is the more acceptable. As in life there are no definitive versions as people construct their own stories – based on their own perceptions. The full truth as always remains beyond human comprehension.

William Trevor is above all a story-teller. His characters are memorable, with strong interior lives. Much of the action in his work takes place in their minds. In translating his narrative into radio plays or television films he is merely using a variety of vehicles to tell the story in different ways. His radio plays remain on the whole very faithful to his narrative style, relying as they do on the power of the word. That style, which includes strong characterisation and good story, is reinforced by the dramatic immediacy that radio can give and the ease with which inner and outer events, past and present can be conveyed almost simultaneously.

Television adds a further dimension to narrative. It presents its stories, not only through word and sound, but very powerfully through moving visual images. In this way Trevor's already well-honed prose can be transferred to the screen with minimum alteration. The result is that both radio and television dramas have retained the atmosphere that permeated the original narrative. The mood he evokes, like the presentation of good and evil in 'Events at Drimaghleen', is not simple – it emanates from situations which are often tragic, and so is characterised by a pervading sadness: but it is also essentially ironic, the tragedy relieved by touches of adroit humour.

*

In forty years of writing William Trevor has created a world which is recognisably his own and which is both varied and complex. His early work introduces us to a miscellany of eccentric characters whom he views from a distance. Later as he engages more closely with his creation, his work becomes increasingly profound, while retaining touches of grotesque comedy – often permeated by nostalgia and gloom. His themes encompass such issues as the operation of grace, the nature of innocence, and the relationship between guilt, evil and madness. Always the outsider, the author began by writing about the old, the marginalised, the bizarre – in an English setting. Subsequently he revisited imaginatively the Irish landscape. From the mid-1970s onwards political events in the country cast a long shadow over his work; in exploring them his outlook darkens and a disturbing vision emerges. He writes too about another Ireland, a grim place, peopled by individuals who experience great tragedies in their small lives. Trevor's genius, however, has never been confined by location or subject matter: whether he writes of England, Ireland, Italy or further afield, his concerns are universal. The hallmark of his work is found in the essential humanity which his characters portray.

The writer's work ranges across both tragic and comic visions of life and is imbued with an inherent hopefulness. His characters, for all their suffering, ordinariness and aberrations somehow arrive at acceptance of life's events, good or evil. They draw strength from one another and continue with the business of living. Their resilience enables them to surmount their troubles, so that they achieve heroism in their bearing of the ordinary vicissitudes of life.

William Trevor is not just a story-teller; he is the master of his craft, the raw material of which is language. His prose moves with a characteristic formality, control and economy. The details, so effective in creating atmosphere, are chosen with consummate precision. Although at times disconcerting and tragic, the world which he creates has an extraordinarily evocative quality, which resonates and lingers in the reader's mind. These features ensure Trevor's position as a distinguished novelist and a major short story writer of the twentieth century.

Interview with William Trevor, Spring 1998

Do you find it difficult to write? Are there times when inspiration doesn't come easily?

Almost all questions put to writers of fiction (or composers, painters, anyone who creates what wasn't there before) cannot be answered with total accuracy. If you asked Piero della Francesca how he did it he would have be shrug and say he didn't know. If you asked Mahler or Dickens or Shakespeare, the honest answer would be that, too.

How long does it take you to write a book – do you rewrite much?

How long it takes to write a book, or how much rewriting there is, or how it is with inspiration? There aren't any firm answers at all. I have spent four years writing a story; I have also spent a single day. I have spent three years over a novel; I have written another in a week. Sometimes I endlessly rewrite; sometimes not at all. I don't ever think about 'inspiration'. I have no rules; it seems to me there aren't any.

Would you say that you enjoy writing?

'Enjoy' isn't quite the word. I certainly don't sit down every morning at half past seven in anticipation of a few hours of enjoyment. I sit down to write another couple of pages or to rewrite the last couple of pages, to discard, to experiment, to hope for the best. If words are your business there is pleasure in using them; but there is also frustration, when they won't do what you want them to do. There's a mystery in the creative process: I still don't understand why a short story – occasionally a novel – seems to write itself or requires the constant use of the whip. When I compare two such stories I have written I can never, after a passage of time, find any difference of quality: each is as successful, or not so, as the other. Such conundrums are repeated in other aspects of creating something out of nothing, and since I value mystery above almost everything else I'm glad they're there.

Do you write much more than the reader gets to read?

A great deal more. You have to know everything about your characters, and the best way to get to know them is to write about them – what they've done, where they've been, all their secrets. Writing is as much concerned with what you leave out as with what you put in. You write, the reader imagines: your task is to control the relationship.

Do you know how a book will turn out as you begin or do the characters ever develop minds of their own?

It is also your task to control your characters. Of course, they develop as the story develops and to you, the author, they begin to feel like real people, but essentially they must do as they're told.

All this is analysis after the event, and this kind of stuff doesn't at all enter into the scheme of things as page follows page – at least not for me. What I do is simply to write stories about people.

Do you ever go on thinking about a book after it is finished?

I *remember* a book (or a short story) after it is finished, but I don't go on thinking about it in the way I believe you mean. There is, after all, the next one to think about.

Do you ever reread your books?

I don't reread my books.

Which do you prefer writing – novels or short stories?

I don't have a preference for writing in one form or the other.

Do you ever read critics of your work?

When I was much younger, writing my first novels, I used to buy all the newspapers on publication day, go to a bar, order a whiskey, drink it, then order another and see what the critics had to say. It was a novelty, it was the curiosity of the beginner; years ago I ceased searching out reviews in that way, and don't much see them now. Occasionally, coming across one by chance, I naturally read it.

Do you think that a writer can be taught?

There is no training for a fiction writer. The clarity and style of writing can be improved as, for instance, drawing can be improved, but no art can be taught.

Do you think that a writer should engage him/herself with the social or political problems of his/her time?

That's up to the particular writer. There is certainly no artistic compulsion to do so.

Are you ever concerned to convey a particular message through your work?

No.

Are you at all aware of an audience when you are writing?

I'm aware of trying to communicate, which is probably the same thing.

Have you any interest in contemporary politics?

I am probably politically naive.

Some people find your work, particularly the short stories somewhat depressing. Do you feel that life is depressing? Are you a happy man?

Life can be melancholy, but that is not the same as depressing. If life were depressing, it would be intolerable; the whole state of existence would be. No storyteller of any worth can be wholly happy. But conversely, no storyteller of any worth can afford to be wholly given over to gloom.

You have had a long and successful relationship with The New Yorker magazine which publishes your short stories. Could you comment on that?

I can refer you to something I have written about it:

Writing stories for *The New Yorker* is a pleasure because every statement made, every sentence, is wondered about. The legal department requires proper reassurance that maligned or libelled persons are fictitious. In what I have always thought of as a small, dusty, high-up room I imagine a couple of indomitable grammarians weeding out hanging particles and *non-sequiturs*. The checking department raises a point or two: what exactly is Tullamore Dew? Am I certain there was a Savoy cinema in Cork in 1939? When I wrote that a named hotel in Venice was pink, the checking department telephoned Venice and Venice said no, it wasn't: it had just been repainted brown. None of this has ever been an irritation, very much the opposite. *The New Yorker's* attention to detail is what authors who like to get things right long for.

After Veronica Geng moved on, my editor was Frances Kiernan, and many years later, when in turn she left the magazine, Roger Angell took her place. Each of them, from time to time, has made suggestions that have nothing to do with the colour of hotels or the difference between our use of the semi-colon and the American. Not once have such suggestions been anything less than constructive, even if, for one reason or another, a few of them weren't adopted. To those three editors, the fiction of mine they have tended over the years owes much. It's good to be able to say so, and to recall as well that in my long love affair with *The New Yorker* there was never a cross word.[1]

Did you grow up in Ireland with the feeling that, in some respects, you and your family were outsiders – belonging neither to the Anglo-Irish gentry nor to the Catholic majority in Ireland?

No. Only in retrospect is that apparent.

How do you think your upbringing shaped your imagination?

I can't answer that because I simply don't know.

Do you see any relationship, in terms of creativity, between your early career as a sculptor and your career as a writer?

No.

Do you see life as farce punctuated by tragedy or, conversely, as tragedy punctuated by farce?

Neither really. I don't think of life in this kind of way at all.

Are you a religious person? Do you believe in the concept of grace in people's lives?

I answered a similar question in the *Independent on Sunday* a few years ago. Whatever I said still stands:

> I'm a God-botherer. Most of my fiction seems to do that. I'm definitely on the side of the Christians, but I don't mind where I go to church, whether it's a Catholic church or a Protestant church.[2]

Having lived in England now for over forty years, how do you view the ongoing strife in Northern Ireland?

With great dismay.

The Ireland you depict in your work is a rather grim place on the whole. Is this the Ireland you remember growing up in or is it the place you visit today – or is it your own fictional country?

The Ireland of my childhood was very far from being a 'grim place'. I developed a profound and lasting affection for it. The Ireland I know today could hardly be described as grim, either.

My stories and novels are essentially about people, I suppose. Neither nationality nor nationalism comes into the scheme of things very much, except when one or other has a distinct part to play in the plot, as for example in the novel *Fools of Fortune* or the short story 'Of the Cloth'.[3]

In your writing which do you find more fascinating as subject matter – evil or goodness?

It is easier to write about what people call 'evil'. Goodness is more interesting.

Do you ever have any qualms about handing over a script to a radio producer or a television director?

The answer depends on who the producer or director is.

Do you like to be involved in radio and/or film production?

Again that rather depends.

You've been living in England for over forty years. Do you ever have a desire to go back to live in Ireland permanently – perhaps to retire there?

I began to live in England purely by chance, driven out of Ireland in the bleak 1950s when emigration – because of lack of employment – was at its height. I have come to like being a foreigner, a stranger in a country that will always be interestingly strange to me. Writers don't really belong anywhere, and being midway between Ireland and the continent suits me geographically.

To retire would be like dying. When I do, I'll be buried in Ireland.

Notes and References

This book was born out of a deep admiration for William Trevor's work and the pleasure it has afforded me over many years. Unless otherwise indicated, the personal insights and information about the author are the fruits of several interviews with him, with members of his family and friends.

All references to page numbers are to the hardback editions of William Trevor's novels and short stories, except for those of *A Standard of Behaviour*, which refer to the Abacus edition, published by Sphere Books Ltd, London: 1982.

Prologue
'Outside the estate gates' (CS 905)

1. Edward MacLysaght. *Irish Families: Their Names, Arms and Origins*, Dublin: Allen Figgis, 957, pp 250-1.

2. Eileen O'Byrne, ed. *The Convert Rolls*. Dublin: Stationary office for the Irish Manuscripts Commission, 1981. See Introduction, p. XIV, Note 19. 'The highest yearly total was in 1783, with 260 enrolments, 95 of them in August, with 75 for 15 August.'

3. Seamus Creighton. 'The Lloyds of Croghan House', *The County Roscommon Historical and Archaeological Society Journal*. Vol 3, 1990, pp 15-17

4. Ibid.

5. Letters written by James McGarry to Guy Lloyd Esq., Bayview Cottage, Dalkey, Kingstown. 9-23 June 1840. The Lloyd Papers, Roscommon County Library.

6. Census of Population of Ireland, Report on Vital Statistics, and Annual Report of the Register General, cited in Kurt Bowen's *Protestants in a Catholic State*. Dublin: Gill & Macmillan, 1983.

7. Ibid., p 88

8. S. Alex. Blair. *County Antrim Characters*, Compiled by Eull Dunlop, Mid-Antrim Historical Group: 19, p 70

Part I

'Behind the lace curtains' (ERW 23)

1. *Tipperary Star*, 8 June 1940, p 4

Part II

Chapter 1. 'How shall we prove we are not dead?' (OB 191)

1. Ronald Hayman. 'William Trevor', *The Times*, 31-7-1971, p 17

2. Venetia Pollock writing in *Punch* ('New Novels', 12-3-1964, p 430) noted that Trevor had 'caught that fierce tenacity of the old, their wiliness and ruthless determination'. Boswell in *The Scotsman* ('An Irish Humour Man', 7-3-1964) observed that the Old Boys were 'people we know or imagine we know outside their existence in the novel'.

3. Michael Radcliffe, 'On Books', *The Tatler*, 1-4-1964, p 14

4. Mandrake, 'Old Boys at bay', *Sunday Telegraph*, 22-3-1964, p 5. Trevor points out that only the old characters speak in staccato dialogue.

5. An anonymous reviewer in an article published in *The Times Literary Supplement*, ('Hanged by a School-Tie', 5-3-1964, p 189) compared *The Old Boys* to both *Tom Brown's Schooldays* and Alec Waugh's *The Loom of Youth*, stating that Trevor's book had 'dealt [English public schools] a blow which for controlled neatness and devastating effect, can rarely be equalled'. Trevor disliked this analysis of the novel and later in an interview with Tim Heald in the *Daily Telegraph* ('An Artist with Words', 26-6-1976, p 20) stated his own view.

Chapter 2. 'A farce in a vale of tears' (LD 294)

1. W.L. Webb. 'Gentle Gerontocrat', *The (Manchester) Guardian*, 1-5-1965, p 7

2. Cf. 'Timothy's Birthday', a much later short story in the collection *After Rain* (1996) which might be seen as a reworking of the same idea and involving a very similar scenario. An elderly Irish couple is visited by a young man who comes in place of their son, Timothy, whom they had expected for the celebration of his birthday. Timothy, who is homosexual, no longer wishes to see his parents and deliberately sends in his

place his rather unsavoury friend who not only exploits the old couple but forces them to acknowledge their son's lifestyle.

3. Benedict Nightingale. 'The Elephant's Foot', *The (Manchester) Guardian*, 22-4-1965.

Chapter 3. 'The best things are complex and mysterious' (CS 111)

1. Francis Stuart. *The Sunday Tribune* 8-3-1981, p 30.

Chapter 4. 'We are the stuff of history' (SA 39)

1. Clare Boylan, 'Trevor's Troubles', *Sunday Press*, 24-4-1983 p 14.

2. *Not Quite among Friends*, BBC Radio 3, 30-9-1981, Producer: Judith Bumpus.

3. Trevor in conversation with Melvyn Bragg, *The South Bank Show*, broadcast by RTE Network 2, 23-4-1983

4. Colm Cronin, 'Frozen scenes from a family album', *The Sunday Tribune*, 16-8-1981.

5. J.M. Synge, 'The Playboy of the Western World', *The Complete Plays*, Eyre Methuen, London: 1981, p 227

6. *The New Yorker*, 15-9-1997, pp 70-80

Chapter 5. 'This pall of distress ...' (CS 1192)

1. Terence DeVere White, Personal Interview, London, June 1991.

2. Melvyn Bragg, 'William Trevor – The Most English of Irishmen', *Good Housekeeping*, December 1984, pp 64-5.

3. Stuart Gilbert, ed. *Letters of James Joyce*, London: Faber & Faber, 1957, p 62.

4. Ibid., p 63.

5. Ibid., p 64.

6. Ibid., p 55.

7. Ibid., p 64.

8. Cf Mark Mortimer, 'William Trevor in Dublin', *Etudes Irlandaises*, November 1975, No 4 (Old Series) pp. 75-85 and Gregory A. Shirmer, "The Weight of Circumstances' – The Irish Fiction' in *William Trevor: A Study of his Fiction*, London: Routledge 1990, pp 122-163.

9. Personal Interview, Dublin, 12-7-1986.

10. Patrick Kavanagh. 'The Great Hunger', *Collected Poems*, London: Martin, Brian & O'Keeffe, 1972, pp 34-55.

11. Ibid., p 51

12. William Trevor. 'Big Bucks', *The New Yorker*, 10-2-1997, pp 68-73.

13. See Wolfgang Sänger. The 'favourite Russian Novelist' in William Trevor's novella '*Reading Turgenev*: A Postmodern Tribute to Realism' in *Irish University Review*, Spring/Summer 1997, pp 182-198.

Chapter 7. 'In a manner of speaking we represent the media' (CS 1092)

1. See Bibliography for details.

2. William Trevor interviewed by Mark Storey on Kaleidoscope, BBC Radio 4, 16-6-1980.

3. Ibid.

4. 'A Gentleman of Substance', William Trevor interviewed by Gail Caldwell, *Boston Globe*, 30-5-1990, Living Section, p 37.

5. Personal Interview, Dublin 20-1-1983.

Interview with William Trevor, Spring 1998

1. William Trevor. 'Best to be young or dead – William Trevor on why he believes that there is no better literary magazine to work for than *The New Yorker*'. *The Daily Telegraph*, 29-9-1993, p 24.

2. Jan Dalley. 'The "God botherer" who just keeps on winning: William Trevor is an exacting novelist', *The Independent on Sunday*, 29-1-1995, Britain 6.

3. William Trevor, 'Of the Cloth', *The New Yorker*, 9-3-1998, pp 76-81.

Bibliography

1. WORKS BY WILLIAM TREVOR

A Standard of Behaviour. London: Hutchinson, 1958. Sphere, 1962. Abacus, 1982.

The Old Boys. London: Bodley Head, 1965. Penguin, 1968. King Penguin, 1966. Published as a play by Poynter Davis 1972.

The Boarding House. London: Bodley Head, 1965. Penguin, 1968. King Penguin, 1981.

The Elephant's Foot (play). Staged at Newcastle-upon-Tyne, 1965. Unpublished.

The Day We Got Drunk on Cake and Other Stories. London: Bodley Head, 1966.

The Love Department. London: Bodley Head, 1966. Penguin, 1981.

The Girl (play). London: Samuel French, 1968.

Mrs Eckdorf in O'Neill's Hotel. London: Bodley Head, 1969. Penguin, 1972. King Penguin, 1982.

Miss Gomez and the Brethren. London: Bodley Head, 1971. Panther, 1978. Penguin, 1997.

The Ballroom of Romance and Other Stories. London: Bodley Head, 1972. Penguin, 1976.

Going Home (play). London: Samuel French, 1972.

A Night with Mrs da Tanka (play). London: Samuel French, 1972.

Elizabeth Alone. London: Bodley Head, 1973. Panther, 1977.

The Last Lunch of the Season. London: Covent Garden Press, 1973.

Angels at the Ritz and Other Stories. London: Bodley Head, 1975. Penguin, 1979.

The Children of Dynmouth. London: Bodley Head, 1976. Heinemann Educ., 1981. King Penguin, 1982.

Marriages (play). London: Samuel French, 1976.

Old School Ties. London: Lemon Tree Press, 1977.

Lovers of their Time and Other Stories. London: Bodley Head, 1978. Penguin, 1980.

The Distant Past and Other Stories. Dublin: Poolbeg Press, 1979.

Other People's Worlds. London: Bodley Head, 1980. King Penguin, 1982.

Beyond the Pale and Other Stories. London: Bodley Head, 1981.

Scenes from an Album (play). Dublin: Co-op Books, 1981.

Fools of Fortune. London: Bodley Head, 1983. Penguin, 1984.

The Stories of William Trevor. London: King Penguin, 1983.

A Writer's Ireland: Landscape in Literature. London: Thames and Hudson, 1984.

The News from Ireland and Other Stories. London: Bodley Head, 1986. Penguin Books, 1986.

Nights at the Alexandra (Novella). London: Century Hutchinson, 1987.

The Silence in the Garden. London: Bodley Head, 1988. Penguin Books 1990.

Family Sins and Other Stories. London: Bodley Head, 1990. Penguin Books, 1991.

Two Lives: Reading Turgenev and My House in Umbria. London: Viking, 1991. Penguin Books, 1992.

Juliet's Story (Children's Fiction). Dublin: The O'Brien Press, 1991.

The Collected Stories. London: Viking, 1992. Penguin Books, 1993.

Outside Ireland: Selected Stories. London: Penguin Books, 1995.

Excursions in the Real World (Autobiographical Essays). London: Hutchinson, 1993. Penguin Books, 1994.

Felicia's Journey. London: Viking, 1994. Penguin Books, 1997.

After Rain. London: Viking, 1996. Penguin Books, 1997.

Death in Summer. London: Viking, 1998.

TELEVISION PLAYS

Walk's End (BBC)*
The Babysitter (BBC) ('In at the Birth')
The Girl (ABC)*
Going Home (BBC)
A Night with Mrs da Tanka (BBC) ('A Meeting in Middle Age')
The Mark-2 Wife (BBC)
The Italian Table (BBC) ('The Table')
The Grass Widows (Anglia)

O Fat White Woman (BBC)
Eleanor (BBC) ('A Nice Day at School')
Marriages (BBC)*
The General's Day (BBC)
Love Affair (Anglia) ('The Introspections of J P Powers')
Mrs Acland's Ghosts (BBC)
The Nicest Man in the World (Anglia)
Afternoon Dancing (ATV)
Last Wishes (Anglia)
Memories (Anglia) (Play *Scenes from an Album*)*
Matilda's England (Trilogy) (BBC)
The Old Curiosity Shop (Dickens) (BBC)*
Secret Orchards (Granada)*
Happy Autumn Fields (Elizabeth Bowen) (BBC)*
Elizabeth Alone (Trilogy) (BBC)
Autumn Sunshine (BBC)
The Ballroom of Romance (BBC/RTE)
The Blue Dress (BBC)
Attracta (BSE/RTE)
Access to the Children (RTE)
One of Our Own (BBC) ('An Evening with John Joe Dempsey')
Miss Smith (ITV)
The Penthouse Apartment (BBC)
August Saturday (BBC)
Events at Drimaghleen (BBC)
Beyond the Pale (BBC)
Broken Homes (BBC)
Teresa's Wedding (RTE)
The Forty-Seventh Saturday (BBC)

DRAMATISATIONS OF WILLIAM TREVOR'S STORIES BY OTHER AUTHORS

The Old Boys — Clive Exton (BBC)
Office Romances — Hugh Whitemore (Granada)
Lovers of their Time — Hugh Whitemore (Granada)
Mrs Silly — Bob Larbey (Granada)

Fools of Fortune — Michael Hirst (Working Title Film/Channel Four)

RADIO PLAYS

The Old Boys (adapted by Pauline Letts)
The Boarding House
The Penthouse Apartment
Going Home
Attracta
Beyond the Pale
Marriages*
The News from Ireland
Travellers*
The Blue Dress
Running Away
Mr McNamara
Events at Drimaghleen
The Piano Tuner's Wives
Matilda's England

*Not adapted from short story

2. SECONDARY WORKS

BOOKS

Morrison, Kristin. *William Trevor*. New York: Twayne Publishers, 1993.

Morrow Paulson, Suzanne. William Trevor: *A Study of the Short Fiction*. New York: Twayne Publishers, 1993.

Schirmer, Gregory A., *William Trevor: A Study of his Fiction*. London: Routledge, 1990.

ARTICLES AND INTERVIEWS: A SELECTION

Aronson, Jacqueline Stahl. 'William Trevor: An Interview', *Irish Literary Supplement*, Spring 1986, pp 7-8.

Bragg, Melvyn. 'William Trevor — the most English of Irishmen', *Good Housekeeping*, December 1984, pp 64-5.

Caldwell, Gail. 'A Gentleman of Substance', *Boston Globe*, 30-5-1990, Living Section, p. 37.

Gitzen, Julian. 'The Truth-Tellers of William Trevor', *Critique* 21, No. 1, August 1979, pp 59-72.

Haymen, Ronald. 'William Trevor', *The Times*, 31-7-1971, p 17.

——. 'William Trevor in Interview', *British Book News*, June 1980, pp 13-14.

Heald, Tim. 'An Artist with Words', *Daily Telegraph*, 26-6-1976, p 20

MacKenna, Dolores. 'William Trevor', *Contemporary Irish Novelists*, Studies in English and Comparative Literature, Vol. 5, Rudiger Imhof (ed.), Türbingen: Narr, 1990, pp 109-23.

——. 'Trevor, William', *Dictionary of Irish Literature*, Robert Hogan (ed.), Westport Ct.: Greenwood Press, 1996, pp 1200-03.

——. 'William Trevor', *La Nouvelle Irlandaise de Langue Anglaise, Literature Irlandaise. Jacqueline Genet (ed.), Presses Universitaires du Septentrion*, 1996, pp 127-37.

Morrison, Kristin. 'Trevor, William.' *Reference Guide to English Literature*, 2nd ed., Vol. 2, 1334-6. London: St James Press, 1991.

——. 'William Trevor's "System of Correspondence"', Massachusetts Review 28, 1987, pp 489-96.

Mortimer, Mark. 'William Trevor in Dublin', *Etudes Irlandaises*, November 1975, No 4 (Old Series), pp 77-85.

——. 'The Short Stories of William Trevor', *Etudes Irlandaises*, December 1984, No 9 (New Series), pp 161-173.

——. 'William Trevor', *Ireland Today*, No 1031, September 1986, pp 7-10.

Ralph-Bowman, Mark. 'William Trevor Interviewed', *Transatlantic Review*, 53-4, February 1976, pp 5-6.

Rhodes, Robert E. 'William Trevor's Stories of the Troubles', *Contemporary Irish Writing*, Iona College Press and Twayne Publishers, 1983, pp 95-114.

——. '"The Rest is Silence": Secrets in Some William Trevor Stories', *New Irish Writing: Essays in Memory of Raymond J. Porter*, James D. Brophy & Eamon Grennan (eds.), Boston: G. K. Hall, 1989, pp 35-53.

Sänger, Wolfgang R. 'The "favourite Russian novelist" in William Trevor's Novella *Reading Turgenev*. A Postmodern Tribute to Realism', *Irish University Review*, Spring/Summer 1997, pp 182-198.

Schiff, Stephen. 'The Shadows of William Trevor', *New Yorker*, 28 December 1992/ 4 January 1993, pp 158-63.

Stinson, John J. 'Replicas, Foils and Revelation in Some "Irish" Short Stories of William Trevor', *Canadian Journal of Irish Studies 11*, No 2 (1985), pp 17-26.

Stout, Mira. 'The Art of Fiction CVIII', *Paris Review* 110 1989, pp 118-51.

Webb, W L 'Gentle Gerontocrat', *(Manchester) Guardian*, 1 May 1965, p 7.

Index

Acknowledgements

Special thanks are due to William Trevor for his help and encouragement throughout the writing of this book. He answered all my enquiries with unfailing patience, courtesy and kindness. I am grateful too to his wife, Jane, for her hospitality and to Mr Alan Cox and Mr Dominic Cox. I extend particular thanks to Ms June Cox for the tremendous interest which she took in the project and for her unstinting support and generosity. I wish to express my gratitude also to Mr and Mrs Ronnie Davison and to the late Dr Mary Emerson and the late Reverend Roy Cox.

I appreciate the help given to me by the late Professor Augustine Martin and the late Professor T.P. O'Neill, by Mr Frank Delaney and Professor Robert Rhodes. I thank Professor Maurice Harmon and Dr Tim O'Neill of University College Dublin for their advice.

Thanks are also due to Ms Helen Kilcline, the staff of Roscommon County Library and Mr Courtney Kenny for access to the Lloyd papers; to the staffs of the National Library of Ireland, the library of University College Dublin, the Berkeley Library, Trinity College Dublin, the library of Reading University, the Bodley Head Publishing Company, the Strokestown Heritage Centre; to Mr G F Platt of the Ulster Bank Staff Magazine, Ms Emer Briody of the Bank of Ireland, Mr Roger Angell and Mr Daniel Menaker of *The New Yorker*, Mr Melvyn Bragg of Independent Television, Ms Mary Curry of RTE, the Loreto Sisters in Youghal, Ms Grainne Devaney and Ms Liz Meldon of Dundrum Books, Mrs Naomi Sim, Ms Elizabeth Skinner, Mr Sean Gallagher, Mr Bill Webb, Mr Magnus Lohkamp, Mr Paul Watson, Mr Anthony Glavin, Mr Cormac Kinsella, Dr Michael Laffan, Ms Jane Bradish-Ellames, Mr Bill Power, Mr Hugh Comerford, Mr Euan Cameron and Mr John Walsh.

Among the many friends who helped in a variety of ways, I wish to express my particular gratitude to Mary Ball — also to Bernadette Comerford, Honor O'Connor, Cecily Laracy,

Stephanie McBride, Michael Cunningham, Maureen and Sean Guyan Lalor; Phyllis and Vincent Madden, Enoch Dillon, Gaye Caird and the late David Caird, Neil Donnelly, Niall MacMonagle and Mary Clayton, Sile Daly, Maurice Flanagan, Rose and Eamonn Giblin, Sr Mary Monaghan IBVM, Margaret Behan, Colette O'Neill Collum, Phil Jordan, Berna McDermott, John MacKenna, Werner Huber, Noel Murphy, Peg Sheehan, Anne Crowley, Patricia Mangan, Jim and Pauline O'Callaghan, Richard and Catherine Rose, Ruth O'Connor, Aideen Cannon, Dympna Tracey and all my former and present colleagues.